History of Universities

VOLUME VI
1986-7

History of Universities

VOLUME VI
1986-7

Oxford University Press

1987

History of Universities is published annually as a single volume.

Editor: Laurence Brockliss (Magdalen College, Oxford).

Acting editor for Vol. VI: Peter Denley (Westfield College, London).

Editorial board:
 J. M. Fletcher (University of Aston in Birmingham)
 W. Frijhoff (Erasmus Universiteit Rotterdam)
 N. Hammerstein (University of Frankfurt)
 D. Julia (Centre de recherches historiques, EHESS, Paris)
 J. K. McConica (St. Michael's College, Toronto University)
 N. G. Siraisi (Hunter College, New York)

Details of subscription rates and terms are available from Oxford Journals Subscription Department, Walton Street, Oxford, OX2 6DP, United Kingdom.

History of Universities, Volume VI, first published in 1987 by Oxford University Press, Oxford, England.

British Library Cataloguing in Publication Data:

History of Universities. - Vol. 6 (1986)
1. Universities and colleges - History - Periodicals
378'.009   LA173

ISBN 0-19-822730-2
ISSN 0144-5138

This volume was prepared using facilities generously provided by the Computer Unit, Westfield College. It was photoset on the Oxford University Computing Service's Monotype Lasercomp phototypesetter, in 10 on 11-point Times Roman. The preparation of the volume has been aided by a grant from the British Academy, for which grateful acknowledgement is made.

Printed in Great Britain at the University Printing House, Oxford

Contents

Articles

Research Note

Book Reviews   143

Zénon Kaluza & Paul Vignaux (eds.), *Preuves et Raisons à l'Université de Paris. Logique, Ontologie et Théologie au XIVe Siècle* (A. George Molland)

Studi e memorie per la storia dell'Università di Bologna, n.s., 4 (Paul Grendler)

Jan Pinborg (ed.), *Universitas Studii Haffnensis. Stiftelsesdokumenter og Statutter 1479* (John M. Fletcher)

Robert Feenstra and Cornelia M. Ridderikhoff (eds.), *Études néerlandaises de droit et d'histoire présentées à l'université d'Orléans pour le 750e anniversaire des enseignements juridiques* (L. W. B. Brockliss)

Astrik L. Gabriel, *The University of Paris and its Hungarian Students and Masters in the Reign of Louis XII and François I* (L. W. B. Brockliss)

James K. Farge, *Orthodoxy and Reform in Early Reformation France. The Faculty of Theology of Paris 1500-1543* (L. W. B. Brockliss)

Acta Nationis Germanicae Iuristarum (1650-1709), ed. Gilda Mantovani (Hilde de Ridder-Symoens)

Christopher Brooke, *A History of Gonville and Caius College* (John Twigg)

J. C. Oates, *Cambridge University Library; a History. From the Beginnings to the Copyright Act of Queen Anne*, and David McKitterick, *Cambridge University Library; a History. The Eighteenth and Nineteenth Centuries* (P. S. Morrish)

P. M. Harman (ed.), *Wranglers and Physicists. Studies on Cambridge Physics in the Nineteenth Century* (W. H. Brock)

J. T. D. Hall, *The Tounis College. An Anthology of Edinburgh University Student Journals, 1823-1923* (R. D. Anderson)

Ferdinand Seibt (ed.), *Die Teilung der Prager Universität 1882 und die intellektuelle Desintegration in den böhmischen Ländern*, and *Acta Universitatis Carolinae. Historia Universitatis Carolinae Pragensis* Vol. XXII (R. J. W. Evans)

Portsmouth Record Series. Records of University Adult Education 1886-1939. A Calendar compiled by Edwin Welch (Alon Kadish)

Geoffrey J. Giles, *Students and National Socialism in Germany* (Carl Landauer)

EDITOR'S NOTE

To be appointed editor of any journal is a great responsibility. To be appointed editor of *History of Universities* in the wake of such an outstanding scholar as Charles Schmitt is also a great honour. Here is not the place to dwell on Charles' vast contribution to the history of ideas in general and the history of universities in particular. A fitting tribute in the form of an obituary notice by Nancy Siraisi appears in this volume. Suffice it to say that Charles belonged to that small group of historians who since the war have turned university history into a respectable discipline by transforming what was often little more than hagiography into a vital branch of the history of ideas. As a university historian, Charles will not just be remembered as the founding father and first editor of this journal. More importantly, he will be remembered as a pioneer in the field who helped to create a need for *History of Universities*.

The appointment of a new editor will not lead to any dramatic alteration in the format of the journal. *History of Universities* will continue as before to comprise a number of articles on different aspects of university history before 1945 and a series of reviews of recent publications concerning the discipline. Potential contributors need not fear that preference will be given to one kind of university history over another. Articles on either the political, social or intellectual history of institutions of higher education are all equally welcome. The cultural role of the university cannot be separated from its pattern of recruitment and relationship with the state.

Nevertheless, the present character of the journal will be modified to a certain extent. In the first place, it is intended that greater weight will be given to work being done post-1800 than has hitherto been the case. In the volumes of the journal published so far, there has been a definite bias towards the Medieval and Renaissance periods. This was not what was originally anticipated by the editorial board, but simply arose from the imbalance in contributions received. This may partly reflect the fact that Charles was primarily a Renaissance historian and his work less well-known among modernists. More probably, it reflects the existence of other less specialised journals (in history, education and sociology), which already offered an outlet for the publication of studies of the nineteenth- and twentieth-century university. A journal, however, that calls itself *History of Universities* must seek to cover the modern as well as earlier periods. A major attempt will be made in future issues, therefore, to extend the present parameters. A start will be made in volume VII. In March of this year I organised a conference at Magdalen College, Oxford, on the theme 'The University in an Age of Revolution 1760-1830'. The next issue will largely be given over to the publication of the papers which were presented at this occasion.

This leads me on to the second change. In order to include as many conference papers as possible, it will be necessary to extend the length of the journal considerably. *History of Universities* will remain an annual but from Volume VII it will be nearly twice as long. This will mean increasing the subscription, but it is felt that a more substantial volume will be greater value for money. Once *History of Universities* is enlarged it will be possible to publish the transactions of other conferences on different aspects of university history, too. At present the editorial board is thinking of organising regular conferences, where scholars (especially young researchers) from different disciplinary backgrounds can meet together to discuss their current work. The journal can promote scholarship by helping to cement social contacts, not just by acting as a forum for publication. University historians need to know the work which is in progress not just the work which has been completed. Indeed, a casual conference conversation often reveals the existence of a research programme of paramount importance to one's own work. A book review, of course, can do the same, but frequently the knowledge comes too late, or at the wrong moment for it to be beneficial.

This is not to deny the utility of the book review. Indeed, the majority of the readers of *History of Universities* almost certainly consult the journal primarily for information about recently published works of interest. In this area, the journal from the beginning has performed creditably, providing reviews of books concerning all aspects and periods of university history. If there has been a problem, it has lain in the failure of continental publishers in particular to send the editor pertinent works to review. Too many doctoral thesis publications on the continent have passed unnoticed. It is hoped, however, that this deficiency, too, will be steadily remedied now that the journal has a genuinely international editorial board and now that it is well established. To offset this difficulty, moreover, it has been decided to publish each year an essay review on the state of university studies in different countries of Europe, beginning in Volume VII with an account of the situation in the Netherlands and Belgium.

Another important innovation will be the replacement of our list of publications received by a full bibliography of work in the field. At the suggestion of Dr John Fletcher, the journal will from Volume VII onwards include the bibliographical section of *The History of European Universities. Work in Progress and Publications*, edited by him and to date published in Birmingham for the International Commission for the History of Universities. Dr Fletcher has kindly agreed to continue as editor of this extremely useful compilation, and entries for it should be sent directly to him at The Department of Modern Languages, University of Aston, Birmingham B4 7ET.

Most of these innovations, it must be said, would have been introduced had Charles lived. Nearly all had been discussed and accepted at the last editorial meeting he chaired. Continuity rather than change, therefore, is the watchword. The publisher of the journal, too, will remain unchanged. The contract with Oxford University Press ensures *History of Universities* a sound future and should attract an even greater number of quality contributors.

In conclusion, a word must be said about the assistant editorship.

Since the journal was founded this role has been manfully filled by Peter Denley. At the expense of his own research, he kindly agreed to see Volume V through the press and edit the whole of Volume VI himself. This has left me free to organise the Magdalen Conference and ensured that my assumption of the editorship will be less traumatic than it would otherwise have been. Peter's contribution to the development and survival of the journal can never be too warmly praised. He should really be described at the second editor of *History of Universities* and I the third. Understandably, he has now resigned the post of assistant editor to get on with his own work on Renaissance Italian universities. I would like to take this opportunity to thank him for his efforts. The assistant editorship is at present vacant but will be filled before the publication of Volume VII.

Laurence Brockliss
Magdalen College
Oxford

Charles B. Schmitt, 1933-86

Charles B. Schmitt, editor and founder of *History of Universities*, died suddenly and unexpectedly in Padua in April, 1986.

Schmitt was born and received his early education in Louisville, Kentucky. After taking a first degree in chemical engineering, he briefly practised that profession. His entry into the field of Renaissance studies came with graduate study at Columbia University, where his mentor was Paul Oskar Kristeller and where he obtained his Ph.D. in philosophy in 1963. After periods spent at Fordham University, the University of California at Los Angeles, and Leeds University, he accepted in 1973 an appointment at the Warburg Institute, London University, where he remained until his death. At the time of his death he was engaged in giving a series of lectures at the University of Padua. The esteem in which he was held by Italian scholarly colleagues was manifested in funeral ceremonies sponsored by the University of Padua and the Istituto di Storia di Filosofia, Padua.

Few scholarly careers of such relative brevity can have been as productive as that of Charles Schmitt. He was the author of a stream of books, articles, and reviews on aspects of the history of philosophy, science, and scholarship during the Renaissance. His knowledge of the learned literature of the period was truly encyclopedic; and his interests encompassed numerous scientific and philosophical subjects, ranging from the revival of skepticism, the topic of his *Cicero Scepticus. A Study of the Influence of the Academica in the Renaissance* (The Hague, 1972), to the varieties of continuity and change in Renaissance Aristotelianisms (to use his own term).[1]

The importance of his contribution to the study of Renaissance Aristotelianism can scarcely be overestimated. Although his massive treatment of Aristotle for the *Catalogus translationum et commentariorum* was unfinished at the time of his death,[2] he had already published both much bibliographic information, the fruit of diligent researches in numerous European libraries, and penetrating analyses of the role of Aristotelianism in Renaissance intellectual life; his views were summed up, and the evidence for them marshalled with graceful cogency in his *Aristotle and the Renaissance* (Cambridge, 1983), which is likely to remain the classic treatment of the theme.

Schmitt emphasised the importance of the connections between areas of study often treated as separate fields: connections across the chronological span 1350-1650; connections between history of philosophy and history of science; and connections among the intellectual milieux of different regions and institutions of Renaissance Europe. As editor of the forthcoming *Cambridge History of Renaissance Philosophy*, he wrote that he envisaged the scope of the volume as 'a broadly based introduction to the intellectual world of the Renaissance'.[3] Furthermore, he was personally very active in fostering both institutional and individual efforts to improve communication between scholars working on different aspects of the history of European learning between the fourteenth and the seventeenth centuries. His frequent visits to Italy, Germany, and France to engage in research and to attend conferences served him as opportunities to multiply contacts between the continental European and Anglo-American scholarly communities. The seriousness with which he took the task of writing book reviews made his prolific output in this genre a valuable guide to modern historical writing on the subjects of his interest. And to a wide circle of scholarly colleagues, students, and friends he was an unfailing source of useful information, sound advice, and generous help.

Throughout Schmitt's work, insistence on the importance for Renaissance culture and intellectual life of the university milieu ran as a linking thread. In an appreciation for this journal, the fruit of his interest in university history, it seems appropriate to focus on this aspect of his scholarship. Some of the papers in the volumes of his collected articles that appeared in 1981 and 1984[4] suggest the scope and themes of his approach to the subject.

In the first place, Schmitt's interest in universities was as centres of intellectual activity. He gave full weight to the influence of social, religious, and political factors on that activity, but he was not personally drawn to the study of the social or administrative history of academic institutions. In terms of intellectual history, however, his approach was fully contextual: he believed that understanding of the intellectual life of any one university in any one generation demanded attentive consideration of the interests, activities, and writings of the teaching faculty, an approach exemplified in his careful studies of 'The Faculty of Arts at Pisa at the Time of Galileo' (1972) and of Paduan medical teaching in the 1490s in 'Thomas Linacre and Italy', (1977).[5] Most recently, he had begun to publish the results of research into the history of the development of philosophy textbooks, works that he showed to be a rich source of information about the cultural formation provided in early modern religious and secular institutions of higher education.

Secondly, he sought to draw attention to the continuing interaction of philosophy and science in the Renaissance university milieu, and to the desirability of a re-evaluation of the wholly negative role often ascribed to universities in regard to the Scientific Revolution. Schmitt emphasized the need to distinguish between different areas of knowledge in weighing the university contribution. For example, writing in 1972 on 'Science in the Italian Universities in the Sixteenth and Early Seventeenth Centuries', he remarked that during the early modern period, 'Unlike the physical sciences, the bio-medical ones advanced nearly wholly within a university context'.[6] His resulting interest in the university faculties of medicine led him to write a number of valuable articles on the intellectual setting of Renaissance and early modern medicine.

Thirdly, and perhaps most importantly, Schmitt advocated a broad and comparative approach to the history of European universities. Like all historians of the subject he had the greatest respect for the collections of documents and narrative histories published over the last two centuries by historians of individual universities, works many of which remain fundamental to the study of university history. Nonetheless, he looked forward to contributions to the history of universities that would not be confined to a single institution, nor even to the universities of a particular geographical region, political unit, vernacular culture or religious confession. As he wrote in 1975: 'The task before us now is to attempt a comparative study of early modern university history without losing sight of individual and local characteristics'.[7]

Given Schmitt's equal insistence on the need for detailed study of the philosophical, scientific, and didactic output of particular intellectual communities, the task he set is no easy one. It is, indeed, work for many hands; and in founding *History of Universities* Schmitt sought to foster and provide a forum for scholarly interest in the role of universities in the history of European learning, science, and culture. His commitment to the importance of the subject may be measured by the energy and enthusiasm that he devoted to establishing and running the journal. At the time of his death he was planning further substantial work of his own on the comparative history of medieval and Renaissance Italian universities.[8]

The loss of Charles Schmitt will be very widely felt in the scholarly community, as various memorial meetings already testify. A memorial lecture by Quentin Skinner was sponsored by the Warburg Institute in June, 1986. A colloquium on 'Aristotelianism 1500-1700' at the Herzog August Bibliothek, Wolfenbüttel, in October, 1986, originally arranged by Charles Schmitt, was held as a memorial to him under the direction of Charles Lohr, Eckhard Kessler, and Walter Sparn. Also in October, 1986, a panel on 'Renaissance Philosophy and Science', organized by Katharine Park at the annual meeting of the History of Science Society (of the United States), held at Pittsburgh, was dedicated to Charles Schmitt's memory. A two-day memorial colloquium organized by Sarah Hutton and John Henry with the help of Constance Blackwell was held at the Warburg Institute in February, 1987. The importance attached by colleagues and friends to Charles Schmitt's scholarly projects is attested by the arrangements that have been made for their completion, some of which are mentioned in the notes to this essay. Others, besides those named and those involved in *History of Universities*, who have been active in the endeavour to secure the continuance or completion of his work include J. B. Trapp, F. Edward Cranz, Constance Blackwell, and Richard Popkin.

Schmitt viewed the superficial or the merely fashionable in historical writing with ironic humor. He himself allied great erudition and a single-minded dedication to fundamental scholarship with a marked originality and independence of mind. The influence of his ideas, work, and personality upon a generation of historians of Renaissance philosophy and science is still growing. The present writer is only one of very many who benefited from his encouragement and friendship. The loss of both the man and the scholar is deeply regretted.

Nancy Siraisi
Department of History
Hunter College and the Graduate School
City University of New York

REFERENCES

1. *Aristotle and the Renaissance* (Cambridge, 1983), pp. 1033.

2. It is being brought to completion under the supervision of Charles Lohr.

3. Draft introduction, supplied by Constance Blackwell. Final editing of the volume has been undertaken by Quentin Skinner and Jill Kraye.

4. *Studies in Renaissance Philosophy and Science* (London, 1981); *The Aristotelian Tradition and Renaissance Universities* (London, 1984).

5. *Studies in Renaissance Philosophy and Science*, IX; *Aristotelian Tradition and Renaissance Universities*, XII.

6. Ibid., XIV, 39.

7. 'Philosophy and Science in Sixteenth Century Universities: some Preliminary Comments', *Studies in Renaissance Philosophy and Science*, V, 487.

8. The project was one on which Paul Oskar Kristeller had first invited him to collaborate and subsequently placed in his hands (the present author was to have contributed sections on medieval university origins and the medical faculties).

JOHN OF SALISBURY AND EDUCATION IN TWELFTH CENTURY PARIS FROM THE ACCOUNT OF HIS *METALOGICON* *

K. S. B. Keats-Rohan

John of Salisbury himself needs no introduction: born between 1115-20, and dying as Bishop of Chartres in 1180, this 'friend and familiar of many of the leading personages of his age', including his one-time employer Archbishop Becket, has long been one of scholarship's favourite humanists and men of letters, whose literary Latin is a model, even for the enlightened age of the Twelfth Century Renaissance. Nor perhaps does his somewhat neglected work, the *Metalogicon*, need an introduction, since, containing as it does John's account of his own education in twelfth-century Paris, it has for long been scrutinised by historians of education anxious to chart the history of this proto-university age. But John was not writing a history of education, or even writing with posterity in mind, when he composed his work, for his primary aim was to write a critique of the educational framework he had experienced, and to sound a strong note of caution to his contemporaries. It is this critique, as well as his examination of Aristotle's logic which was itself quickly superseded by the advent of new, and other, translations of the Aristotelian corpus, that rapidly dated the *Metalogicon*, and accounts for its having been little read in the Middle Ages. This is not to say that it was not read at all, but the fact nonetheless remains that I know at present of only six manuscript copies of the *Metalogicon*,[1] of which two are unreliable secondary copies; nor did it make its first appearance in print until 1610, while by contrast John's other great work, the very popular *Policraticus*, is extant in manifold copies, and was first printed around 1475.

In recent years scholars have attempted to redress the balance by which the *Metalogicon* was plundered of the historiographical information it contains, while its context was comparatively neglected, by reappraising the content of the work in its entirety. Dr. B. P. Hendley has pointed out the theory of knowledge which is expounded in the *Metalogicon*,[2] for instance, and I shall take this theory as my starting point, for I shall be hoping to show how John's critique of contemporary education and his concomitant warning to educationalists is woven into the fabric of this theory, although to attempt so vast a survey here will necessarily mean the omission of some details, and consequent superficiality. This theory and this critique must then be utilised in the interpretation of John's autobiographical chapter 10 in Book II, which has occasioned so many debates among modern scholars, and in presenting my own interpretation of this chapter I shall be obliged to refer again to the 'school of Chartres' debate, and to hope that this will not add to the tedium of so unwieldy an enterprise as I now propose.

The *Metalogicon* is a defence of logic on John's own testimony,[3] but a defence of the entire *triuium* underlies it and forms John's starting point. The defence of the *triuium* consists in elaborating the search for wisdom, the legitimate end of every inquiry, and its culmination, by grace, in the understanding of the divine, that is, true *sapientia* as distinct from *scientia*,[4] the worldly knowledge of natural philosophy; since the entire quest for wisdom utilises the speech or written words by which man is distinguished from the beasts, the verbals arts of the *triuium* are essential to success. Indeed, they are the foundations of the civilisation made possible when the social contract has been formed verbally. To neglect them is to imperil not merely civilised values but the whole of civilisation itself.[5] Grammar is the beginning of all philosophy; eloquence is both its accomplishment and its acutest tool, and the end of philosophy is wisdom. Wisdom in part arises from the world of sense, and to interpret sense-perception in order to arrive at the understanding of the truth, or the divine, by harnessing reason to speech, the search for wisdom utilises logic and dialectic, in order by reasoning to distinguish the true from the false. Probable logic most helpfully achieves this distinction since it neither asserts (demonstration) nor deceives (sophistry). It is itself comprised of dialectic and rhetoric, the one the art of fine persuasive speech, while the other, at its best, impartially assesses the truth of two propositions 'in a ready and tempered balance of probability'.[6] 'Grammar primarily examines the words used to express thoughts, dialectic the thoughts expressed in words'.[7] Eloquence, the product of grammar and trained natural ability (whether great or small), mediates between the man who is trained to use words in the reasoned pursuit of philosophy, or wisdom, and his attainment of his goal, the knowledge of the divine, the true wisdom, by his manipulation of the rational techniques of logic and dialectic, since it endows him with the ability the most aptly to express his mental perceptions. The goal of *sapientia* is attained only when the forces of the entire *triuium* have been marshalled in its pursuit, so that grammar is the cradle of all philosophy[8] which trains our faculties of sight and hearing when it imparts the fundamentals of language.[9] This nurse itself should be nurtured by a wide reading of the Latin *auctores* who not only impart good style and eloquence by example, but also, if one carefully examines the works of Vergil or Lucan, 'no matter what your philosophy, you will find therein its seed or seasoning', as John says in I.24.[10] This remark, itself a part of John's humanist manifesto, is preceded by another which not merely refers to John's humanist beliefs but summarises his whole practice as a man and a thinker, and that is: 'Of all branches of learning that which confers the greatest beauty is Ethics, the most excellent part of philosophy, without which the latter would not even deserve its name'.[11] John's thought has a very marked ethical bias, and one which is firmly directed to the world of practical affairs wherein it must pursue its search for the higher truths of revelation and earn the merit of grace which alone can ultimately fructify it. He is, therefore, impatient of the demonstration of the self-evident[12] as he is equally impatient of the apodictic assertion of truth for one of two propositions, the truth of neither of which is evident.[13] John prefers, as a pragmatist and a moralist the thesis-antithesis-synthesis approach to a two-sided problem by which a balance of probable truth is preserved, rather than that one proposition, possibly having a valid claim to share in the truth, should perforce be argued to — sophistical — oblivion.[14] This explains both John's preference for probable logic as opposed to demonstration, and his definition of true dialectic as that which weighs the truth in a balance of probability. It explains also his solution to the problem of universals, and his impatience with some of its manifestations in contemporary scholastic debate. His mistaken belief that Nominalism was but a passing fancy of some schoolmen,[15] whereas in fact it went on to a distinguished career in the University of Paris, for instance, also reflects John's preference for the Realists' use of logic when approaching the mysteries of faith to the Nominalist attitude that the use of logic is permissible, indeed desirable, in every inquiry, which he anyway condemned as lacking in balance. Strongly influenced as he was by Aristotelian syncretism, John held that universals could be viewed as fictions (whereby material things are the only substances) or as substantial truths (whereby material things become mere accidents), but that to distinguish between them is unnecessary since we usually take universal forms together with material objects as useful or true fictions or ideas.[16] Indeed, to separate their functions and assert only one to be true in isolation is not merely to controvert

Aristotle, but also to deny the cognitive processes of sense-perception and imagination, tempered by reason, whereby scientific knowledge — *scientia* — evolving from these earlier opinions and itself the first landmark on the journey towards *sapientia*, is both acquired and assimilated.[17] This nascent *scientia* is brought forth when its memory of the forms and outward qualities of things is turned into the perception of their true nature, and this is achieved by reading (*lectio*), learning (*doctrina*), meditation (*meditatio*), and assiduous application (*assiduitas operis*):[18] of these reading may refer to the activity of teaching and being taught, or to the occupation of studying written things by oneself.[19] Since the whole of knowledge is communicated by the spoken or written word, the man who neglects grammar is hampered in his search for wisdom as one who is blind or deaf,[20] and if he should have wisdom but has neglected to strive for the felicitous self-expression conferred by eloquence, his wisdom will be likewise feeble and maimed.[21] Eloquence is more than a natural facility, since assiduous reading of the *auctores* can confer this accomplishment on even those of limited natural ability if only they possess diligence,[22] and this attractive relative of prudence or truth[23] most aptly suits those who seek to discover or expound philosophical truth since they must perforce use words, and their success will be the greater in proportion to their verbal facility and to their knowledge.[24] But eloquence is undirected and misdirected if it is ignorant of the techniques of reasoning inculcated by logic and dialectic which distinguish between truth and falsehood in that desideratum, the balance of probability. Indeed, eloquence is harmful when it departs from wisdom,[25] just as wisdom is enfeebled or mute without eloquence, but the eloquent man who attains wisdom through the proper exercise of balanced rational inquiry attracts to himself the blessings of both temporal and spiritual rewards.[26]

Most of John's *Metalogicon* deals, as I have said, with Aristotelian logic in what is an able exposition of Aristotle's position, but the substance of its importance for John remains as I have described it, as the reasoning technique which seeks with controlled and economical impartiality to distinguish the truth about the world of sensible reality, and to discover the medial probable truth of two apparently contradictory propositions concerning this reality. It is clear from this pursuit of the Golden Mean, so to speak, that the underlying theme of John's critique of twelfth-century education will be a castigation and rejection of all forms of excess, or nimiety. Indeed, John's purpose in composing the *Metalogicon* — which was not at all to fuel the debates of the twentieth-century historians — was to undertake the defence of the *triuium*, grammar, rhetoric, and dialectic, which for John were at once the representatives of the totality of civilised values and the guardians of the storehouse of truth. Any nimiety in the exposition of these verbal arts imperils the delicate preservation of the truth about sensible reality enshrined in both the civilised complex of post-contract human society and in nature, and further imperils the equally delicate balance of equity in the political organism which directs civilised society. Faith and morals are merely the first victims of either the deprivation or the depredation of the gift of speech which distinguishes man from brute creation.[27] In this respect nimiety subsumes that part of excess which is guilty of expending an excessive parvitude, or too little, of its attention on that which is important, as is true of those who neglect the essential study of grammar in their haste for specious progress.[28] 'He is a public enemy who tries to thrust asunder the fruitful union of reason and speech which God ordained for the common good'[29] either by an excess of verbiage or by that paucity of words which fails adequately to communicate, since these produce the nonsense by which the lying sophist perverts the commonwealth of men. If one remembers that wisdom is derived in part from sense-perception rationalised by dialectical reasoning and most aptly communicated by the previously acquired skill of eloquence, thus utilising all the verbal arts in a world of speech, one can see that if the sequence grammar-eloquence-wisdom is neglected in any of its parts then this will, in John's view, threaten the very fabric of human society and hence civilisation: to degrade language by verbal sophistry or quibbling, or opacity, or pretentiousness of other kinds, leads to the same result; to pervert logic by rational sophistry or verbal sophistry, degrades wisdom and so attacks eloquence or good speech, and leads to the same result; arrogance, and the false philosophy which seeks to seem better than it is, perverts eloquence and prostitutes wisdom, and so virtue, to falsehood, and leads to the same result; materialism and utilitarianism prostitute wisdom and so degrade all the verbal arts, and are thus the selfsame threat to civilisation. For John the castigation of nimiety which pervades his book, and his likewise pervasive plea for moderation in the dialecticians' assessment of truth, are concordant aspects of his concern for the preservation of both *scientia* and *sapientia*. Their content as the preservers of truth is obviously ethical, as is self-evidently the castigation of an increasing utilitarianism in contemporary education. The wise man is also the virtuous man if he has earned grace. Since the man seeking virtue is aware of the brotherhood of men and because he has been taught to turn the other cheek,[30] this man must direct his conservative and anti-revolutionary critique against either a pseudonymous rival, or a personification of his vices, and thus John created his Cornificius, and his school the Cornificians, named after the cawing detractor of Vergil,[31] who were, amongst other things, guilty of 'carnal excesses that would shame an Epicurean pig'.[32]

Part of this utilitarian's utility for John is that he can mercilessly excoriate this masquerader and so temper his criticisms of his own masters who appear in John's pages under their own names. Part of Cornificius's utility for us is that he and his followers attacked some of John's own masters and mentors, or their students, personally, such as Abelard, William of Conches, and Hugh of St. Victor,[33] as well as attacking the liberal studies which alone preserve civilised values, and this is itself partly responsible for the biographical and autobiographical interludes in the *Metalogicon* in which modern scholars are so interested. But the more important occasion of the autobiographical interlude in *Met*. II. 10 is that it furnishes John with the opportunity to relate a cautionary tale, and that tale concerns how he himself had nearly fallen victim to the snares of the nimiety he so strongly opposes. It was in particular the false brilliance of some contemporary dialectic by which he was so nearly undone: only a thorough (remedial) grounding in grammar and rhetoric, the correct use of language, could reveal the specious errors of the sophists, and of those dialecticians who demonstrated the truth of their favoured contention by totally refuting that of their opponents, but which antithesis had for John a legitimate claim to share in the truth, or the understanding of truth, so that its refutation was itself in part sophistical. Another of the many aspects of this speciousness and this nimiety, was the tendency, noticed also by Hugh of St. Victor,[34] for lecturers to read the whole of philosophy into an incipit and thus either to acquire a false veneer of learning, or anyway by such excess of knowledge to confuse and so impede the progress of the student. The latter was hindered additionally by not merely those masters such as Cornificius whose nonsensical speech was like a windy bellows buffeting the air,[35] but those masters also who sought to cloak their meaning in verbal obscurity, like Adam du Petit Pont, who may thereby have given the desired impression of great learning[36] but could not in John's view have imparted much learning to their students who benefitted best from simplicity.[37] John's impatience with the debate concerning universals probably stemmed from his own unhappy experience of contemporary dialectic, but it is interesting to note in this respect that it is Abelard who, despite one sharp rebuke in *Met*. II. 17[38] receives the largest single number of favourable mentions in the *Metalogicon*, concerning those masters of

John himself.[39] Nor should the impression be given that John is without praise for contemporary masters, or that he is merely worried by the trends in contemporary education as a whole. R. W. Southern has pointed out that the unobtrusive hero of the *Metalogicon* is the able and temperate schoolmaster Bernard of Chartres[40] whom John could not have known personally since he died before John reached France, but whose teaching, as he understood it from his own masters, he took to be inspired. John gives a full description of Bernard's exacting methods in *Met.* I. 24[41] where the thorough, disciplined, moderate, but above all humane and fruitful education of Bernard's young charges is described. A boy trained in Latin by Bernard's methods should have had little to fear from a failure to recognise sophistry, but above all his love of humane learning would have been awakened and nourished both by reading and imitation. In this connexion John is eventually led in *Met.* III. 4 to make the optimistic observation about human reason which we might expect from a twelfth-century scholar: 'Our own generation enjoys the legacy bequeathed to it by that which preceded it. We frequently know more, not because we have moved ahead by our own natural ability, but because we are supported by the strength of others, and possess riches that we have inherited from our forefathers. Bernard of Chartres used to compare us to dwarfs perched on the shoulders of giants. He pointed out that we see more and farther than our predecessors, not because we have keener vision or greater height, but because we are lifted up and borne aloft by their gigantic stature'.[42] The balance of this optimistic chapter against the perhaps prevailing pessimism of Book I, for example, is also seen in the alternately laudatory and critical references made to John's own masters, as well as to Bernard himself. Bernard, in fact, is criticised for attempting to reconcile Plato and Aristotle, who failed to agree in their own lifetimes.[43] Perhaps John is afraid that to harmonise these irreconcilable philosophers would be to obliterate the fundamental concord between them, but it more importantly demonstrates that John's common-sense did not permit his judgement to be clouded by his admiration — neither does his friendship with Adam du Petit Pont blind him to Adam's vice of verbal opacity.[44]

Having said all of which, and remembering that we are in the middle of both a critique of contemporary education and an exposition of the possible remedies, we come now to the cautionary tale of *Met.* II. 10. John's account of his own schooling, equivalent to our tertiary education, in that fluid situation in the mid-Twelfth Century, which prefigured, if it was not the prototype of, the thirteenth-century University of Paris, is the personal account of a very distinguished twelfth-century humanist, and as such *Met*. II. 10 has naturally and inevitably attracted a great deal of attention from historians of education and the Twelfth Century.[45] The information it contains from the pen of so distinguished a witness is obviously of the first importance to historians, who are also justifiably dismayed by the information it neglects to give us. But such as it is, it has engendered a fair amount of debate about such details as it does contain, and about which there is little agreement among modern scholars. Perhaps this is itself a cautionary tale. Much of the debate has centred upon the issue of the so-called 'School of Chartres', whose existence was seriously questioned first in 1965 by R. W. Southern.[46] In fact Southern sought to demolish the school of Chartres, largely successfully, but we must concern ourselves again with this issue because Southern described John of Salisbury as one of the (unlikely) corner-stones of this 'school', along with Bernard of Chartres, Thierry of Chartres, Gilbert de la Porrée, and William of Conches,[47] although I do not propose to rehearse the Chartres debate — which is well-known to have caused strong feeling — in any detail, and shall merely allude to the issue when giving details concerning the four masters to whom I have just referred. Since I cannot provide this debate with an epiphonema of my own, I shall instead cite the happy example of Charles Schmitt's compendious and genial dismissal of the idea that the School of Padua was preeminent among the schools of the Veneto, when he said: 'All things considered, however, there was much more similarity among Italian universities than is evident in much which has been written about the uniqueness of Padua. This is not a failure to recognise the genuine brilliance of Padua from any of a number of different perspectives, but merely an attempt to bring a balance back into the discussion. Padua was a *primus* or at least a *secundus inter pares* from the fourteenth century onward. It was not, however, unique',[48] for since to be a second among equals is to be nowhere at all, the case against Paduan preeminence was closed thereby — at the start of his paper — in a rich and economical vein of humour such as has not been granted to the case for and against Chartres.

The association of John of Salisbury with Chartres was never more than circumstantial, to say the least, and it arose in the first place from the observation made in 1843 by Christian Petersen, the editor of John's *Entheticus*, that since John uses the word 'reuersus', meaning 'I returned', in the course of his account, he must previously have left Mont-Sainte-Geneviève in Paris where he tells us that he spent at least two years from 1136-8 at the start of his studies (and his chapter) and must in consequence be found a home for the period in question,[49] that is, from 1138-41, for which Chartres became a popular, if, in Southern's view, unevidenced candidate. It has since been learned that John could never have known Bernard of Chartres, who seems to have retired from the chancellorship of Chartres after 1124, and to have died before 1130, that is, six years before John's arrival in Paris.[50] Moreover, the evidence of John's *Met.* I. 24 demonstrates that Bernard was an extremely able grammar-school master, and not the head of a school such as Abelard and Thierry presided over, and whose services John would presumably therefore not have needed.[51] This is not to deny that Bernard formed his pupils in the liberal arts to the highest and most exacting standards which enabled them eventually to become masters in advanced studies of the highest calibre, such as Gilbert de la Porrée, who is known to have been his pupil, and William of Conches, whom John's text suggests to have been another of his pupils. There is nothing to associate William of Conches with Chartres after his grammar-school training (if that is indeed where he received it), but that Gilbert de la Porrée was chancellor of Chartres from at least 1126-37 is evidenced by contemporary charters of Chartres Cathedral. That Gilbert was in Paris in 1141 is the evidence of John's text, but where he was at other intervals in this period is a matter for conjecture, except to say that his presence in Chartres is not recorded after 1137. John's remark in *Met.* I. 5[52] that 'when he was chancellor of Chartres Gilbert was wont to say ... ' together with the words 'repperi magistrum Gilebertum'[53] — I sought out master Gilbert — with reference, as I understand it, to 1141, have been taken to mean that John must have met Gilbert in Chartres in the period 1138-41, particularly if one unnecessarily takes *repperi* to mean 'I found again'. Even if the initial period of John's studies in Paris were contracted to overlap with the last recorded period of Gilbert's presence in Chartres as chancellor, in 1137, in contradiction of what John himself says, we should have still to reconcile the remainder of John's text with this dubious and tenuous link to Chartres. Master Bernard was wont to say that which John could not have heard, and indeed the future Bishop of Poitiers could well have borrowed his former plumage to make his wonted remarks to John, if he had indeed surrendered his chancellorship at that date, which is not at all certain.[54] We do know, however, that Gilbert became bishop of Poitiers in 1142, and died in 1154.[55]

Thierry, who seems to have died after 1150, became chancellor of Chartres in 1142, a fact which John of Salisbury ignores in the *Metalogicon* by nowhere giving him the appellation *Carnotensis*, and this brings me to an observation I am uncertain how to elucidate, and that concerns the distinct ambiguity of John's references to one who

was another of the most celebrated masters of his time.[56] In the
context of his praise of contemporary masters who fell victim to the
malice of the Cornificians, in *Met*. I. 5, John names in the same
sentence as 'amatores litterarum' Thierry, William of Conches, and
Abelard. Where William is 'gramaticus post Bernardum
Carnotensem opulentissimus', and Abelard is one 'qui logice
preripuit omnibus coetaneis suis', Thierry is 'artium studiosissimus
inuestigator', an observation which in the context is bland to the
point of irony.[57] Nor does John describe Thierry as the brother of
Bernard of Chartres, as he is popularly supposed to have been,
although they both appear in the sentence just cited, and although a
few lines later he refers to Anselm and Ralph of Laon as 'fratres
theologos',[58] and in the only other reference to both Anselm and
Ralph in his work that I know of, in the *Historia Pontificalis*,[59] he
again refers to them as brothers. Thierry is known to have taught in
Paris from the evidence of his disciple Clarembald, also a pupil of
Hugh of St. Victor, and William of Tyre, who recalls that in around
1145 Peter Helias, Bernard Brito, and Ivo of Chartres, had for long
been pupils of Thierry,[60] but he is not known to have been in Chartres
before the 1140s. Gilbert de la Porrée, on the other hand, is known to
have been in Chartres, and to have held a class of four there. Otto of
Freising provides us with our information concerning Gilbert's
education in his *Gesta Friderici* where he says: 'Iste enim ab
adolescentia magnorum uirorum discipline se subiciens magisque
illorum ponderi quam suo credens ingenio, qualis primo fuit Hylarius
Pictauiensis, post Bernhardus Carnotensis, ad ultimum Anselmus et
Radulfus Laudunenses, germani fratres, non leuem ab eis sed grauem
doctrinam hauserat',[61] that is, Gilbert submitted the forming of his
judgement to the teaching of great men, first Bernard of Chartres and
Hilary of Poitiers, then to the 'brother theologians' Anselm and
Ralph of Laon, from whom he heard matters of weight. However one
views the phrase 'non leuem ab eis', and I take it on the evidence of
Met. I. 24[62] more accurately to refer to Anselm and Ralph only, this
is clear evidence that Gilbert received his first training from Bernard
of Chartres. Our next witness is Everard of Ypres in his *Dialogus Ratii
et Everardi* where he says of Gilbert: 'Ad quem audiendum mater
mea, cuius nomen Ratio Atheniensis, consilio Sophiae, meae sororis,
me in Franciam misit. Cui Carnoti quartus in lectionem, Parisius in
aula episcopi fere tercentesimus assedi. Et ipsi episcopo Pictauis
adhaesi usque ad ipsius obitum, qui me docente Graecam nouerat
linguam, ego quoque ipso Latinam',[63] that he was fourth in a class
held by Gilbert in Chartres, then the two hundred and ninety-ninth in
a class in Paris,[64] and that he continued as Gilbert's pupil until the

latter's death as bishop in Poitiers, during which time Gilbert had learned Greek from Everard,[65] just as Everard had learned Latin from Gilbert. Everard obviously derived a substantial part of his education from Gilbert, from the first things to the last. I cannot avoid the conclusion that at the time this eternal student heard Gilbert in Chartres he was learning from Gilbert in much the same way as Gilbert must have learned from Bernard of Chartres, for Everard implies that he had pursued his lengthy — and profound — study of Latin, the most elementary requirement of a mediaeval scholar, under Gilbert, just as he also seems, in a scholarly *quid pro quo*, to have taught Gilbert Greek, although I do agree with Dronke's dating of this episode to not much before 1126,[66], since Everard was still active in the 1190s, when he wrote the *Dialogus*.

There is no evidence associating William of Conches with Chartres in his adult career, but the remark, previously quoted, by John, that he was 'gramaticus post Bernardum Carnotensem opulent-issimus'[67] closely associates the two, and in *Met.* I. 24 John says: 'Ad huius magistri (sc. Bernard) formam preceptores mei in gramatica, Willelmus de Conchis et Ricardus, cognomento Episcopus, officio nunc archidiaconus Constantiensis, uita et conuersatione uir bonus, suos discipulos aliquandiu informauerunt',[68] which again links the two and strongly suggests that William received his grammar-schooling from Bernard. It also suggests that Richard did too. John goes on to describe how William and Richard were worsted in their attempt to teach grammar properly by the onslaught of an ignorant mob demanding to possess instant knowledge, and that they ceased in consequence to teach this discipline. In addition to this link between William and Richard, there is the evidence of John's second, and only other, laudatory reference to Richard in *Met.* II. 10,[69] and these taken together with the fact that Richard died as the respected and loved bishop of Avranches in 1182, as Robert of Torigny testifies,[70] prompt me to wonder whether Richard was not a fairly near contemporary of John himself, for whom the latter had a sincere affection as well as admiration, as an undated letter of his, written in exile, suggests.[71] John was Richard's pupil in 1141, when Richard might perhaps have been in his middle or late twenties, not too young to have been a master, nor so old as to have created any distance between himself and John. If this were so, and Robert of Torigny does not record that Richard died at any very venerable age, then it would make most sense to suppose that Richard had been a pupil of William of Conches, and had learned Bernard's method from him; although it is not of course impossible that Richard should have been a pupil of Bernard of Chartres before 1124, nonetheless there is no more evidence associating Richard's teaching career with Chartres after that date than there is for that of William of Conches.

From what has been said it is evident that I am not about to find John of Salisbury in Chartres as a student any more than I have found his masters to be there. I might even say that the quality of John's command of the Latin language has been overlooked in this debate, and that the result of my scrutiny of the text of *Met*. II. 10 has been the discovery of a perfectly logical and coherent account of twelve years spent by John as a student at the schools of Paris, and nowhere else. I am certain that Professor Southern did not mean to impugn the quality of John's language, or the coherence of his account, when he said in his essay 'Humanism and the School of Chartres', that 'John tells us something, though in a rather confused way, about the other masters with whom he apparently studied in the years from 1138-41',[72] but he correctly implied that John's account of his studies is inconsequential. Indeed, while it is not possible always to agree with Southern, it is surely possible not consistently to misunderstand or to misquote his admirably lucid essay, as has been the case not least in Häring's otherwise well-researched article,[73] and if this is indeed so, what must be the final catalogue of the misinterpretation of John's text itself? This being said, and mindful of it myself, I must repeat that John's autobiographical interlude is part of his purpose in examining and criticising aspects of twelfth-century education, and that it must be read primarily in this context in fairness to John's intentions, although we may nevertheless legitimately take it together with the historiographical subtext which most concerns us at present, for although it is not primarily autobiographical or topographical in its content, it can nonetheless be read as both.

John begins by saying: 'Cum primum adolescens admodum studiorum causa migrassem in Gallias, anno altero postquam illustris rex Anglorum Henricus, Leo iusticie',[74] that is, when a young man he went to France in order to study, in the year after the death of Henry I of England, 1136. He continues 'contuli me ad Peripateticum Palatinum qui tunc in monte sancte Genouefe clarus doctor et admirabilis omnibus presidebat',[75] that is, he went to Mont-Sainte-Geneviève where Abelard, the admiration of everyone, presided. He tells us that he received the rudiments of the art of dialectic (the subject of his previous chapter appears as *artis huius*) to the moderate capacity of his abilities at the feet of Abelard, who did, however, too hastily depart — 'ibi ad pedes eius prima artis huius rudimenta accepi et pro modulo ingenioli mei quicquid excidebat ab ore eius tota mentis auiditate excipiebam'.[76] Although in *Met* II. 17 Abelard is described as one ensnared by Nominalism and who tortures his students with it,[77] John's references to Abelard as a logician usually commend his clarity and good sense.[78] After Abelard departs, fairly soon afterwards, John hears master Alberic de Monte and master Robert of Melun,[79] which latter was, John explains, an Englishman by birth, who had acquired his reputation in his school at Melun, and who had previously been himself a pupil of Abelard. He died as bishop of Hereford in 1167, in which capacity he lost his claim to John's respect, to judge by the evidence of four of John's letters.[80] Of Alberic de Monte we are told that he was reputed to be the best of the other dialecticians, and that he vigorously opposed the Nominalists, and so, presumably, Abelard, and he is perhaps, as Häring has suggested,[81] to be identified with a chancellor of Ste. Geneviève of that date; William of Tyre was later a pupil also of both Alberic and Robert.[82] From these masters John hears more dialectic, but these are imperfect teachers. Alberic found so many subtle questions to ask in the course of his disputation that he would have found knots in need of untying in a very bulrush (ei cirpus non esset enodis . . .).[83] Robert, on the other hand, was most facile with his answers, and had at least the virtue of demonstrating that there was more than one reply to any given question (doceret unam non esse responsionem).[84] Of these two John asserts that were the qualities of Alberic and Robert to have been combined in one person their equal in disputation could not have been found; moreover, had either of them possessed a broad foundation in literary studies, or had followed in the footsteps of their predecessors as closely as they delighted in their own discoveries, then they would have been truly illustrious natural philosophers.[85] But while Robert went on to acquire a reputation as a theologian,[86] Alberic went to Bologna and unlearned what he had taught and then returned to unteach it, whether for the better his students before and after must judge (nam postea unus eorum, profectus Bononiam, dedidicit quod docuerat; siquidem et reuersus dedocuit. An melius, iudicent qui eum ante et postea audierunt)[87] — but notice that John is quite explicit concerning whence Alberic returned to unteach what he had unlearned. John twice says that he heard Alberic and Robert for two years on the Mont, 'sic ferme toto biennio conuersatus in monte'[88] and 'apud hos toto exercitatus biennio',[89] and since he heard Abelard only long enough to be impressed and not critical, we may assume that this takes the period of John's studies down to at least the end of 1137, and most probably to 1138.

At this point John realised that he had mistaken his familiarity with the rudiments of dialectic for the expertise of these acknowledged, if flawed, masters, and had erroneously believed himself to be quite a little scholar who could readily repeat what he had learned.[90] He had, he admits, become conceited: he had in fact been led astray by the false brilliance of contemporary dialectic. But he recovered his senses and took stock of his powers, at some unelaborated prompting, and decided to transfer his course, with the blessing of his preceptors, to the grammarian of Conches: 'Deinde reuersus in me, et metiens uires meas, bona preceptorum meorum gratia, consulto me ad gramaticum de Conchis transtuli',[91] for he had perceived the necessity of placing his dialectic on a surer foundation by means of a thorough grounding in grammar and rhetoric with a solid instructor, and so he remains a pupil of William of Conches for three years, 'ipsumque triennio docentem audiui'.[92]

John's transfer to William of Conches involved no stated significant removal, nor, I believe, is more than a localised removal implied. He then remarks: 'interim legi plura, nec me unquam penitebit temporis eius'[93] — 'Meanwhile I read many texts, nor will I ever regret the time thus spent'. To say simply that he read or studied many books might seem to be a somewhat redundant statement on the part of a serious scholar until we remind ourselves of the opening of *Met*. 1.24: 'The word reading is equivocal. It may refer either to the activity of teaching and being taught, or to the occupation of reading written things by oneself'.[94] However, John is here further reinforcing his main aim, that is to point out the pitfalls and potential sterility of dialectic, for which he himself had neglected those other arts, grammar and rhetoric, which alone can lay a sure foundation for dialectic. The false display of his own aptitudes as a pupil of the dialecticians, in neglect of these disciplines, had necessitated his transfer to the grammarian of Conches the more thoroughly to acquire them. For both a humanist of John's stature, and a scholar whose theory of knowledge emphasises the fundamental importance of the verbal arts, this was the most important aspect of his studies, as every page of his writings witnesses. John is then led naturally to state: 'Postmodum uero Ricardum cognomento episcopum, hominem fere nullius discipline expertem, et qui plus pectoris habet quam oris, plus scientie quam facundie, plus ueritatis quam uanitatis, uirtutis quam ostentationis, secutus sum; et que ab aliis audieram ab eo cuncta relegi, et inaudita quedam ad quadruuium pertinentia, in quo aliquatenus Teutonicum preaudieram Hardewinum. Relegi quoque rethoricam, quam prius cum quibusdam aliis a magistro Theodorico tenuiter auditis paululum intelligebam. Sed eam postea a Petro Helia plenius accepi'.[95] After John had completed his studies with William of Conches during 1138-41, he hears Richard L'Evêque, a man of wide learning and modest bearing (as Robert of Torigny will also describe him upon his death[96]) who takes him over ground previously covered by Hardewin the German, to whom John's is our only reference and about whom nothing is known, pertaining to the *quadriuium*; they also refresh together rhetoric which John had previously heard from Thierry of Chartres, among others, without, however, having understood very much, another of John's ambiguous references to this otherwise reputable master. These last two (i.e. Hardewin and Thierry) he must have heard between 1136 and 1141. Later still he goes over rhetoric again with Peter Helias — this is presumably after Richard's instruction in 1141 — and this time he learns more fully what Thierry had failed to teach him. Interestingly enough, as I have previously remarked, from the evidence of William of Tyre, another of his pupils, we know Peter Helias to have been a pupil of the very Thierry who had failed to impart rhetoric to John.[97] These lines, which take us from Richard L'Evêque to Peter Helias, form a digression the point of which is again to emphasise the importance of grammar and rhetoric in themselves, and, secondarily, as essential means to the right use of dialectic in debate.

Then John says: 'Et quia nobilium liberos qui michi, amicorum et cognatorum auxiliis destituto, paupertati mee solatiante Deo, alimenta prestabant, instruendos susceperam . . . '.[98] The phrase 'et quia' here is resumptive and takes us back to the period of John's studies with William of Conches in the triennium, that is, 1138-41. John was forced during that time by the circumstances of poverty and the dearth of friends able to assist, to earn his living — and pay for his own studies — by himself assuming the office of tutor to the scions of noble families. The word *officium*, with its onerous implication of duty rather than vocation, will be used again by John when he returns to the subject later. John continues: 'ex necessitate officii et instantia iuuenum urgebar quod audieram crebrius reuocare. Vnde ad magistrum Adam, acutissimi uirum ingenii et, quicquid alii sentiant, multarum litterarum, qui Aristotili pre ceteris incumbebat, familiaritatem contraxi ulteriorem; ut, licet eum doctorem non habuerim, michi sua benigne communicaret, et se, quod aut nulli faciebat aut paucis alienis, michi patentius exponebat. Putabatur enim inuidia laborare'.[99] Prompted by the insistent questions of his young pupils John was obliged frequently to recall to mind what he had previously learned, but perhaps because he himself needed answers to practical questions, or moral support, he contracted a close friendship with Adam du Petit Pont, an enthusiastic Aristotelian who was kind enough to explain his own doctrines to John, despite a reputation for jealously guarding his knowledge, although John was not a pupil of Adam, as he presumably could not afford to be.[100] Adam is probably no longer to be identified with a later bishop of St. Asaph of the same name, although John tells us elsewhere that he was the author of the *Ars disserendi* which John admires for its learning, but condemns for the verbal opacity in which it was written.[101] John reports Adam, in *Met*. III. 3,[102] as saying that were he to teach logic with the simplicity it deserved he would have few or no listeners, with the implication that Adam's obscurity was the result of consumer demand. He observes that Adam was a widely learned man, despite what his envious detractors say, and he is himself grateful to Adam for his kindness, despite the fact that he addled William of Soissons' brains, and controverted Aristotle, which John cannot approve of. For at this time, that is, during 1138-41, John did have one pupil to whom he taught the first principles of logic. William of Soissons is the only pupil John mentions by name, and the only one whom he appears to have taught more than preparatory exercises: his teaching of young nobles was obviously not at an exalted level itself, as is indicated by the use of *officium* to describe it. 'Interim Willelmum Suessionensem, qui ad expugnandam, ut aiunt sui, logice uetustatem et consequentias inopinabiles construendas et antiquorum sententias diruendas machinam postmodum fecit, prima logices docui elementa et tandem iam dicto preceptori apposui. Ibi forte didicit idem esse ex contradictione, cum Aristotiles obloquatur, quia idem cum sit et non sit, non necesse est idem esse, et item, cum aliquid sit, non necesse est idem esse et non esse. Nichil enim ex contradictione euenit et contradictionem impossibile est ex aliquo euenire. Vnde nec amici machina impellente urgeri potui ut credam ex uno impossibili omnia impossibilia prouenire'.[103] It must be borne in mind again at this point that John is attacking the barrenness of some kinds of dialectic throughout the *Metalogicon*, for we learn that William was a disappointment who afterwards devised a system of false logic, *machina*. John sent him on to Adam (one good turn deserves another — and the irony is implied by John himself) who seems not to have straightened William's thinking, but indeed to have encouraged his false logic. John observes gently that not even the (false) logical system devised by a friend could make him believe that all impossibilities originate from one impossibility. Perhaps John's pupil was that William of Soissons whom William of Tyre later found expounding Euclid in Bologna, and of whom he observes that he was 'impeditioris lingue uirum, sed acute mentis et ingenii subtilioris hominem'[104] — a man of rather unclear speech, but with a penetrating and quite subtle intelligence.

John's next sentence, 'Extraxerunt me hinc rei familiaris angustia, sociorum petitio, et consilium amicorum, ut officium docentis aggrederer. Parui. ',[105] is firstly a restatement of how he came to be teaching in the years from 1138 to 1141, but secondly, and more importantly, he is saying that he was 'rescued' from the endless and fruitless discussions of logical paradoxes which had resulted from his association with William, or anyway prevented from wasting any more time on William's form of idiocy, that is, fallacious reasoning, by the aforementioned straitened circumstances, and the advice of the friends and colleagues who were alarmed by his lack of practicality and urged him to begin to take his humbler teaching duties seriously and thereby pay attention to the practicalities of life, a lesson which obviously made a lasting impression on John, who saw the wisdom of this and complied (*parui*).[106] This 'parui' is a lapidary statement of 'Well, there you are; I was again in a mess because of dialectic, and I needed simple arguments of pressing needs to recall me to a sense of duty, to my young pupils and to myself'. I take the whole utterance from *extraxerunt me hinc* to *parui* to imply 'Look where dialectic can lead you!'. The restatement of how he came to teach in the first place gives John the chance further to reinforce his point about the potential fruitlessness of misdirected dialectic: William of Soissons was not the only victim — it had wasted John's own time, probably to his literal as well as to his metaphorical cost.

At last, 'Reuersus itaque in fine triennii repperi magistrum Gilebertum':[107] at the end of this difficult and demanding three years, during which he had been the pupil of William of Conches, a teacher himself, and also a colleague of Adam du Petit Pont, John then went to Gilbert de la Porrée. I would point out that in my reading of John's text he is a teacher, himself a student, and also a colleague of Adam du Petit Pont contemporaneously, and this must imply (or, if you prefer, must mean) that John heard William of Conches teach in the near vicinity of where Adam du Petit Pont was teaching, that is, presumably, by the Petit Pont in Paris. The use of *consulto me* and *transtuli*, referring to William of Conches, and *apposui*, referring to Adam du Petit Pont, in neither case means or even implies that great distances were involved. The episode is localised. I am aware that there is no other evidence associating the teaching career of William of Conches with Paris, but I believe that John's text makes best sense if that is where we find William during 1138-41. Moreover, those other masters once associated with the 'school of Chartres', where they cannot be firmly linked to the teaching of higher studies, Thierry of Chartres and Gilbert de la Porrée, are known to have taught in Paris, and since these three masters have been demonstrated by some commentators closely to share some common philosophical speculations,[108] the suggestion is not unreasonable that they were most easily able to read each other's work, or to exchange views on their common interests, in Paris, where both Gilbert and Thierry are known to have taught in their most productive years, so that it is likewise not unreasonable to find William of Conches, whose teaching cannot be linked to Chartres either, teaching in Paris also. I may also briefly observe that R. W. Southern has suggested that William of Conches had given up his regular teaching by 1138-9[109] when John became William's pupil, a suggestion he bases on William's remarks in his *Dragmaticon*, and which is reinforced by John's remark in the *Metalogicon* when he says that William and Richard L'Evêque ceased to teach grammar when overwhelmed by the onslaught of an ignorant mob:[110] that he was still teaching to some extent in 1138 is the evidence of *Met.* II. 10, but John was able obviously to fit much else besides into his years spent as William's part-time pupil.

The statement *reuersus itaque in fine triennii* is again resumptive. *Itaque* underlines the sequential nature of 'I returned' when at the end of a difficult and demanding, but academically important three years, John could now resume his formal — and full time — studies in the *triuium*. This time he takes up the study of theology in addition to formally resuming dialectic, which was a step up the academic ladder, having put his dialectic on a very sure foundation, or, to put it another way, having served his academic apprenticeship. I take the force of *reuersus itaque* to be not merely 'I returned' either from afar or from a not very considerable distance, but rather, 'at the end of this triennium — 1138-41 — I returned to the course of study I had begun with Abelard, Alberic, and Robert of Melun, and sought out Gilbert de la Porrée', who like the forementioned was both a logician and a theologian. John used the phrase *reuersus in me* when he began to talk about the triennium, and there it had the force of 'I recovered my senses' or 'I returned to my senses'. The reappearance of *reuersus* with the force 'I recovered or returned to my former status as a formal 'full-time' student of the logicians', gives the episode a roundness and a unity which derive from a rhetorical and not merely a literal use of language, as John as a consummate artist well knew. 'Repperi magistrum Gilebertum, ipsumque audiui in logicis et in diuinis; sed nimis cito subtractus est';[111] John now became a pupil of Gilbert de la Porrée, one of the most distinguished scholars of the day. This was not necessarily a reunion, as has been thought.[112] It is, I believe, quite simply saying that John sought out, or otherwise went to, Gilbert, who had a good reputation attractive to a student of John's abilities, but he was unfortunately too quickly removed from Paris on becoming bishop of Poitiers in 1142. Quite where he taught is a matter for debate, but it was possibly at Notre Dame, or even at Mont-Sainte-Geneviève. John then went to Robert Pullen, 'quem uita pariter et scientia commendabant',[113] a man equally commended by his morals and his learning. Robert Pullen was archdeacon of Rochester from 1138 to 1143, and had been supported in his determination to teach in Paris, in defiance of his bishop, because of the recognised soundness of his teaching by Bernard of Clairvaux.[114] He ceased to teach in Paris in 1144 on being elevated to the cardinalate. John reports in *Met.* I. 5 that he would have been the object of the Cornificians' scorn if they had not been restrained by deference to the Apostolic See.[115] But John's last master, Simon of Poissy, is probably that Simon of Paris mentioned also in *Met.* I. 5 as one whom the Cornificians did not hesitate to vilify.[116] Simon is not known to have written anything that has lasted. He was, according to John, a reliable lecturer, but a rather dull disputator (fidus lector, sed obtusior disputator), [117] so that John's student days, which began with the bright flare of Abelard's brilliance, ended with the rather damp squib that was Simon's. John says little concerning his years spent studying theology as they are simply not germane to his subject, that is, the virtues of grammar and rhetoric and the vices of false dialectic. John concludes his history by observing: 'sic fere duodennium michi elapsum est diuersis studiis occupato'.[118] We have no firm date for the end of John's studies in Paris, but if he indeed spent nearly twelve years engaged in various studies and scholarly occupations, it could not well have been before mid-to-late 1147. But John concludes this chapter, as distinct from his account of his student days, by telling us of a visit he made to his former associates on Mont-Sainte-Geneviève, when he discovered that his former friends and colleagues had added not one iota to their dialectical propositions, thereby demonstrating again by personal experience to John the fruitlessness of dialectic when it is pursued in isolation from the nourishing sun of other liberal studies.[119] Since John was anyway in Paris or its suburbs throughout the years from 1136 to 1147, I fail to see any particular force in placing this visit to Mont-Sainte-Geneviève at the end of his studies in *c.* 1147. John does not state when the visit took place, nor does he mention any particular circumstances of the visit. He merely wished to compare notes about the relative progress made by himself and his former associates, and to confer with them concerning their old problems, presumably so as the more accurately to estimate this progress. But he discovered them to have advanced not at all in philosophy. As a peripatetic ecclesiastical administrator, and so one who had had to put his learning to practical, worldly, use, John could have made his visit to his former colleagues on Mont-Sainte-Geneviève at any time, and since the point of describing this visit is to conclude his demonstration from personal experience of his contention that dialectic will always be sterile when unfructified by other liberal studies, it would presumably have most point for John himself if the visit were to have been later than the time his own studies ended, and nearer to that of the composition of the *Metalogicon*, since his grief for the waste of his friends and justifiable pride in his own progress would be intensified.

John's unifying purpose in this chapter has been to expose the pitfalls of contemporary dialectical techniques which cannot, in his view, lead to true philosophy, or wisdom, when pursued in isolation from other liberal studies. The two masters who have been most clearly criticised in this account are Alberic de Monte and Robert of Melun, who instructed John in the two years preceding his transfer to William the grammarian. Both are accused of a form of nimiety, and so a lack of balance. Alberic the subtle questioner was for John a verbal quibbler; even Bernard of Chartres does not escape the taint of this charge when in *Met*. III. 2 John dismisses impatiently the hair-splitting he has just described.[120] Robert, on the other hand, concentrated too particularly on his answers, and so too his dialectic failed to achieve balance. Both Alberic and Robert lacked sufficient grounding in humane letters, which neatly explains their other deficiencies. William of Soissons fell victim to his own sophistry, and that despite John's instruction, but John also suggests that not only was his sophistry not discouraged, but that William also heard some perverted forms of Aristotelian doctrine from Adam du Petit Pont, to whom he had sent him, and so John has to convict his friend Adam of both offences, in addition to the charge of verbal obscurity. Quite how Thierry of Chartres failed John as a teacher of rhetoric is unclear, but perhaps John's dissatisfaction with Thierry is elucidated in *Met*. IV.24 where he observes that Thierry derided the *Topics* of Aristotle as the work of one Drogo of Troyes, although he sometimes lectured on them; the disciples of Robert of Melun also contemned the *Topics*, while John himself found great merit in Aristotle's little book, and seriously questioned the sense of its contemporary critics.[121] William of Conches, only briefly referred to here, suffers no detraction from the reference to him in *Met*. I.5,[122] and Richard L'Evêque, with whom he is associated in *Met*. I.24,[123] receives in *Met*. II.10[124] his second laudatory mention, and one has the clear impression from these references that these two of John's masters were those from whom he derived the greatest benefit. Certainly, the literary studies he pursued with these two masters were those having the greatest relevance to this humanist and man of letters, who strives to express the diffuse thoughts of his perceptive and inquiring mind in Latin which takes Cicero as its model, and it is this, together with his undoubted admiration for Aristotle, which most clearly demonstrates John's own scholarly bent as a humanist having a strong ethical bias, just as it distinguishes him from the accomplished speculative philosophers of his time. John is not a philosopher in the sense that Abelard, for instance, is, but rather in much the sense that Cicero was, and he seems deliberately to have eschewed the opportunity to become such a philosopher because he considered that he would have had to abandon his own clear-headed and commonsense attitude to the ethical problems that concerned him in order to achieve it, and his ethics are accordingly directed firmly to the world of practical affairs.

It is important to remember that John has not rejected dialectic in this chapter, but he has related his own misfortunes consequent on his exposure to and, in part, seduction by the false brilliance of contemporary dialectic. John has drawn a fine distinction between sophistry, or false dialectic, and genuine dialectic by means of exemplary autobiographical reminiscences from which an obvious moral is to be inferred. In fact, genuine dialectic makes only an oblique appearance as that which is to be desired, and the quest of which necessitated his transfer to the grammarian of Conches, described by John as the first in his three-stage autobiographical exemplification of the futility of the dialectic which is ignorant of other liberal arts, followed by Richard L'Evêque and Peter Helias, so that he might the more thoroughly acquire a solid base in the verbal arts, grammar and rhetoric, without which no scholar's dialectic could hope to achieve its most fruitful, and chief legitimate, function as the balance of probable truth. This turning point in John's own search for wisdom, in embarking on a profound study of grammar and rhetoric, heightens the implicit condemnation of his earlier masters in dialectic, Alberic de Monte and Robert of Melun: because Alberic and Robert lacked a broad base in the *litterae humanae* so too their dialectic could not hope to achieve its true end, with the result that their subtle questions and facile answers, for all their brilliance, were in the last analysis little better than imbalanced sophistry. The second stage of exemplification concerns William of Soissons in the difficult three years when John was not merely trying to salvage his own academic quest for wisdom, but having to convert his learning into practical use as a tutor to the children of the Parisian nobiity, as a remedy for the exigencies of poverty, and perhaps it was the difficulty of this experience, and the disappointment of his failure to salvage William of Soissons from a later career as a devoted sophist, which not only contributed to the forming of his theory of knowledge, but also ensured that John's ethics would in future bear the impress of a determined pragmatism. Indeed, pragmatism is itself the hallmark of John's description of the lengthy acquist of wisdom or *sapientia*, from the time when the study of grammar 'trains our faculties of sight and hearing when it imparts the fundaments of language',[125] preparing the foundations of the dialectical reasoning which will sift the data of, first, sense-perception and imagination (opinion), and then the gains of *scientia* or natural philosophy, to determine the likely truth 'in a ready and tempered balance of probability'[126] of those things which are (*ea quae sunt*) by means of the true dialectic that utilises probable logic, the results of which will lead ultimately to *sapientia*; and this last, the desired end, by its very definition as the divine truth (*diuinas rationes*) of things which are, gives the final seal of the moralist to John's ethical and pragmatic theory of knowledge. The value to John's purpose of *Met.* II. 10 is precisely that it teaches by personal example, so that he can best vindicate the claims of his book by the moral inference of the experience he had himself gained, as it were, in the field. The later visit to Mont-Sainte- Geneviève is the final stage of exemplification wherein it is implied, although he would hesitate to say so, that he has succeeded in acquiring true dialectic — and, moreover, acquired it as an empirical practitioner in the uncomfortably mundane world of ecclesiastical administration: at all events John's progress strongly contrasts with the futility of the misdirected endeavours of his former friends which has caused their sophistical, because false, dialectic completely to atrophy, allowing John to conclude by enunciating the underlying contention of his chapter of warning and illustration that: 'Expertus itaque sum, quod liquido colligi potest, quia, sicut dialectica alias expedit disciplinas, sic, si sola fuerit, iacet exanguis et sterilis, nec ad fructum philosophie fecundat animam, si aliunde non concipit'.[127] This is a contention which has already been adumbrated with *Met.* II. 9, a chapter which is most significant for its intense pragmatism, for John says: 'The utility of eloquence is, in fact, directly in proportion to the measure of wisdom a person may have attained. On the other hand, eloquence becomes positively harmful when it departs from wisdom. It is accordingly evident that dialectic, the highly efficient and ever-ready servant of eloquence, is useful to anyone in proportion to the degree of knowledge he possesses. It is of greatest advantage to a person who knows much, and of least use to one who knows little . . . So also, if it is bereft of the strength which is communicated by the other disciplines, dialectic is in a way maimed and practically helpless; but if it derives life and vigour from other studies, it can destroy all falsehood, and at least enables one to dispute with probability concerning all subjects. Dialectic, however, is not great, if, as our contemporaries treat it, it remains forever engrossed in itself, walking 'round about and surveying itself, ransacking (over and over) its own depths and secrets: limiting itself to things that are of no use whatsoever in a domestic or military, commercial or religious, civil or ecclesiastical way, and that are appropriate only in school. For in school and during youth, many things are permitted within certain limits, and for the time being, which are to be speedily sloughed off when one advances to a more serious study of philosophy. Indeed, when one has become intellectually or physically mature, the treatment of philosophy becomes more earnest. It not only divests itself of puerile expressions and speech that were (formerly) permitted by indulgent concession, but even frequently discards all books . . . It is easy for an artisan to talk about his art, but it is much more difficult to put the art into practice. What physician does not often discourse at length on elements, humours, complexions, maladies, and other things pertaining to medicine? But the patient who recovers as a result of hearing this jargon might just as well have been sickened by it. What moral philosopher does not fairly bubble over with laws of ethics, so long as these remain merely verbal? But it is a far different matter to exemplify these in his own life. Those who have manual skills find no difficulty in discussing their arts, but none of them can erect a building or fight a boxing match with as little exertion. The like holds true of other arts. It is a simple matter, indeed, to talk about definitions, arguments, genera, and the like; but it is a far more difficult feat to put the art (of logic) into effect by finding the aforesaid in each of the several branches of knowledge. One who has the sad misfortune of being in want of the other disciplines, cannot possess the riches that are promised and provided by dialectic'.[128] Pursuant, in strong part, to these remarks concerning the practice of that which one preaches, there ensues the exemplary Chapter 10, that cautionary tale of both illustration and warning, which John can then follow with the elegantly compendious Chapter 11 wherein dialectic by itself is said ironically to be able to resolve questions relative to itself although this is of limited practical use: 'Est tamen quod solitaria pollicetur et prestat, solius gramatice subnixa presidio; propositas enim de se expedit questiones, sed ad alia non consurgit; quale est: An affirmare sit enuntiare, et: An simul extare possit contradictio. Hoc autem quid ad usum uite conferat, si non est adminiculans alii, quisque diiudicet';[129] but, more interestingly, John describes the fruitful functions of logic when informed by other disciplines by the use of a neat parallel drawn from the natural world: 'Fere ergo ut spiritus animalium ea disponit et uegetat, et humores regit et fouet ad uitam animalem, ab ipsis tamen humoribus nascitur, et subtilitate sua et uigore magnam molem agitat et ad se disponit, quantum non noxia tardant corpora; sic logica ab aliis ducit originem easque disponit et mouet, quantum inertie et ignorantie nocumento non retardatur. Quod planum est his qui et artem disserendi nouerunt et alias disciplinas',[130] which, by its very economy, gives the best theoretical summary account of his contention, which has been elaborately and conclusively proved, that logic and dialectic are the tools of the liberal arts, put into the hands of the man (pragmatically) seeking wisdom who has mastered these verbal arts in order that he may best shape the ultimate success of his quest.

However, in addition to criticising the sophistical and nonsensical verbal prolixity, opacity, and quibbling, which corrupt language, the basis of human society, and pervert the reasoning processes which would otherwise lead to wisdom, and thus misguide human society, along with other forms of excess which lead to a perilous imbalance both in scholarship and in individual moral character, John castigates the excess of pretentious arrogance among the Cornificians which had induced a lack of virtue in their teaching, which was empty of contents, and in their morals, which made 'any vulgar villain seem but an amateur in crime'.[131] 'Their excesses would shame an Epicurean pig'[132] — while this statement may be read as pure vilification on John's part, much more sinister is his suggestion in *Met.* I. 4 that the Cornificians are the invidious corruptors of monasteries and medical schools.[133] To point to carnal excesses may well be an inevitable line of attack from a twelfth-century scholar and cleric, but it is part of a more substantial cause of concern to John, and that is the increasing utilitarianism of the liberal education of his day. The students of Cornificius stay in school no longer 'than it takes a baby bird to sprout its feathers'[134] and demand to leave giving the impression that they know everything. Their emphasis on a speedy and superficial acquisition of learning[135] goes hand in hand with their desire speedily to make themselves masters of a lucrative profession.[136] John sums up the cynicism of this attitude in the words of some enterprising doctors, 'dum dolet accipe'[137] — take your fee while the patient suffers! Gilbert de la Porrée noticed the same trend, which he derided or deplored, and he predicted that such students would finish as bakers, the easy subsidiary trade which could accommodate all those who, quite unskilled, concerned themselves more with bread, or material possessions, than with any skill itself,[138] while William of Conches and Richard L'Evêque were forced to cease their sound teaching of grammar when the onslaughts of the ignorant mob demanding instant learning overwhelmed them.[139] John is sufficiently idealistic to abhor utilitarianism and materialism among scholars, but he is also a pragmatist and had himself discovered that the need to earn one's own living could be very pressing. In an ironically moralising passage in *Met.* I. 7 he observes: 'One who can with facility and adequacy verbally express his mental perceptions is eloquent. The faculty of doing this is appropriately called eloquence. For myself I am at a loss to see how anything could be more generally useful, more helpful in acquiring wealth, more reliable for winning favour, more suited for gaining fame, than is eloquence . . . Who are the most prosperous and wealthy among our fellow citizens? Who are the most powerful and successful in all their enterprises? Is it not the eloquent?'[140] For John it is legitimate for material benefits to accrue to an educated man in the form of a reward, but that these benefits should be acquired in the form of profit he is bound to anathematise.

John received his schooling in the intensely competitive and fluid atmosphere of twelfth-century Paris, and he found abhorrent the prevailing climate of utilitarianism in this enterprising and informal situation. One might, therefore, speculate as to how he would have received the institutionalisation of education in the thirteenth-century universities, whose large student populations dictated that these should be trained for (lucrative) professions, in accordance also with the increasingly complex needs of society. He would, I believe, have condemned the gradual supersession of the emphasis on the *triuium* by that on more advanced and increasingly specialised studies. Such specialisation he would have seen as imbalance, and he would have doubted how efficacious the specialised pursuit of philosophy and theology could have been with such a comparatively narrow base in the *litterae humanae*. Nonetheless, John was a pragmatist who would have realised the need for what might be termed vocational training in such a situation; he had himself pursued a career as an ecclesiastical administrator upon leaving the schools of Paris. The threat to civilisation posed by the neglect of the verbal arts did not materialise, but it may be doubted that John would have found much to commend in the literarily austere prose of those thirteenth-century speculative theologians and philosophers who perhaps for us represent the greatest achievement of mediaeval philosophy. It has seemed to some, wrote Southern, that humanism died with Abelard and Thierry of Chartres between 1140 and 1150,

'Certainly some freshness and charm died with them'.[141] It seems that John of Salisbury might have been prepared to agree, although his statement of twelfth-century humanist optimism was not written until 1159.[142] He mentions that William of Conches and Richard L'Evêque were forced to abandon their teaching of grammar, and we know that William of Conches joined the household of Geoffrey of Normandy before the latter's death in 1151, and is thought to have died himself in 1154, while Richard L'Evêque became archdeacon of Coutances in 1159, and bishop of Avranches in 1171. These two have been associated with the advancing tide of materialism by John,[143] master Gilbert's comments have been cited from *Met.* I. 5,[144] while Thierry of Chartres, in company with Abelard and William of Conches, have been described as ones rendered temporarily insane by the insanity of their time, although they did recover, and went on to win further glory for themselves and for their arts.[145] But perhaps the freshness and charm of their approach to their teaching had been dealt a severe blow, for we find that Thierry, who became chancellor of Chartres in 1142, had left Paris by the middle of the decade, as had Gilbert de la Porrée, who became bishop of Poitiers in 1142; in 1156 Peter Helias is found witnessing a charter of Poitiers, and perhaps he too had left his teaching career behind; Robert Pullen left for the Apostolic See in 1144, but perhaps he only with reluctance surrendered his controversial career as a Parisian master. However, all these masters left Paris and their teaching careers in a remarkably short space of time, and all went on to some other kind of employment, predominantly in the Church which had anyway long embraced them, but not for all of them was this a promotion such as might be seen as a reward. Perhaps this is unsurprising: with the probable exception of Richard L'Evêque, who did not die until 1182, and Peter Helias, a pupil of Thierry of Chartres, these were not especially young men such as might have seen their preferments in the light of a well-earned rest; but nevertheless perhaps the reason for this exodus is after all to be sought in a blemishing of the complexion of humanism in face of a gathering momentum in the advance of utilitarianism. Certainly the account of John of Salisbury's *Metalogicon* makes this a reasonable hypothesis. Indeed, it might also be said that the greatest hour of literary medieval humanism was passing at this moment also: there are few literary humanists of towering stature after this point, such as John himself was and would have approved of. I myself find the greatest glory of medieval humanism in the work of the thirteenth-century theologians, but it must be conceded that these would have been unlikely to have passed John's acid test of humanism, a wide knowledge of the Classical Latin *auctores*, and thus his critique of twelfth-century education was vindicated. More important, perhaps, for John himself, as a moralist and lover of wisdom such as I have described, was the vindication of his own life and ideals contained in the obituary notice upon him written by the chronicler Robert of Torigny, who described him simply as 'uir honestus et sapiens' — a wise and upright man.[146]

c/o Department of Classics
Royal Holloway and Bedford New College
Egham, Surrey TW20 0EX

REFERENCES

* I would like to express my gratitude to Sir Richard Southern, Professor N. Rubinstein, and my supervisor Dr J. B. Hall, for their invaluable comments on drafts of this paper, and also the various members of the Warburg seminar for the interesting discussion which followed my reading of the paper to them on April 25 1986. Finally, I should like here particularly to thank Dr Charles Schmitt, at whose invitation I was privileged to write this paper, for the inspiration of his teaching, and the patient guidance I have benefitted from over these past years, by dedicating this paper to his memory: in the last analysis, such imperfections as remain in these pages remain because Charles did not live to remove them, and I am emboldened to present them here only because he himself asked me so to do.

1. Being: Lond. Bibl. Reg. 13 D IV (s. xii), Oxon. Bodl. lat. misc. c. 16 (s. xii), Cantabrig. Coll. Corp. Christi 46 (s. xii), Lond. Bibl. Reg. 12.D.I (s. xii-xiii), Charleville Bibl. Mun. 151 (s. xii), Cantabrig. Bibl. Vniu. Ii. II. 31 (s. xiv), Oxon. Bodl. 315 (s. xv). Dr J. B. Hall and I are re-editing the *Metalogicon*.

2. B. P. Hendley, 'John of Salisbury's defense of the Triuium', in *Arts Libéraux et Philosophie au Moyen Age. Actes du Quatrième Congrès International de Philosophie Médiévale. Montréal 1967* (Paris, 1969), pp. 753-762.

3. *Ioannis Saresberiensis Episcopi Carnotensis Metalogicon*, ed. C. C. J. Webb, (Oxford, 1929), Prol. p. 3 11.16-17. All subsequent references to the *Metalogicon* will refer to Webb's edition, simply giving the page and line number, as in *Met.* Prol. 3.16-17, the Latin will usually follow: 'Et quia logice suscepit patrocinium, METALOGICON inscriptus est liber . . . ' (MSS *suscepit* for *suscepi* 3.16).

4. John's account of the hierarchical ascent to wisdom from the world of sense-perception is summarised in *Met.* 4.18-9, 184.3- 185.1: Qua uero proportione ratio transcendit sensum, ea, sicut Plato in Politia auctor est, excedit intellectus rationem. Nam intellectus assequitur quod ratio inuestigat, siquidem in labores rationis intrat intellectus et sibi ad sapientiam thesaurizat quod ratio preparans adquisiuit. Est itaque intellectus suprema uis spiritualis nature, que humana contuens et diuina, penes se causas habet omnium rationum naturaliter sibi perceptibilium. Sunt enim que exuperant omnem sensum tam hominum quam angelorum diuine rationes et nonnulle aliis plus aut minus pro diuine dispensationis decreto innotescunt. Hunc solius Dei esse

et admodum paucorum hominum, scilicet electorum, asserit Plato . . . Sapientia uero sequitur intellectum, eo quod diuina de his rebus quas ratio discutit, intellectus excerpsit, suauem habent gustum et in amorem suum animas intelligentes accendunt. Nam et ex eo sapientiam dici reor, quod boni saporem habeat in diuinis. Vnde Patres scientiam referunt ad actiuam, ad contemplatiuam uero sapientiam. Patet ex his quod, si quis premissos gradus recenseat, de scaturigine sensuum etiam sapientiam, preeunte et opitulante gratia, uidebit emanare. (I have replaced Webb's *continens et diuinas* (184.9) and *selectorum* (184.14) with true MSS readings.) For the definition of *sapientia* cf. Boethius, *De arithmetica* I. 1; PL 63.1081 C: Est enim sapientia earum rerum quae uere sunt cognitio et integra comprehensio; and Thierry of Chartres, *Prologus in Eptatheucon*, ed. E. Jeauneau, *Mediaeval Studies* xvi (1954), 171-5, on p. 174: Phylosophya autem est amor sapientie: sapientia uero est integra comprehensio ueritatis eorum que sunt, quam nullus uel parum adipiscitur nisi amauerit.

5.   *Met.* 1.1, 7.5 *ad fin.* : Licet enim quandoque aliquatenus sibi prodesse possit sapientia elinguis ad solatium conscientie, raro tamen et parum confert ad usum societatis humane. Nam ratio, scientie uirtutumque parens altrix et custos, que de uerbo frequentius concipit et per uerbum numerosius et fructuosius parit, aut omnino sterilis permaneret aut quidem infecunda si non conceptionis eius fructum in lucem ederet usus eloquii, et inuicem quod sentit prudens agitatio mentis hominibus publicaret. Hec autem est illa dulcis et fructuosa coniugatio rationis et uerbi que tot eggregias genuit urbes, tot conciliauit et federauit regna, tot uniuit populos et caritate deuinxit, ut hostis omnium publicus merito censeatur quisquis hoc quod ad utilitatem omnium Deus coniunxit, nititur separare. Mercurio Philologiam inuidet et ab amplexu Philologie Mercurium auellit qui eloquentie preceptionem a studiis philosophie eliminat, et quamuis solam uideatur eloquentiam persequi, omnia liberalia studia conuellit, omnem totius philosophie impugnat operam, societatis humane fedus distrahit, et nullum caritati aut uicissitudini officiorum relinquit locum. Brutescent homines si concessi dote priuentur eloquii, ipseque urbes uidebuntur potius pecorum quasi septa quam cetus hominum nexu quodam societatis federatus ut participatione officiorum et amica inuicem uicissitudine eodem iure uiuat. Quis enim contractus rite celebrabitur? Que fidei aut morum disciplina uigebit? Quenam erit obsecundatio aut communicatio uoluntatum subtracto uerbi commercio? Non ergo unam, non paucas, sed omnes simul urbes et politicam uitam totam aggreditur Cornificius noster, studiorum eloquentie imperitus et improbus impugnator. (My punctuation: the MSS reading *paucas* replaces *paucos* at 7.32).

6.   *Met.* 2.3, 65,19-20: sed prompta et mediocri probabilitate uerum examinat: translated J. B. Hall. My previous résumé of the functions of logic and dialectic is found in *Met.* 2.3, 64.13-18 and 64.23 *ad fin.*: Inchoantibus autem philosophiam prelegenda est eo quod uocum et intellectuum interpres est, sine quibus nullus philosophie articulus recte procedit in lucem. Qui uero sine logica philosophiam doceri putat, idem a sapientie cultu omnium rerum exterminet rationes, quoniam eis logica presidet . . . Pro eo namque logica dicta est, quod rationalis, id est rationum ministratoria et examinatrix est. Diuisit eam Plato in dialecticam et rethoricam; sed qui efficaciam eius altius metiuntur, ei plura attribuunt: siquidem ei demonstratiua, probabilis et sophistica subiciuntur. Sed demonstratiua a disciplinalibus uiget principiis et ad eorum consecutiua progreditur, necessitate gaudet, et quid cui uideatur, dum tamem ita esse oporteat, non multum attendit; decet hec philosophicam recte docentium maiestatem, que suo citra auditorum assensum roboratur arbitrio. Probabilis autem uersatur in his que uidentur omnibus aut pluribus aut sapientibus, et his uel omnibus uel pluribus uel maxime notis et probabilibus aut consecutiuis eorum; hec quidem dialecticam et rethoricam continet, quoniam dialecticus et orator persuadere nitentes, alter aduersario, alter iudici, non multum referre arbitrantur uera

an falsa sint argumenta eorum, dummodo ueri similitudinem teneant. At sophistica, que apparens et non existens sapientia est, probabilitatis aut necessitatis affectat imaginem, parum curans quid sit hoc aut illud, dum phantasticis imaginibus et uelut umbris fallacibus inuoluat eum cum quo sermo conseritur. Profecto quam pre ceteris omnes ambiunt sed pauci meo iudicio assequuntur, dialectica est, que neque ad docentium aspirat grauitatem, nec undis ciuilibus mergitur, nec seducit fallaciis, sed prompta et mediocri probabilitate uerum examinat. (Hall's punctation: Hall's *autem* for *enim* 64.13; MSS *neque* for *nec* 65.17.)

7.   *Met.* 2.4, 66. 6-8: Vt enim gramatica de dictionibus et in dictionibus, teste Remigio, sic ista (sc. dialectica) de dictis et in dictis est. Illa uerba sensuum principaliter, sed hec examinat sensus uerborum . . . (punctuated Hall).

8.   *Met.* 1.13, 31.15-22: Est enim gramatica scientia recte loquendi scribendique et origo omnium liberalium disciplinarum. Eadem quoque est totius philosophie cunabulum et, ut ita dixerim, totius litteratorii studii altrix prima, que omnium nascentium de sinu nature teneritudinem excipit, nutrit infantiam, cuiusque gradus incrementa in philosophia prouehit, et sedulitate materna omnem philosophantis producit et custodit etatem . . . (my punctuation).

9.   *ibid.* 32.14-17: Tradit ergo prima elementa sermonis ars ista, oculorum et aurium iudicium instruit, ut non facilius queat aliquis preter eam philosophari quam inter philosophos eminere qui semper cecus fuit et surdus. (My punctuation.)

10.   *Met.* 1.24, 55.7-9: Excute Virgilium aut Lucanum, et ibi, cuiuscumque philosophie professor sis, eiusdem inuenies condituram. (My punctuation.) Translated D. McGarry, (California, 1955), p. 67.

11.   *ibid.* 55.4-7: Illa autem que ceteris philosophie partibus preminet, ethicam dico, sine qua nec philosophi subsistit nomen, collati decoris gratia omnes alias antecedit. (My punctuation.) Translated McGarry, *loc. cit.*

12.   *Met.* 4.32, 200.17-22: Vnius, inquit, ad duo et duorum ad quattuor uerissima ratio est; nec magis fuit heri ratio illa uera quam hodie; nec magis cras aut post annum erit uera. Nec si omnis mundus iste concidat, poterit ista ratio non esse. Simili modo substantiam esse, si sit corpus, non esse non potest.

13.   *Met.* 2.13, 85.22-30: Sed demonstratiua necessarias metodos querit, et que illam rerum inherentiam docent, quam impossibile est dissolui; hoc enim dumtaxat necessarium est, quod aliter esse impossibile est. Ceterum quia uires nature aut nullus pene scrutatur aut rarus, et numerum possibilium solus Deus nouit, de necessariis plerumque non modo incertum, sed et temerarium iudicium est. Quis enim nouit penitus quid esse possit aut non possit? Here and note 12 above, cf. *Met.* 2.8, 75.25-76.7: Debuerat Aristotiles hanc compescuisse intemperiem eorum qui indiscretam loquacitatem dialectice exercitium putant. Et sane compescuerat, si audiretur. Non oportet, inquit, omne problema nec omnem positionem considerare, sed quam dubitabit aliquis rationis egentium et (non) pene uel sensus. Nam qui dubitant utrum oporteat deos uereri et parentes honorare uel non, pene indigent; qui uero utrum nix alba est uel non, sensus. Neque uero quorum propinqua est demonstratio, neque quorum ualde longe; nam hec quidem non habent dubitationem, illa autem magis quam secundum exercitatiuam. Hec ille. (MSS *omne* omitted by Webb at 75.28.)

14.   John's position might be best expressed in the problematic syllogism: if A may be B (= thesis), and if B may be C (= antithesis), then A may be C (= synthesis), by which the middle term B unites the two extremes in a problematically true conclusion, which itself, in uniting A and C, preserves the balance of probable truth. Cf. *Met.* 3.9, 152. 9-20: Versatur in his inuentionis materia, quam hilaris memorie Willelmus de Campellis, postmodum Catalanensis episcopus, diffiniuit, etsi non perfecte, esse scientiam

reperiendi medium terminum et inde eliciendi argumentum. Cum enim de inherentia dubitatur, necessarium est aliquod inquiri medium, cuius interuentu copulentur extrema; qua speculatione an aliqua subtilior uel ad rem efficacior fuerit, non facile dixerim. Medium uero necessarium est, ubi uis inferentie in terminis uertitur; si enim inter totas propositiones sit, ut potius sit obnoxia complexioni partium quam partibus complexis, medii nexus cessat.

15.   *Met.* 2.17, 91.25- 92.2: Naturam tamen uniuersalium hic omnes expediunt, et altissimum negotium et maioris inquisitionis contra mentem auctoris explicare nituntur. Alius ergo consistit in uocibus; licet hec opinio cum Rocelino suo fere omnino iam euanuerit. For John's review of the discussion of universals in his time see *Met.* 2.17 *passim*, followed by his comment at the beginning of *Met.* 2.18, 96.5-9: Longum erit et a proposito penitus alienum, si singulorum opiniones posuero uel errores; cum, ut uerbo comici utar, fere quot homines, tot sententie. Nam de magistris aut nullus aut rarus est qui doctoris sui uelit inherere uestigiis. Vt sibi faciat nomen, quisque proprium cudit errorem . . .

16.   *Met.* 2.20, 114.10 *ad fin.* : Quod si nec subici res sensibilis potest, Aristotilem nullus esse mentitum ambigit aut nugatum. Itaque hic, sicut et alibi, executus est quod decet liberalium artium preceptorem, agens, ut dici solet, Minerua pinguiori, ut intelligeretur; nec in generibus et speciebus hanc statuit difficultatem quam ipsi doctores nequent intelligere, nedum sufficiant aliis explanare. Ex hac Minerue pinguedine dictum est illud in Topicis: Differentie omnes aut species aut indiuidua erunt; siquidem sunt animalia; nam unumquodque animalium aut species est aut indiuiduum. Similiter et illud Boetii: Omnis species est suum genus. Nam omnis homo animal, omnis albedo color. Quid ergo prohibet iuxta hanc licentie rationem ea que sunt sensibilia uel predicari uel subici? Nec opinor auctores hanc uim imposuisse sermoni, ut alligatus sit ad unam in iuncturis omnibus significationem, sed doctrinaliter sic esse locutos, ut ubique seruiant intellectui qui commodissimus est et quem ibi haberi pre ceteris ratio exigit. Hoc ipsum ergo quod dicitur predicari, ab adiunctis plures significandi contrahit modos. Poterit tamen forte ubique aliquam quodammodo conuenientiam uel inherentiam designare. Nam cum sermo de sermone iungibilitatem quandam terminorum uere affirmationis innuit, cum de re sermo dicitur predicari, ostenditur quod ei talis nuncupatio aptatur. Rem uero de re predicari interdum notat, quoniam hoc est hoc, puta Plato homo; interdum quoniam hoc participat hoc utpote subiectum accidente. Nec erubesco confiteri quod res de re predicetur in propositione, etsi res in propositione non sit; cum hoc in mente michi uersetur quod res significetur predicato termino uere affirmationis, cuius subiecto aliqua de re agitur aut res aliqua significatur. Itaque non aduersandum littere arbitror, sed amicandum, eique mos gerendus est in admittenda licentioris uerbi indifferentia; nec ad omnem translationem aut usurpationem discole, ut creditur, dictionis lectorem uel auditorem decet dentem caninum exercere. Quod male fers, assuesce, feres. Et plane ingratus est et tam impudentis quam imprudentis ingenii qui ad omnia se docentis uerba mouetur et ei in aliquo obtemperare detrectat. Sequamur ergo figuras auctorum, et singula dicta pensemus ex causis dicendi; inde enim fidelis sumenda est intelligentia. Sed et rei nomen latius pateat, ut possit uniuersalibus conuenire, que sic auctore Aristotile intelliguntur abstracta a singularibus, ut tamen esse non habeant, deductis singularibus; hoc enim, sicut ait, illi asserunt qui genus unum numero esse dicunt. Id autem faciunt qui formas solas ponunt, ideas scilicet, quas cum auctore suo Platone, quotiens datur occasio, uehementer impugnat. Vnde licet Plato cetum philosophorum grandem et tam Augustinum quam alios plures nostrorum in statuendis ideis habeat assertores, ipsius tamen dogma in scrutinio uniuersalium nequaquam sequimur; eo quod hic Peripateticorum principem Aristotilem dogmatis huius principem profitemur. Magnum quidem est et quod Boetius in secundo

commento super Porphirium nimis arduum fatetur tantorum uirorum diiudicare sententias sed ei qui Peripateticorum libros aggreditur, magis Aristotilis sententia sequenda est; forte non quia uerior, sed plane quia his disciplinis magis accommoda est. Ab hac autem longissime uidentur abcedere tam illi qui genera et species uoces esse constituunt aut sermones, quam alii qui premissis de rerum inuestigatione opinionibus distrahuntur. Et quidem omnes ab Aristotile puerilius aut stolidius euagantur quam Platonici, cuius sententiam agnoscere dedignantur. Hec opinor debere sufficere, quod nec fideliter cum Porphirio nec utiliter cum introducendis uersantur qui omnium de generibus et speciebus recensent opiniones, omnibus obuiant, ut tandem sue inuentionis erigant titulum; cum hoc a proposito auctoris omnino dissideat et retundat ingenia auditorum et aliis articulis eque necessariis scitu locum inquisitionis esse non sinat.

17.   *Met.* 4.13, 178.17-179.2: Inde est quod maiores prudentiam uel scientiam ad temporalium et sensibilium notitiam retulerint; ad spiritualium uero, intellectum uel sapientiam. Nam de humanis scientia, de diuinis sapientia dici solet. Adeo autem de sensu scientia pendet, ut eorum que sensu sciuntur non scientia sit, rebus a sensu subductis. Constat enim hoc ab Aristotile. Potest tamen esse fidelis opinio; ut cum post noctem sol creditur rediturus. Vnde, quia humana transitoria sunt, certum opinionis de eisdem nequit esse iudicium, nisi raro; si autem, quod non usque quaque certum est pro certo statuatur, fit accessus ad fidem, quam Aristotiles diffinit esse uehementem opinionem.

18.   *Met.* 1.23, 52.18-53.6: Precipua autem sunt ad totius philosophie et uirtutis exercitium lectio, doctrina, meditatio, et assiduitas operis. Lectio uero scriptorum preiacentem habet materiam, doctrina et scriptis plerumque incumbit et interdum ad non scripta progreditur, que tamen in archiuis memorie recondita sunt aut in presentis rei intelligentia eminent. At meditatio etiam ad ignota protenditur, et usque ad incomprehensibilia sepe seipsam erigit et tam manifesta rerum quam abdita rimatur. Quartum, operis scilicet assiduitas, etsi a preexistente cognitione formetur scientiamque desideret, uias tamen parat intelligentie, eo quod intellectus bonus est omnibus facientibus eum. Et precones ueritatis, ut scriptum est, adnuntiauerunt opera Dei et facta eius intellexerunt. Ceterum operationem cultumque uirtutis scientia naturaliter precedit, neque enim uirtus currit in certum aut in pugna quam exercet cum uitiis aerem uerberat, sed uidet quo tendit et quo dirigit arcum. Nec passim coruos sequitur testaque lutoque. At lectio, doctrina et meditatio scientiam pariunt. (My punctuation: MS reading *archiuis* for *archanis* 52.22.) Cf. Hugh of St. Victor, *Didascalicon*, 3.6-7, trans. J. Taylor, (Columbia, 1961), pp. 90-1.

19.   *Met.* 1.24, 53.21- 54.1: Qui ergo ad philosophiam aspirat, apprehendat lectionem, doctrinam et meditationem cum exercitio boni operis, nequando irascatur Dominus et quod uidebatur habere auferatur ab eo. Sed quia legendi uerbum equiuocum est, tam ad docentis et discentis exercitium quam ad occupationem per se scrutantis scripturas, alterum, id est quod inter doctorem et discipulum communicatur, ut uerbo utamur Quintiliani, dicatur prelectio, alterum, quod ad scrutinium meditantis accedit, lectio simpliciter appelletur. (My punctuation.) Cf. Hugh of St. Victor, *Didascalicon* 3.7, *op. cit.* p. 91.

20.   *Met.* 1.13,32.14-17; *v. supra* n. 9.

21.   *Met.* 1.1, 7.2-5: Sicut enim eloquentia non modo temeraria est sed etiam ceca quam ratio non illustrat, sic et sapientia que usu uerbi non proficit non modo debilis est sed quodam modo manca. (My punctuation.)

22.   *Met.* 1.8, 25.28, 29.5: Prodest utique natura sed eatenus aut nunquam aut raro ut sine studio culmen optineat; nichil enim est tam ualidum tam robustum quod negligentia non eneruet, nichil tam erectum quod non deiciat; sicut e contra quamlibet

humilem gradum cura diligens erigit et conseruat. Ergo si natura propitia est, contemni non debet sed excoli ut facile prosit, si aduersa, eo diligentiorem cultum exigit ut ope uirtutis felicius et gloriosius inualescat. (My punctuation; MSS *negligentia* for *diligentia* (25.30.).)

23. *Met.* 2.3, 64.18-23: Vt diuertamus ad fabulas, Fronesim, sororem Alitie, nec sterilem reputauit antiquitas, sed egregiam eius sobolem castis Mercurii iunxit amplexibus. Est enim soror ueritatis prudentia, et amorem rationis et scientie per eloquentiam fecundat et illustrat. Siquidem hoc est Philologiam Mercurio copulari. (Hall's punctuation.)

24. *Met.* 2.9, 76.16-18: Ex quo liquet dialecticam, que inter ministras eloquentie expeditissima est et promptissima, unicuique prodesse ad mensuram scientie sue.

25. *ibid.* 76.14-16: Ergo et pro modulo sapientie quam quisque adeptus est eloquentia prodest; nocet enim hec, si dissocietur ab illa.

26. *Met.* 1.7, 22.15- 23.10: Ergo cui facilitas adest commode exprimendi uerbo quidem quod sentit, eloquens est. Et hoc faciendi facultas rectissime eloquentia nominatur. Qua quid esse possit prestantius ad usum, compendiosius ad opes, fidelius ad gratiam, commodius ad gloriam, non facile uideo. Nichil enim dotem istam nature et gratie antecedit aut rarum. Siquidem cum uirtus et sapientia, que forte, sicut Victorino placet, uerbis potius quam substantia differunt, in appetendis locum primum obtineant, secundum sibi eloquentia uendicat, tertius autem cedit bonis corporeis, eique ad materiam gerendorum cohabitantium fauor et rerum copia quarto loco succedunt. Secutus est hunc ordinem ethicus, uotorumque seriem in ordine expetendorum eleganter expressit:

> Quid uoueat dulci nutricula maius alumno
> quam sapere et fari possit que sentiat, et cui
> gratia, fama, ualitudo contingat habunde
> et mundus uictus non deficiente crumena.

Si ergo rationis et uerbi usu aliorum animantium naturam humana dignitas antecedit, quid conducibilius ad omnia, quid ad claritatem conciliandam potentius quam in eo nature preuenire consortes et generis in quo solus homo cetera uincit? Hec autem cum omnem etatem deceat et exornet, clariorem efficit iuuentutem, eo quod etas tenerior gratie quodammodo lenocinatur ut ingenium uendicet. Qui sunt enim qui florent inter conciues, qui sunt qui opibus pollent, qui sunt qui preualent uiribus et in omnibus negotiis obtinent nisi eloquentes? (My punctuation: MSS *locum* for *locis* (22.23); MSS *cedit bonis corporeis* for *cedit locus bonis corporeis* (22.25); MSS *rationis et uerbi* for *uerbi et rationis* (23.1); Hall's *deceat* for *doceat* (23.5).) *v. infra* p. 18: *Met.* 4.17, 183.23-28: Habet autem terrenam et mortalem Philologia originem; sed, cum ad diuina transit, immortalitate quadam deificatur. Quia cum prudentia, que de terrenis est et rationis amor, ad incorrupte ueritatis diuinorumque archana consurgit, in sapientiam transiens, quodammodo a mortalium conditione eximitur. (MSS *autem* for *enim* 183.23)

27. *Met.* 1.1, 7.13-18; *v. supra n.* 5.

28. For the castigation of verbal nimiety and pretentiousness see especially *Met.* 1.3, 10.12 -11.13, and *ibid.* 11.24 *ad fin.* : Eo autem tempore ista Cornificius didicit que nunc docenda reseruat, audienda quidem felicibus et, ut dici solet, auribus Iouis, quando in liberalibus disciplinis littera nichil erat et ubique spiritus querebatur qui, ut aiunt, latet in littera. Ylum esse ab Hercule, ualidum scilicet argumentum a forti et robusto argumentatore, potestates uocalium quinque, iura regnorum et in hunc modum docere omnia studium illius etatis erat. Insolubilis in illa philosophantium scola tunc temporis questio habebatur, an porcus qui ad uenalicium agitur ab homine an a funiculo teneatur. Item an capucium emerit qui cappam integram comparauit. Inconueniens

prorsus erat oratio in qua hec uerba 'conueniens' et 'inconueniens', 'argumentum' et 'ratio' non perstrepebant, multiplicatis particulis negatiuis et traiectis per 'esse' et 'non esse', ita ut calculo opus esset quotiens fuerat disputandum, alioquin uis affirmationis et negationis erat incognita. Nam plerumque uim affirmationis habet geminata negatio, itemque uis negatoria ab impari numero conualescit, siquidem negatio iterata plerumque seipsam perimit, et contradictioni sicut regulariter proditum est coequatur. Vt ergo pari loco an impari uersetur deprehendi queat, ad disceptationem collectam fabam et pisam deferre qui conueniebatur consilio prudenti consueuerat; ita quidem si intellectui rerum que uidebantur in questione uersari operam dabat, sufficiebat enim ad uictoriam uerbosus clamor, et qui undecumque aliquid inferebat ad propositi perueniebat metam. Poete historiographi habebantur infames, et si quis incumbebat laboribus antiquorum, notabatur . . . Sed quid docebant noui doctores et qui plus somniorum quam uigiliarum in scrutinio philosophie consumpserant, et facilius instituti quam illi iuxta narrationes fabulosas qui somniantes in Parnaso repente uates progrediebantur, aut citius quam hi qui de Castalio fonte Musarum hauriebant munus poeticum, aut quam illi qui, uiso Phebo, Musarum nedum musicorum meruerant ascribi consortio? Nunquid rude aliquid aut incultum, nunquid aliquid uetustum aut obsoletum? Ecce noua fiebant omnia, innouabatur gramatica, dialectica immutabatur, contemnebatur rethorica, et nouas totius quadruuii uias euacuatis priorum regulis de ipsis philosophie aditis proferebant. Solam 'conuenientiam' siue 'rationem' loquebantur, 'argumentum' sonabat in ore omnium, et asinum nominare uel hominem aut aliquid operum nature instar criminis erat aut ineptum nimis aut rude et a philosopho alienum. Impossibile credebatur 'conuenienter' et ad 'rationis' normam dicere quicquam aut facere nisi 'conuenientis' et 'rationis' mentio expressim esset inserta. Sed nec argumentum fieri licitum nisi premisso nomine argumenti. Ex arte et de arte agere idem erat. Docebunt hi forte quod poeta uersifice nichil dicet nisi cognominet uersum, quod faber lignarius scannum facere nequeat nisi scannum aut lignum uoluat in ore. Inde ergo hec sartago loquendi in qua senex insulsus exultat, insultans his qui artium uenerantur auctores, eo quod nichil utilitatis in his repperit, cum se eis dare operam simularet. (My punctuation: MSS *nunquid* for *numquid* throughout; MSS *qui* for *que* 11.7; MSS *hauriebant munus* for *munus hauriebant* 11.29.)

29.   *Met.* 1.1, 7.13-18; *v. supra* n. 5.

30.   Cf. *Met.* 2. prol., 60.13-15: Vtique ueritatis amatori non placent iurgia, et ultro, nedum sponte, se subtrahit contentioni quisquis amplectitur caritatem.

31.   *V.* Donatus, *Vita Vergilii*, in *Vitae Vergilianae*, ed. J. Brummer (Leipzig, 1933).

32.   *Met.* 1.2, 9.11-12: Vt libet ergo ille stertat in dies medios, cotidianis conuiscerationibus ingurgitetur ad crapulam, et in illis immunditiis uolutatus incumbat que nec porcum deceant Epicuri. (My punctuation.) Trans. McGarry *op. cit.* p. 13.

33.   *Met.* 1.5,17.16-18 and *ibid.* 18.10-19.5: Inde ergo ire, hinc lacrime, hinc indignatio quam aduersus discipulos memoratorum sapientium (sc. Abelard, William of Conches, and Thierry of Chartres) concepit Cornificii domus . . . Willelmus de Campellis errasse conuincitur scriptis propriis. Vix parcitur magistro Hugoni de Sancto Victore, et hoc quidem magis propter reuerentiam scientie aut doctrine. Deo enim in ipso deferunt non persone. (My punctuation.)

34.   Hugh of St. Victor, *Didascalicon*, 3.5, trans. Taylor *op. cit.* p. 89; *Met.* 2.19, 97.7-13: Primum quod onera importabilia teneris auditorum humeris imponunt. Deinde quod, docendi ordine pretermisso, diligentissime cauent ne
singula queque locum teneant sortita decenter;
finem enim artis, ut sic dixerim, legunt in titulo, et non modo Topicorum, sed Analecticorum et Elenchorum uim Porphirius predocet.

35. *Met.* 1.3, 9.27-30: Nescio quid arduum et ignotum omnibus sapientibus tumenti uentosi pulmonis folle concepit, unde alicui respondere aut patienter audire quempiam dedignatur. (My punctuation.)

36. *Met.* 3.3, 134.11-17: Deridebat eos noster ille Anglus Peripateticus Adam, cuius uestigia sequuntur multi, sed pauci prepediente inuidia profitentur; dicebatque se aut nullum aut auditores paucissimos habiturum, si ea simplicitate sermonum et facilitate sententiarum dialecticam traderet, qua ipsam doceri expediret.

37. *Met.* 1.24, 55.9-19: Ergo pro capacitate discentis aut docentis industria et diligentia constat fructus prelectionis auctorum. Sequebatur hunc morem Bernardus Carnotensis, exundantissimus modernis temporibus fons litterarum in Gallia, et in auctorum lectione quid simplex esset et ad imaginem regule positum ostendebat, figuras gramatice, colores rethoricos, cauillationes sophismatum, et qua parte sui proposite lectionis articulus respiciebat ad alias disciplinas proponebat in medio, ita tamen ut non in singulis uniuersa doceret, sed pro capacitate audientium dispensaret eis in tempore doctrine mensuram. (My punctuation.) Cf. Hugh of St. Victor, *Didasc.* 3.5, trans. Taylor *op. cit.* p. 90.

38. *Met.* 2.17, 92.2-9: Alius sermones intuetur et ad illos detorquet, quicquid alicubi de uniuersalibus meminit scriptum; in hac autem opinione deprehensus est Peripateticus Palatinus Abaelardus noster, qui multos reliquit et adhuc quidem aliquos habet professionis huius sectatores et testes. Amici mei sunt; licet ita plerumque captiuatam detorqueant litteram ut uel durior animus miseratione illius moueatur. (MSS *moueatur* for *mouetur* 92.9.)

39. *Met.* 1.5,17.1-3: . . . et Peripateticus Palatinus, qui logice opinionem preripuit omnibus coetaneis suis . . . (*v. supra* p. 10 and *infra* n. 57); *Met.* 2.10,78.2-4: . . . ad Peripateticum Palatinum qui tunc in monte sancte Genouefe clarus doctor et admirabilis omnibus presidebat. (*v. supra* p. 12 and *infra* n. 75); *Met.* 3. prol., 119.1-4: Et illud idem reprobabit eo quod a Gileberto, Abailardo, et Adam nostro sit prolatum? Vtique non sum ex eis qui bona temporis sui oderint et coetaneos suos inuideant commendare posteritati. (*oderunt* Webb 1.3); *Met.* 3.1,120:6-14: Equidem ex animi mei sententia sic omnem librum legi oportet, ut quam facillime potest eorum que scribuntur habeatur cognitio. Non enim occasio querenda est ingerende difficultatis, sed ubique facilitas generanda. Quem morem secutum recolo Peripateticum Palatinum. Inde est, ut opinor, quod se ad puerilem de generibus et speciebus, ut pace suorum loquar, inclinauit opinionem; malens instruere et promouere suos in puerilibus quam in grauitate philosophorum esse obscurior. (MSS *se* for *sed* 120.11); *ibid.* 123.5-9: Nec tamen ob hoc esse incorporeum sequitur; quoniam, ut aiebat Abaelardus, negatio uehementior est. Figuratiue quoque locutionis progressum inhibebat; eo quod figuras non licet extendere, que ipse non recipiuntur, nisi cum expedit. ; *Met.* 3.4, 136.10-18, *v infra* n. 42.

40. R. W. Southern, 'Humanism and the School of Chartres', in *Mediaeval Humanism and Other Essays*, (Oxford, 1970), p. 79.

41. *Met.* 1.24, 55.11-57.6: Sequebatur hunc morem Bernardus Carnotensis, exundantissimus modernis temporibus fons litterarum in Gallia, et in auctorum lectione quid simplex esset et ad imaginem regule positum ostendebat, figuras gramatice, colores rethoricos, cauillationes sophismatum, et qua parte sui proposite lectionis articulus respiciebat ad alias disciplinas proponebat in medio, ita tamen ut non in singulis uniuersa doceret, sed pro capacitate audientium dispensaret eis in tempore doctrine mensuram. Et quia splendor orationis aut a proprietate est, id est cum adiectiuam aut uerbum substantiuo eleganter adiungitur, aut a translatione, id est ubi sermo ex causa probabili ad alienam traducitur significationem, hoc sumpta occasione inculcabat mentibus auditorum. Et quoniam memoria exercitio firmatur,

ingeniumque acuitur ad imitandum ea que audiebant, alios admonitionibus, alios flagellis et penis urgebat. Cogebantur exsoluere singuli die sequenti aliquid eorum que precedenti audierant, alii plus, alii minus; erat enim apud eos precedentis discipulus sequens dies. Vespertinum exercitium, quod declinatio dicebatur, tanta copiositate gramatice refertum erat ut siquis in eo per annum integrum uersaretur, rationem loquendi et scribendi, si non esset hebetior, haberet ad manum, et significationem sermonum qui in communi usu uersantur ignorare non posset. Sed quia nec scolam nec diem aliquem decet esse religionis expertem, ea proponebatur materia que fidem edificaret et mores, et unde qui conuenerant quasi collatione quadam animarentur ad bonum. Nouissimus autem huius declinationis, immo philosophice collationis, articulus pietatis uestigia preferebat, et animas defunctorum commendabat deuota oblatione psalmi qui in penitentialibus sextus est, et oratione Dominica Redemptori suo. Quibus autem indicebantur preexercitamina puerorum in prosis aut poematibus imitandis, poetas aut oratores proponebat et eorum iubebat uestigia imitari, ostendens iuncturas dictionum et elegantes sermonum clausulas. Si quis autem ad splendorem sui operis alienum pannum assuerat, deprehensum redarguebat furtum, sed panem sepissime non infligebat. Sic uero redargutum, si hoc tamen meruerat inepta positio, ad exprimendam auctorum imaginem modesta indulgentia conscendere iubebat, faciebatque ut qui maiores imitabatur, fieret posteris imitandus. Id quoque inter prima rudimenta docebat et infigebat animis, que in economia uirtus, que in decore rerum, que in uerbis laudanda sint, ubi tenuitas et quasi macies sermonis, ubi copia probabilis, ubi excedens, ubi omnium modus. Historias et poemata percurrenda monebat diligenter quidem et qui uelut nullis calcaribus urgebantur ad fugam, et ex singulis aliquid reconditum in memoria, diurnum debitum, diligenti instantia exigebat. Superflua tamen fugienda dicebat, et ea sufficere que a claris auctoribus scripta sunt; siquidem persequi quid quis unquam uel contemptissimorum hominum dixerit, aut nimie miserie aut inanis iactantie est, et detinet atque obruit ingenia melius aliis uacatura; quod autem melius tollit, eo usque non prodest quod nec boni censetur nomine; omnes enim scedas excutere et euoluere scripturas etiam lectione indignas non magis ad rem pertinet quam anilibus fabulis operam dare. (My punctuation: MSS *hoc* for *hec* (55.23); MSS *et oratione* for *et in oratione* (56.10); Hall's *historias et poemata* for *historias poemata* (56.24).

42. In full, *Met.* 3.4,136.10-137.11: Dixisse recolo Peripateticum Palatinum quod uerum arbitror, quia facile esset aliquem nostri temporis librum de hac arte componere, qui nullo antiquorum quod ad conceptionem ueri uel ad elegantiam uerbi, esset inferior; sed ut auctoritatis fauorem sortiretur aut impossibile aut difficillimum. Hoc ipsum tamen asserebat maioribus ascribendum, quorum floruerunt ingenia, et inuentione mirabili pollentes: laboris sui fructum posteris reliquerunt. Itaque ea, in quibus multi sua tempora consumpserunt, in inuentione sudantes plurimum, nunc facile et breui unus assequitur; fruitur tamen etas nostra beneficio precedentis et sepe plura nouit, non suo quidem precedens ingenio, sed innitens uiribus alienis et opulenta doctrina patrum. Dicebat Bernardus Carnotensis nos esse quasi nanos gigantum humeris insidentes, ut possimus plura eis et remotiora uidere, non utique proprii uisus acumine aut eminentia corporis, sed quia in altum subuehimur et extollimur magnitudine gigantea. Et his facile adquieuerim, quia artis preparatitia et multos articulos ueritatis tradunt artium preceptores, etiam in Introductionibus suis, eque bene antiquis et forte commodius. Quis enim contentus est his que uel Aristotiles in Periermeiniis docet? Quis aliunde conquisita non adicit? Omnes enim totius artis summam colligunt, et uerbis facilibus tradunt. Vestiunt enim sensus auctorum quasi cultu cotidiano, qui quodammodo festiuior est, cum antiquitatis grauitate clarius insignitur. Sunt ergo memoriter tenenda uerba auctorum, sed ea maxime que plenas sententias explent, et que commode possunt ad multa transferri; nam et hec

integritatem scientie seruant, et preter hoc a seipsis tam latentis quam patentis energie habent plurimum. (MSS *uel ad elegantiam* for *uel elegantiam* (136.13); MS *opulenta doctrina patrum* for *opulenta patrum* (136.22-23); MSS *gigantum* for *gigantium* (136.24); MSS *Et* for *ex* (136.27).)

43. *Met.* 2.17, 94.22-26: Egerunt operosius Bernardus Carnotensis et auditores eius ut componerent inter Aristotilem et Platonem, sed eos tarde uenisse arbitror et laborasse in uanum ut reconciliarent mortuos qui, quamdiu in uita licuit, dissenserunt.

44. *Met.* 4.3, 167.15-23: Vnde qui Aristotilem sequuntur in turbatione nominum et uerborum et intricata subtilitate, ut suum uenditent, aliorum obtundant ingenia, partem pessimam michi preelegisse uidentur, quo quidem uitio Anglicus noster michi pre ceteris uisus est laborasse in libro quem Artem Disserendi inscripsit. Et utinam bene dixisset bona que dixit; et licet familiares eius et fautores hoc subtilitati asscribant, plurimi tamen hoc ex desipientia uel inuidentia uani, ut aiunt, hominis contigisse interpretati sunt.

45. For example: C. Schaarschmidt, *Johannes Saresberiensis nach Leben und Studien, Schriften und Philosophie*, (Leipzig, 1862); H. Liebeschutz, *Medieval Humanism in the Life and Writings of John of Salisbury*, (London, 1950); R. L. Poole, 'The Masters of the Schools of Paris and Chartres in John of Salisbury's Time', *E.H.R.* 35 (1920), 321-342; and recently, O. Weijers, 'The Chronology of John of Salisbury's Studies in France (Metalogicon 11.10)', in *The World of John of Salisbury*, ed. M. Wilks, (Oxford, 1984), and K. S. B. Keats-Rohan, 'The Chronology of John of Salisbury's Studies in France: A Reading of *Metalogicon* 11.10', forthcoming in *Studi Medievali*, where the argument of pp. 12-20 below appears in note form.

46. Southern, *op. cit.* pp. 61-85 *passim*. The most notable replies were P. Dronke, 'New Approaches to the School of Chartres', *Annuario de estudios medievales* 6 (1971), 117-140, and N. Häring, 'Chartres and Paris Revisited', in *Essays in Honour of A. Ch. Pegis*, (Toronto, 1974), pp. 268-329. Southern refers to the issue also in his 'Platonism, Scholastic Method and the School of Chartres', Stenton Lecture 1979, (Reading University Press), and 'The Schools of Paris and the School of Chartres', in *Renaissance and Renewal in the Twelfth Century*, ed. R. L. Benson and G. Constable, (Oxford, 1982), pp. 113-137.

47. Southern 1970, p. 62.

48. C. B. Schmitt, 'Aristotelianism in the Veneto and the Origins of Modern Science: Some Considerations on the Problem of Continuity', in *The Aristotelian Tradition and Renaissance Universities*, (Variorum Reprints, London, 1984), I p. 108.

49. Chr. Petersen, edition of *Entheticus*, (Hamburg, 1843), pp. 68-78.

50. Here and throughout I have largely taken my account of historical fact from secondary sources, relying for the most part on Häring's carefully researched account of the careers of the masters with whom I am concerned in the article cited in note 46.

51. *v. supra* n. 41.

52. *Met.* 1.5, 16.7-15: Solebat magister Gilebertus, tunc quidem cancellarius Carnotensis et postmodum uenerabilis episcopus Pictauorum temporis eius nescio ridens aut dolens insaniam, cum eos uidebat ad studia que predicta sunt euolare, eis artem pistoriam polliceri, quoniam illa est, ut aiebat, in gente sua que sola excipere consueuit omnes aliis opibus aut artificio destitutos; ars enim facillime exercetur et subsidiaria est aliarum, presertim apud eos qui panem potius quam artificium querunt. (My punctuation: MSS *excipere* for *accipere* (16.12); MSS *opibus* for *operibus* (ib.).)

53. *Met.* 2.10, 82.6-7, *v. infra* pp. 17-20.

54. Häring (*op. cit.* p. 274) suggested that Gilbert was replaced as chancellor of Chartres after 1137 by one Guido. This is denied by Southern in 'The Schools of Paris and the School of Chartres', p. 125 n. 31, in which he points out that Guido appears as

Guido cancellarius in a transcript of a charter of 1136, when Gilbert is known to have been in office; further an original document of 1139 is extant wherein Guido appears as *Guido cancellarii,* so that in the earlier document a mistaken transcription of *cancellarius* for *cancellarii,* which would be easy, seems the only explanation'.

55.   Robert of Torigny, *Chronicon,* ed. R. Howlett, Rolls Series 82, vol. 4, (London, 1889), p. 181: Moritur etiam Gislebertus, episcopus Pictauensis, uir religiosus et multiplicis doctrinae, qui psalmos et epistolas Pauli luculenter exposuit.

56.   Thierry himself apparently made some curious — and disputed — observations concerning his own career in both the introduction to his commentary on Cicero's *De inuentione,* and at the end of the commentary on the first book of this work. I give the text as printed by N. Häring *op. cit.* pp. 292-4:

Vt ait Petronius, nos magistri in scolis relinquemur soli nisi multos palpemus et insidias auribus fecerimus. Ego uero non ita. Nam medius fidius paucorum gratia multis mea prostitui. Sic tamen meum consilium contraxi ut uulgus profanum et farraginem scole petulcans excluderem.

Nam simulatores ingenii exsecrando studium et professores domestici studii dissimulando magistrum tum etiam scolastice disputationis histriones inanium uerborum pugnis armati tales quidem mea castra secuntur sed extra palatium quos sola nominis aura hinc detulit ut in partibus suis studio pellacie Theodoricum mentiantur. Sed, ut ait Persius (4,21): Esto dum non deterius sapiat pannuncia Baucis.

Atque hec hactenus ne, cui prefacio incumbit, is eam prolixitatis arguens forte rescindat . . .

At the end of the first book of Cicero's *De inuentione* Thierry suddenly interrupts his commentary to insert a passage in which *Inuidia* addresses *Fama.* The story Envy has to tell is not a pleasing one:

Inuidia falso uultu dyaletice subornata Famam sic alloquitur et fallacibus uerbis, ut solet, aggreditur:

Diua potens! Notum est cunctis quantum rerum in te consistat momentum. Nam — ut taceam quod auctoritate tui iudicii rerum humanarum pretium libretur — illud singulare tuum totus predicat orbis quod celitum gestamina uicissim assumas: Saturni falcem, fulmen Iouis, Archadis alas, Gradiui frameam, tum spicula ceca Dione tum Phebi citharam tum spicula certa Diane.

Te omnes poete ac oratores sequuntur. Te quidam ex sectatoribus meis summum bonum esse reputant. To mundus omnis timet offendere. Te etiam ego ipsa ueneror tum propter antiquam familiaritatem et amicitiam tum presertim quia sine te scola nostra tepesceret. Cum igitur et in diuinis et in humanis tam potens appareas, quid est quod tam patienter opprobria sustines?

Ecce Theodoricus Brito, homo barbarice nationis, uerbis insulsus, corpore ac mente incompositus, mendacem de se te uocat quod ei nomen meum super omnes non scribas. Idcirco igitur te uerbis turpissimis persequitur ille superbus inuidus detractor, inimicis supplex, amicis contumeliosus, sicut etiam sui discipuli de eo adtestantur. Quare ergo et quod maxime de tuis bonis appetit aut meretur, illud ei subtrahe ut ne promeruisse uideatur.

Talibus Inuidie uerbis Fama permota alas concutit, sonos multiplicat, urbes et nationes duce Inuidia peragrat, rumoribus implet, Theodoricum ubique accusat, ignominiosis nominibus appellat. Cum uero rudibus et indiscretis loquitur, Boetum crasso tunc iurat in aere natum. Quando uero religiosis tunc nicromanticum uel hereticum uocat. At inter conscios ueritatis tacet. Et si de eo mentio fiat, aliam hystoriam inceptat.

In scolis uero et scolarium conuentibus mentes conmutat ut ignominiam eius lucretur. Platonem ei concedit ut rethoricam auferat. Rethoricam uero uel gramaticam quasi per ypothesim donat ut dyaleticam surripiat. Quidlibet uero potius quam dyaleticam tum mores eius improbos tum negligentiam in studio tum longas interpositiones inculcat. Ad ultimum, cum cetera deficiunt, obicit eum legere prouectis ut nouos detineat uel potius corrumpat ut ulterius non possint apud eum proficere.

Hactenus Inuidie respondi.

57.   *Met.* 1.5, 16.15-17.4: Sed et alii uiri amatores litterarum, utpote magister Theodoricus, artium studiosissimus inuestigator, itidem Willelmus de Conchis gramaticus post Bernardum Carnotensem opulentissimus, et Peripateticus Palatinus, qui logice opinionem preripuit omnibus coetaneis suis, adeo ut solus Aristotelis crederetur usus colloquio, se omnes opposuerunt errori. (My punctuation.)

58.   *ibid.* 18.1: . . . Lauduni gloriam, fratres theologos Ansellum et Radulfum . . .

59.   John of Salisbury, *Historia Pontificalis*, ed. M. Chibnall, (London, 1956), pp. 18-19: Audierat enim, ut dicebat, in scolis clarissimorum doctorum fratrum Anselmi et Radulfi Laudunensium . . .

60.   For William of Tyre's account of his own education c. 1145-63 see R. B. C. Huygens, 'Guillaume de Tyre Étudiant: Un chapitre (XIX, 12) de son "Histoire" retrouve', *Latomus* 21 (1962), 811-29; 822.14-20: . . . magister Bernardus Brito, qui postea (fuit) in patria unde ortus fuerat episcopus Cornualenssis, magister Petrus Helie, natione Pictauenssis, magister Iuo, genere et natione Carnotenssis. Hii omnes magistri Theodorici senioris uiri litteratissimi per multa tempora auditores fuerunt; horum tamen nouissimus, magister Iuo, magistri Gilleberti Porrea Pictauenssis episcopi, quem post magistrum Theodoricum audierat, doctrinam profitebatur.

61.   Otto of Freising, *Gesta Friderici* I,52: MGH Sr G 46,74.

62.   *v. supra* n. 41.

63.   Everard of Ypres, *Dialogus Ratii et Everardi*, ed. N. M. Haring 'A Latin Dialogue on the Doctrine of Gilbert of Poitiers', *Medieval Studies*, xv (1953), p. 252.

64.   This statement seems to demonstrate the relative unimportance of Chartres as a teaching centre in contradistinction to Paris. I note the following passage in Peter Dronke's very interesting article (*op. cit.* n. 46, p. 128): 'This is precisely the myth of Paris that had reached the ears of a young Englishman, Daniel of Morley, who came there on his first trip abroad, around 1150, in search of wisdom. The reality, as he saw it, was sadly different: Cum dudum ab Anglia me causa studii excepissem et Parisius aliquamdiu moram fecissem, uidebam quosdam bestiales in scolis graui auctoritate sedes occupare . . . Qui, dum propter inscitiam suam locum statuae tenerent, tamen uolebant sola taciturnitate uideri sapientes, sed tales, cum aliquid dicere conabantur, infantissimos repperiebam. Cum hec, inquam, in hunc modum se habere deprehenderem, ne et ego simile damnum incurrerem, artes, que scripturas illuminant, non in transitu salutandas uel sub compendio pretereundas mecum sollicita deliberatione tractabam. Sed quoniam doctrina Arabum, que in quadruuio fere tota existit, maxime his diebus apud Toletum celebratur, illuc, ut sapientiores mundi philosophos audirem, festinanter properaui. In northern Europe it was Chartres, rather than Paris, that first showed itself exceptionally receptive to the *doctrina Arabum*, the knowledge being furthered *apud Toletum*. If it had occurred to Daniel to visit Chartres, he would have found, not all the riches of Toledo, but certainly some books of Arab science and some open-minded men to discuss them with', and I would only observe that it did not after all occur to Daniel to visit Chartres, a perhaps eloquent omission.

65.   N. M. Haring, in 'The Cistercian Everard of Ypres and His Appraisal of the Conflict between St. Bernard and Gilbert of Poitiers', *Medieval Studies* 17 (1955) 143-

72, writes (pp. 147-8): 'However, if Gilbert's handling of the Greek in the *Opuscula* is any indication of what he was taught, Everard had little of which to be proud'.

66. Dronke *op. cit.* p. 120.

67. *v. supra* n. 57.

68. *Met.* 1.24, 57.23-27.

69. *v. infra* pp. 10-11.

70. Robert of Torigny, *Chronicon, op. cit.* p. 304: Obiit pater noster Richardus, Abrincensis episcopus, uir magnae litteraturae tam secularis quam diuinae, morum honestate uirgo ab utero laudandus.

71. *The Letters of John of Salisbury: Volume Two, The Later Letters* (1163-1180), ed. W. J. Millor, S.J. and C. N. L. Brooke, (Oxford, 1979), Letter 201, pp. 292-4.

72. Southern 1970, p. 73.

73. To give one unfortunate example, on p. 295 of his article Häring writes: 'After posing this question R. W. Southern states: 'Apart from this relationship he (= Bernard) would scarely have begun to have a place in the early history of the school'. In other words, we are told that 'Bernard of Chartres owes most of his renown to his *brother* Thierry', whereas in fact on p. 69 of 'Humanism and the School of Chartres', Southern's remark clearly refers to the subject — Thierry — of his preceding question: 'To begin with: was Thierry the brother of Bernard of Chartres?' Bernard, indeed, so far from having a place in the early history of the 'School of Chartres', has an honoured place in its late history.

74. *Met.* 2.10, 77.31-78.1.

75. *ibid.* 78.2-4.

76. *ibid.* 78.4-6.

77. *v. supra* n. 38.

78. *v. supra* n. 39.

79. For the following paraphrase see *Met.* 2.10, 78.6-79.22: Deinde post discessum eius, qui michi preproperus uisus est, adhesi magistro Alberico, qui inter ceteros opinatissimus dialecticus enitebat et erat reuera nominalis secte acerrimus impugnator. Sic ferme toto biennio conuersatus in monte, artis huius preceptoribus usus sum Alberico et magistro Rodberto Meludensi (ut cognomine designetur quod meruit in scolarum regimine, natione siquidem Angligena est); quorum alter, ad omnia scrupulosus, locum questionis inueniebat ubique, ut quamuis polita planities offendiculo non careret et, ut aiunt, ei cirpus non esset enodis. Nam et ibi monstrabat quid oporteat enodari. Alter autem, in responsione promptissimus, subterfugii causa propositum nunquam declinauit articulum, quin alteram contradictionis partem eligeret aut determinata multiplicitate sermonis doceret unam non esse responsionem. Ille ergo in questionibus subtilis et multus; iste in responsis perspicax, breuis et commodus. Que duo si pariter eis alicui omnium contigissent, parem utique disputatorem nostra etate non esset inuenire. Ambo enim acuti erant ingenii et studii peruicacis; et, ut reor, magni preclarique uiri in phisicis studiis enituissent, si de magno litterarum niterentur fundamento, si tantum institissent uestigiis maiorum quantum suis applaudebant inuentis. Hec pro tempore quo illis adhesi. Nam postea unus eorum, profectus Bononiam, dedidicit quod docuerat; siquidem et reuersus dedocuit. An melius, iudicent qui eum ante et postea audierunt. Porro alter in diuinis proficiens litteris etiam eminentioris philosophie et celebrioris nominis assecutus est gloriam.

80. Because as Bishop he supported Henry II against Archbishop Becket of Canterbury, whose exile John shared; *Letters of John of Salisbury Vol. Two, op. cit.*, Letters 171, pp. 126-7; 174, pp. 142-3; 175, pp. 156-7, 162-3; 176, pp. 172-3.

81.   Häring *op. cit.* pp. 317-8. For the preceding paraphrase see n. 79 above (*Met.* 2.10, 78.6-79.1).

82.   William of Tyre, ed. Huygens *op. cit.* 822.21-823.26: Audiuimus et alios etsi non assidue, tamen sepius et maxime disputationis gratia, uiros eximios et omni laude prosequendos magistrum Albericum de Monte, magistrum Robertum de Meleuduno, magistrum Mainerum, magistrum Robertum Amiclas, magistrum Adam de Paruo Ponte, qui uidebantur quasi *maiora luminaria.*

83.   *Met.* 2.10, 79.3-4; *v. supra* n. 79.

84.   *ibid.* 79.8; *v. supra* n. 79.

85.   Latin at *ibid.* 79.10-16, *v. supra* n. 79.

86.   *ibid.* 79.20-22, *v. supra* n. 79.

87.   *ibid.* 79.17-20, *v. supra* n. 79.

88.   *ibid.* 78.10.

89.   *ibid.* 79.22.

90.   *ibid.* 79.22-29: Apud hos, toto exercitatus biennio, sic locis assignandis assueui et regulis et aliis rudimentorum elementis, quibus pueriles animi imbuuntur, et in quibus prefati doctores potentissimi erant et expeditissimi, ut hec omnia michi uiderer nosse tanquam ungues digitosque meos. Hoc enim plane didiceram, ut iuuenili leuitate pluris facerem scientiam meam quam esset. Videbar michi sciolus, eo quod in iis que audieram promptus eram.

91.   *ibid.* 79.29-80.2.

92.   *ibid.* 80.2.

93.   *ibid.* 80.2-3.

94.   *v. supra* n. 19.

95.   *Met.* 2.10, 80.3-13.

96.   *v. supra* n. 70.

97.   *v. supra* n. 60.

98.   *Met.* 2.10, 80.13-81.3.

99.   *ibid.* 81.3-11.

100. *ibid.* 81.8-10.

101. *Met.* 4.3, *v. supra* n. 44.

102. *v. supra* n. 36.

103. *Met.* 2.10, 81.11-82.3.

104. William of Tyre *op. cit.* 823.39-41.

105. *Met.* 2.10, 82.3-6.

106. On the occasion of my reading this paper to the Warburg seminar it was put to me that the lines 'Extraxerunt . . . Parui' might be interpreted to mean that it was suggested to John by his friends that he should prepare himself for a teaching career at a more advanced level, and that by agreeing to do this (*Parui*), and thus advancing the argument of his text, he was rescued from teaching the likes of William of Soissons at the end of his period of part-time study with William of Conches (*Extraxerunt me hinc*). The fact that John resumes his full-time education at a higher level of study, involving theology, (*Reuersus itaque . . . logicis et diuinis*) is adduced in support of this contention. While this interpretation is certainly very attractive, I find myself wondering whether the teaching of higher studies would be described as *officium docentis*, even in contradistinction to an earlier implied *officium instruendi*, which in fact I have taken to be a reinforcement of the previous appearance of *officium*. There is

no further evidence in John's text that he ever did undertake such advanced teaching, nor do I know of any compelling evidence elsewhere that he did so. It might also be noted that I have translated *aggrederer* as meaning not merely 'I should begin (to teach)', but as having the sense of 'get to grips with', or, as I have written, 'to begin to take his humbler teaching duties seriously' — and it might be borne in mind that another sense of the verb is 'to attack'! I agree that the lines in question are somewhat syncopated, but I believe that my interpretation allows the text to be fully logical and coherent, without resorting to any emendation of the Latin, as it is surely meant to be, and that we should not hesitate to expand the meaning of these lines by interpreting fully the parable of William of Soissons' later career. The sorry story of William of Soissons, as I see it, fits into a chronological digression in John's account, the linguistic unity of which is signalled by the two appearances of *officium*, and itself advances the argument by providing another powerful illustration, from personal experience, of John's primary contention that misdirected dialectic will always be without fruit. It is not impossible, however, that the truth ultimately lies somewhere between these two interpretations, and I am happy to record this divergency from my own interpretation.

107.   *Met.* 2.10, 82.6-7.

108.   They are particularly distinguished by their Platonism, which has contributed to their being linked together in a 'school of Chartres': see T. Gregory, *Anima Mundi: la filosofia di Guglielmo di Conches e la scuola di Chartres*, (Florence, 1955), and compare, for example, William of Conches *Philosophia mundi, P. L.*, 172, 41-102, and Thierry of Chartres, *De sex dierum operibus*, ed. N. M. Haring, *A. H. D. L. M. A.*, 22, (1955), pp. 137-226.

109.   Southern, 1979, p. 16 n. 16: 'The only evidence that William of Conches was a pupil of Bernard of Chartres is John of Salisbury's statement (*Metalogicon*, ed. C. C. J. Webb, pp. 57-8) that William whom he elsewhere (pp. 16-17) calls 'grammaticus post Bernardum opulentissimus', and Richard Bishop both followed the teaching method of Bernard, until the demand of students for quicker results made them give up ('impetu multitudinis imperite uicti cesserunt'). There are two problems here: 1. Does this statement imply that William of Conches and Richard Bishop, besides following the method of teaching of which Bernard was the chief exponent in the earlier generation, were his pupils? No clear answer can be given, but the implication that they were pupils seems likely. 2. Does he mean that they gave up teaching altogether on account of the changed demand of the students, or that they merely changed their method of teaching? The natural sense of *cesserunt*, as well as perhaps the natural impulse of teachers out of tune with their time, would be that they went out of business. If so, and if William had given up regular teaching by 1139, his statement (which he made in dedicating his *Dragmaticon* to the Duke of Normandy in 1144-50) that he had taught the subjects comprised in his treatise 'for twenty years and more' would be easier to understand: it is impossible to construct a plausible chronology of William's career on the basis of a twenty-year teaching career beginning in about 1125 and continuing to 1145-50, but a regular teaching career from c. 1115 or a little earlier to c. 1135, would be consistent with all the evidence. (See A. Wilmart, *Analecta Reginensia, Studi e Testi* 59, 1933, p. 264 for the dedicatory letter of the *Dragmaticon*.)'.

110.   *Met.* 1.24, 57.23-58.4: Ad huius magistri formam preceptores mei in gramatica, Willelmus de Conchis et Ricardus, cognomento episcopus, officio nunc archidiaconus Constantiensis, uita et conuersatione uir bonus, suos discipulos aliquamdiu informauerunt. Sed postmodum, ex quo opinio ueritati preiudicium fecit, et homines uideri quam esse philosophi maluerunt, professoresque artium se totam philosophiam breuius quam triennio aut biennio transfusuros auditoribus pollicebantur, impetu multitudinis imperite uicti cesserunt.

111.   *Met.* 2.10, 82.6-8.

112.   *v. supra* p. 9, and nn. 45, 46.

113.   *Met.* 2.10, 82.9.

114.   Bernard of Clairvaux, *Epistola* 205, PL. 182.372.

115.   *Met.* 1.5, 19.5-20.2: Rodbertus Pullus, cuius memoria bonis omnibus iocunda est, diceretur filius subiugalis nisi sedi apostolice deferretur, que ipsum de doctore scolastico cancellarium fecit. (My punctuation.)

116.   *ibid.* 18.4-10: Nam de Alberico Remensi et Symone Parisiensi palam loquuntur et prouerbium nullum dicunt, et sequaces eorum non modo philosophos negant, immo nec clericos patiuntur, uix homines sinunt esse, sed boues Abrahe uel asinos Balaamitas dumtaxat nominant, immo derident, aut si quid scomatice magis aut ledorice in eos dici potest. (My punctuation: MSS *Balaamitas*, for *-tos* (18.8).)

117.   *Met.* 2.10, 82.10-11.

118.   *ibid.* 82.12-13.

119.   *ibid.* 82.13 *ad. fin.* : Iocundum itaque uisum est ueteres quos reliqueram et quos adhuc dialectica detinebat in monte reuisere socios, conferre cum eis super ambiguitatibus pristinis, ut nostrum inuicem ex collatione mutua commetiremur profectum. Inuenti sunt qui fuerant et ubi; neque enim ad palmum uisi sunt processisse. Ad questiones pristinas dirimendas neque propositiunculam unam adiecerant. Quibus urgebant stimulis, eisdem et ipsi urgebantur, profecerant in uno dumtaxat, dedidicerant modum, modestiam nesciebant; adeo quidem ut de reparatione eorum posset desperari. Expertus itaque sum, quod liquido colligi potest, quia, sicut dialectica alias expedit disciplinas, sic, si sola fuerit, iacet exanguis et sterilis, nec ad fructum philosophie fecundat animam, si aliunde non concipit. (MSS *palmum* for *palmam* (82.18), and *dedidicerant* for *dedicerant* (82.21).)

120.   *Met.* 3.2, 124.21-125.19: Aiebat Bernardus Carnotensis quia albedo significat uirginem incorruptam, *albet* eandem introeuntem thalamum aut cubantem in thoro, *album* uero eandem, sed corruptam. Hoc quidem quoniam *albedo* ex assertione eius simpliciter et sine omni participatione subiecti ipsam significat qualitatem, uidelicet coloris speciem, disgregatiuam uisus. *Albet* autem eandem principaliter, etsi participationem persone admittat. Si enim illud excutias, quod uerbum hoc pro substantia significat, qualitas albedinis occurret, sed in accidentibus uerbi personam reperies. *Album* uero eandem significat qualitatem, sed infusam commixtamque substantie et iam quodammodo magis corruptam; siquidem nomen ipsum pro substantia subiectum albedinis, pro qualitate significat colorem albentis subiecti. Videbatur etiam sibi tam de Aristotile quam de multorum auctoritatibus niti. Ait enim: *Album* nichil aliud significat quam qualitatem. Multa quoque proferebat undique conquisita, quibus persuadere nitebatur res interdum pure, interdum adiacenter predicari, et ad hoc denominatiuorum scientiam perutilem asserebat. Habet hec opinio sicut impugnatores, sic defensores suos. Michi pro minimo est ad nomen in talibus disputare, cum intelligentiam dictorum sumendam nouerim ex causis dicendi. Nec sic memoratam Aristotilis aliorumue auctoritates interpretandas arbitror, ut trahatur istuc quicquid alicubi dictum reperitur.

121.   *Met.* 4.24, 191.4-12: Satis ergo mirari non possum quid mentis habeant (si quid tamen habent) qui hec Aristotilis opera carpunt, que utique non exponere propositum fuerat sed laudare. Magister Theodoricus, ut memini, Topica non Aristotilis sed Trecasini Drogonis irridebat; eadem tamen quandoque docuit. Quidam auditores magistri Rodberti de Meliduno librum hunc fere inutilem esse calumniantur. Alii detrahunt Cathegoriis. Vnde in commendatione eorum diutius moratus sum . . .

122.   *v. supra* n. 57.

123. *v. supra* n. 110.

124. *v. supra* p. 14 and n. 95.

125. *v. supra* n. 9.

126. *v. supra* n. 6.

127. *Met.* 2.10, 82.23 *ad fin.*

128. *Met.* 2.9, 76.14-20, 76.23- 77.8, 77.14 *ad fin.* : Ergo et pro modulo sapientie quam quisque adeptus est eloquentia prodest; nocet enim hec, si dissocietur ab illa. Ex quo liquet dialecticam, que inter ministras eloquentie expeditissima est et promptissima, unicuique prodesse ad mensuram scientie sue. Ei enim prodest plurimum qui habet notitiam plurimorum et ei qui pauca nouit minimum prodest . . . sic dialectica, si aliarum disciplinarum uigore destituatur, quodammodo manca est et inutilis fere. Si aliarum robore uigeat, potens est omnem destruere falsitatem; et, ut minimum ei ascribam, sufficit de omnibus probabiliter disputare. Neque enim magnum est si more nostrorum iugiter in se rotetur, se circumeat, sua rimetur archana, et in illis dumtaxat uersetur que nec domi, nec militie, nec in foro, nec in claustro, nec in curia, nec in ecclesia, immo nusquam nisi in scola prosunt; ibi enim teneriori etati plura indulgentur ad modum et modicum, que mox magis serius philosophie tractatus eliminat. Siquidem hic, cum ad maturam scientie uel uite uenitur etatem, non modo uerba puerilia et licentioris indulgentie, sed totos plerumque reicit libros . . . Est autem cuique opifici facillimum de arte sua loqui; sed ex arte quod artis est facere difficillimum est. Quis est enim medicus qui non de elementis et humoribus et complexionibus et morbis et ceteris pertinentibus ad phisicam sepe loquatur et multum? Sed qui ad hoc conualescit, magis poterat egrotare. Quis ethicus morum regulis, dum in lingua uersantur, non habundat? Sed plane longe difficilius est ut exprimantur in uita. Mecanici opifices facile singuli loquuntur de artibus suis, sed nemo eorum tam leui opera architectum exercet aut pugilem. Idem est et in reliquis. Sic de diffinitione aut argumentis aut genere et similibus loqui facillimum est; sed eadem ad artis explendum officium in singulis facultatibus inuenire longe difficilius. Ergo qui disciplinarum inopia premitur, copiam, quam dialectica pollicetur et prestat, non habebit. Transl. McGarry, *op. cit.* pp. 93-5.

129. *Met.* 2.11, 83.5-10.

130. *ibid.* 83.16 *ad fin.*

131. *Met.* 1.4, 16.2-4: . . . adeo quidem ut sic proficientium philosophorum, aut ut uerius dixerim deficientium, collatione quiuis in turba prophane multitudinis rudis ad flagitia uideretur. (My punctuation.) Transl. McGarry *op. cit.* p. 20.

132. *v. supra.* n. 32.

133. *Met.* 1.4, 12.22-14.6: Ceterum huius secte damnum temporis rerumque iacturam et spes deceptas et propositi sui solatio destitutas multiplex usus emersit. Alii namque monachorum aut clericorum claustrum ingressi sunt et plerumque suum correxerunt errorem, deprehendentes in se et aliis predicantes quia quicquid didicerant uanitas uanitatum est et super omnia uanitas. Plerumque, inquam, eo quod quidam in sua perdurantes insania, tumide uetusta peruersitate, malebant desipere quam ab humilibus quibus Deus dat gratiam fideliter erudiri; erubescebant enim formam discipuli qui magisterii presumpserant fastum. Si michi non credis, claustra ingredere, scrutare mores fratrum, et inuenies ibi superbiam Moab et eam intensam ualde ut arrogantia absorbeat fortitudinem eius. Miratur Benedictus et queritur quod se quodammodo auctore latet lupus in pellibus agninis; utique tonsuram et pullam uestem a supercilio distare causatur. Et ut rectius dixerim, supercilium arguit eo quod tonsure uestibusque non consonet. Ritus obseruationum contemnitur, et sub imagine philosophantis spiritus fallacis elationis obrepit. Nota sunt hec et in omni ueste ac professione uulgata. Alii autem suum in philosophia intuentes defectum, Salernum uel

ad Montem Pessulanum profecti, facti sunt clientuli medicorum, et repente, quales fuerant philosophi, tales in momento medici eruperunt. Fallacibus enim referti experimentis in breui redeunt, sedulo exercentes quod didicerunt. Hippocratem ostentant aut Galienum, uerba proferunt inaudita, ad omnia suos loquuntur afforismos et mentes humanas uelut afflatas tonitruis sic percellunt nominibus inauditis. Creduntur omnia posse quia omnia iactitant, omnia pollicentur. Duo tamen deprehendi eos fideliori tenuisse memoria et frequentius in eorum operatione uersari. Alterum quidem Hipocratis est, sed ibi uergit ad alium intellectum: ubi, inquit, indigentia, non oportet laborare. Et reuera hi inopportunum et inofficiosum opinantur dare operam indigentibus et his qui nolunt aut nequeunt uel solis uerbis eorum plene gratiam referre mercedis. Alterum profecto est non quod meminerim Hipocratis sed diligentium adiectio medicorum: dum dolet accipe. (My punctuation: MSS readings *plerumque* for *plerique* (12.28); *tumide* for *tumidi* (13.1); *opinantur* for *opinantes* (14.2); 1610 editio princeps's *loquuntur* for *loquitur* (13.20-1).

134.   *Met.* 1.3, 11.19-22: Fiebant ergo summi repente philosophi, nam qui illiteratus accesserat fere non morabatur in scolis ulterius quam eo curriculo temporis quo auium pulli plumescunt. (My punctuation.) cf. *supra* n. 28.

135.   *ibid.* 11.22-12.1; *v. supra* n. 28.

136.   *Met.* 1.4, 15.5-9, and *ibid.* 15.11 *ad. fin.* : Alii profecto, similes mei, se nugis curialibus mancipauerunt, ut magnorum uirorum patrocinio freti possent ad diuitias aspirare quibus se uidebant et iudicio consciente, quicquid lingua dissimulet, fatebantur indignos . . . Alii autem Cornificio similes ad uulgi professiones easque prophanas relapsi sunt, parum curantes quid philosophia doceat, quid appetendum fugiendumue denuntiet, dummodo rem faciant, si possunt, recte, si non, quocumque modo, rem. Exercent fenebrem pecuniam, alternis uicibus inequalia rotundantes et adiectione multiplici quod rotundauerant abequantes. Nichil enim sordidum putant, nichil stultum nisi paupertatis angustias, et solas opes ducunt esse fructum sapientie. Siquidem celebre est in corde eorum quod ait ethicus, etsi hoc eum quia contemnitur dixisse non nouerint:
    Et genus et formam regina Pecunia donat,
    et bene nummatum decorat Suadela Venusque.
Hoc autem quasi quadruuio, sibi utique necessario, euadebant illi repentini philosophi et cum Cornificio non modo triuii nostri sed totius quadruuii contemptores. Nam ut dictum est, aut sub pretextu religionis mergebantur in claustris, aut sub imagine philosophandi et utilitatis publice confugiebant ad phisicam, aut sub honestatis uelamine quo splenderent et sublimarentur se preclaris domibus ingerebant, aut sub obtentu necessitatis exercendique officii, dum lucrum sitiebant, multiplicis auaritie uoragine absorbebantur, adeo quidem ut sic proficientium philosophorum, aut ut uerius dixerim deficientium, collatione quiuis in turba prophane multitudinis rudis ad flagitia uideretur. (My punctuation.)

137.   *Met.* 1.4, 14.5-6; *v. supra* n. 133.

138.   *v. supra.* n. 52.

139.   *v. supra* n. 110.

140.   *Met.* 1.7, 22.9-20 and *ibid.* 23.7-10; *v. supra* n. 26; transl. McGarry, *op. cit.* pp. 26-7.

141.   Southern, 1970, p. 41.

142.   *v. supra.* p. 5 and n. 42.

143.   *v. supra.* n. 110.

144.   *v. supra* n. 52.

145.   *Met.* 1.5, 16.15-17.10: Sed et alii uiri amatores litterarum, utpote magister

Theodoricus, artium studiosissimus inuestigator, itidem Willelmus de Conchis gramaticus post Bernardum Carnotensem opulentissimus, et Peripateticus Palatinus, qui logice opinionem preripuit omnibus coetaneis suis, adeo ut solus Aristotelis crederetur usus colloquio, se omnes opposuerunt errori. Sed nec uniuersi insanientibus resistere potuerunt; insipientes itaque facti sunt dum insipientie resistebant, et erronei diutius habiti dum obuiare nitebantur errori. Verumtamen fumus ille cito euanuit, et predictorum opera magistrorum et diligentia redierunt artes, et quasi iure postliminii honorem pristinum nacte sunt et post exilium gratiam et gloriam ampliorem. (My punctuation.)

146. Robert of Torigny, *op. cit.* p. 271: . . . in Carnotensi urbe Iohannis Saresberiensis, uir honestus et sapiens, qui prius fuerat clericus Thebaldi, Cantuariensis archiepiscopi, et postea sancti Thomae martyris, successoris eiusdem Thebaldi.

CAREER TRENDS OF PARISIAN MASTERS OF THEOLOGY, 1200-1320 *

Reuven Avi-Yonah

Studies on the relation of the medieval university to society have usually focused on the social origins of students and masters,[1] and on late medieval universities.[2] The impact of the university on society in the early period (c.1200-1350) is usually discussed in general, vague terms.[3] In this article, an attempt will be made to study this question in a more precise manner, by discussing the careers of the Masters of Theology (M.T.'s) of the University of Paris from its origins to around 1320.

The degree of M.T. at the University of Paris in the thirteenth century was difficult to obtain, requiring a course of study extending over at least fifteen years.[4] After receiving his degree the new master had to lecture in the Faculty of Theology for two years (*magister regens*), but after that he was free either to stay on and teach, or else to move elsewhere. A study of the careers of M.T.'s after their regency may tell us something about the opportunities open to M.T.'s in thirteenth century society. It may also provide some conclusions about their status and the impact of the newly established university on the church and through it on society as a whole.

The basis for this study is Palemon Glorieux's *Répertoire des Maîtres en Théologie de Paris au XIIIe siècle*, with the additions of Victorin Doucet.[5] For each M.T. Glorieux supplies a brief biography including the known facts regarding his career.[6] In all Glorieux lists 131 secular and 155 regular M.T.'s, who obtained their degree between 1167 and 1320. Before presenting and analyzing the data drawn from this work, some methodological questions are in order.

First, how complete is the evidence? Glorieux and Doucet have attempted to be as exhaustive as possible, but it is probable that some M.T.'s have left no trace of their existence. This is indicated by the fact that our knowledge of several M.T.'s depends upon a single document, e.g., the list of members of the commission to investigate the Talmud in 1248, which contains two M.T.'s not known from elsewhere.[7] Nevertheless, there is reason to believe that we have some information regarding most M.T.'s. For the regulars there are lists compiled by the various orders of all their M.T.'s.[8] Yet even for the seculars it is likely that a man who spent many years at the university and obtained the degree of M.T., composing at least one work, would leave some trace. The number of chairs, and so of regent masters, was limited to eight since 1207 and twelve since 1218.[9] Glorieux was able to compile a chart which tells us who occupied each chair for almost every year of the period under consideration in this study.[10]

We probably have more information on those M.T.'s who had successful careers either inside the university or outside it. Our sample is thus somewhat skewed in the direction of successful masters, and the number of undistinguished careers was probably somewhat higher in reality than that known to us. As will be seen below, we are more interested in general trends than in specific careers. Therefore, while the exact numbers might be inaccurate, their interrelations should broadly be correct — especially for trends within each category of careers, where the same factors limit our knowledge throughout.

Another methodological problem is the possibility that two M.T.'s with similar names may in fact be the same person. Glorieux several times raises such a possiblity.[11] Nevertheless, our sample is large enough to prevent such cases from significantly distorting the results. With these considerations in mind we may now proceed to analyse the information derived from Glorieux regarding the post-regency careers of M.T.'s from the University of Paris in the thirteenth century.

Secular Masters' Careers, 1167-1320

Table 1 gives a broad classification of the careers of secular M.T.'s arranged by the decade in which they received their degree. Each column gives the number of masters in each category.

The first column includes those masters who devoted most of their post-regency career to teaching, either at Paris or elsewhere. For example, Odo of St Denis, M.T. *c.*1248, who taught at Paris for over thirty years until his death in 1284.[12] The second column lists M.T.'s who left the university to return to their home town or elsewhere, usually serving in low ecclesiastical posts, yet getting no higher than dean, archdeacon or chancellor of a cathedral: for instance Stephen of Rheims, M.T. *c.*1214, who served as dean of Rheims from 1226 to his death in 1239.[13] The numbers in this column were probably larger in reality, as indicated above. The third column lists M.T.'s who

Table 1: Secular Masters' Careers, 1167–1320

Date of M.T.	University Career	Extra University	High Eccles.	Unknown	Total
–1200	5	0	2	0	7
1201–10	4	2	3	1	10
1211–20	3	2	2	1	8
1221–30	4	2	11	0	17
1231–40	4	1	1	2	8
1241–50	5	1	1	3	10
1251–60	7	1	1	2	11
1261–70	5	1	1	3	10
1271–80	7	1	3	0	11
1281–90	8	0	1	5	14
1291–00	2	0	1	1	4
1301–10	8	4	1	2	15
1311–20	3	0	1	2	6
Total	65	15	29	22	131

Source: P. Glorieux, *Répertoire des Maîtres en Théologie de Paris au XIIIe siècle* (Paris, 1933-34), *passim*.

succeeded in reaching high ecclesiastical posts, from bishop to cardinal. Such, for instance, was Guiard of Laon, M.T. 1226, teacher at Paris until 1236, chancellor in 1236-38, and then bishop of Cambrai until his death in 1247.[14] It should be noted that no secular M.T. became pope in our period, though John XXI (Peter of Spain) was a former Master of Arts. Finally, there are some masters about whom nothing is known beyond their regency.

From the total figures it appears that almost half of all 131 known secular M.T.'s stayed in Paris, or occasionally elsewhere, to teach throughout the period. This figure is significantly high in view of the fact that not more than twelve at the most could occupy chairs at a time; actually six chairs were reserved for the regulars from 1254 onward.[15] Thus other M.T.'s apparently were successful in obtaining benefices which enabled them to continue their scholarly career. In the fourteenth century it became the custom for the university to send to the pope "rolls of candidates for benefices" on special occasions, such as the accession of a new pontiff.[16] In the thirteenth century this system was not as well organized, but apparently M.T.'s succeeded in finding sources of support. Some obtained such benefices in their home town, e.g. Simon of Tournai, M.T. *c*.1184, teaching at Paris till his death in 1203, and canon of Tournai throughout.[17] Others managed to get them elsewhere, for instance Odo of St Denis, M.T. *c*.1248 and teacher at Paris for over thirty years, who had benefices in St Omer, Rouen and Paris.[18] This case also illustrates the multiplication of benefices, which was a heated subject of discussion at the university in the 1280s and '90s. The ability of those active M.T.'s to obtain benefices may indicate the high prestige they enjoyed and the recognition by the popes that their contribution was valuable and they should have the means to pursue their teaching and studies.

Nevertheless, there are substantial changes in the relative numbers of M.T.'s who remained at the university. The founding generation of masters largely consisted of men who devoted a lifetime to the university, such as Peter of Poitiers, teacher for thirty-eight years from 1167 to 1205, Simon of Tournai, regent master of Theology from *c*.1184 to 1203, and Raoul Ardent, who taught from 1175 to 1215.[19] Stephen Langton also was *magister regens* at Paris for over twenty years before becoming Archbishop of Canterbury in 1206.[20] The two decades 1201-1210 and 1211-1220, however, saw an increasing number of M.T.'s turn to extra-university careers, and a corresponding decline in the number of masters staying to teach. This process reached its peak in the decade of 1221-1230, when of seventeen known masters, the largest number known of any decade in the century, only four had inter-university careers; of these two, Stephen Berout and Godfrey of Poitiers, probably had their careers cut short, and a third, John Blount, was in 1233 candidate for Archbishop of Canterbury.[21] Only William of Auxerre, the well-known theologian, can be said to have truly chosen the university. On the other hand thirteen masters are known to have pursued extra-university careers, and of those eight became bishops, one archbishop, and two, Odo of Chateauroux and Peter of Bar, became cardinals.[22] Later on, we see a sharp decline in the number of masters succeeding outside the university, and a corresponding rise in the number of those remaining to teach, stabilizing around half the total. This phenomenon will be discussed below.

The number of M.T.'s who did not obtain either teaching posts or high ecclesiastical office, in the second column of Table 1, is surprisingly small — only fifteen in all. These masters usually obtained some secure position as chancellor or dean and teacher in a cathedral school. Their "failure", thus, is relative, and on the whole one can say that most of those who succeeded in obtaining the M.T. were normally assured of a good position; almost three quarters of those known to us succeeded in remaining at a major university or reaching a high position in the church. Several of the future bishops, archbishops and cardinals started out as deans or chancellors, e.g. Peter of Bar, M.T. *c.*1227, regent master till 1231, and dean of St Marlo in his native diocese until his elevation to cardinal in 1244.[23] They had the luck, connections or ability, while others were left behind.[24]

Twenty-nine of the 131 known secular M.T.'s succeeded in reaching positions of power and influence in the church, which in the thirteenth century meant in society at large. This is a high figure, indicating that the popes valued the knowledge and ability of M.T.'s and wished to use them in governing the church. Some were promoted after many years of teaching, e.g. Robert of Courçon, M.T. before 1200, who taught for over twelve years until his friend and classmate Innocent III made him cardinal in 1212.[25] Others were promoted quickly, for instance Master Ardengus, M.T. from 1227 to 1230, and Bishop of Florence from 1231 to his death in 1249.[26]

The most interesting fact observable in Table 1 is the fall in the number of secular M.T.'s appointed to high ecclesiastical posts between 1221-30 and 1231-40 from eleven to just one, Walter of Chateau-Thierry, M.T. *c.*1240, who served as chancellor in 1246-49 and was made bishop of Paris in 1249, dying the same year.[27] Moreover, only one secular M.T. reached high ecclesiastical office from each decade between 1231 and 1320, with the exception of three during the turbulent decade of 1271-80.

What is the reason for the decline in the number of secular M.T.'s reaching high ecclesiastical posts from *c.*1231 onward? The explanation seems to me complex, and partially has to do with the regular masters, who will be discussed below. Here, however, it is possible to mention three relevant factors.

The first is that the fall in the number of known masters who obtained high ecclesiastical appointments coincides with a rise in the number of M.T.'s who stayed to teach. Moreover, the relative number of teaching masters remains high for the rest of the period, while that of masters in church careers remains low.[28] On the face of it, this would simply indicate that as the M.T.'s were unable to obtain extra-university posts, they were forced to remain at Paris. This is undoubtedly part of the explanation, but not all of it. For in no less than six cases, all dating from 1231 onward, we have information about secular M.T.'s *refusing* high ecclesiastical appointments offered to them. For example, Godfrey of Fontaines, scion of a noble family of Liège, taught at Paris from 1285 to 1304 while holding numerous benefices, yet refused to become bishop of Tournai in 1300.

He bequeathed his books to the Sorbonne.[29] Some M.T.'s went to extremes to avoid the office thrust upon them: John des Alleux, M.T. 1264 and chancellor from 1271 to 1280, entered the Dominican order in the latter year to avoid becoming bishop of Paris, and taught for twenty-six years at St Jacques.[30] Another example is Adenulf of Anagni, M.T. 1272, who was Gregory IX's nephew and thus destined to highest church ranks, and served as chaplain to the pope (a benefice) from 1250 to 1286, but refused to become bishop of Narbonne in 1287 and of Paris in 1288, and escaped to St Victor, where he died the following year. He bequeathed his books to the Sorbonne.[31] It seems that we have here a group of men who saw university life as their vocation, and refused to leave it even when seemingly destined by birth to the highest of church ranks.

This phenomenon has to be tied to a development in the nature of the university itself and in the attitude of both masters and popes towards this institution. In 1231, the year which marks the beginning of the sharp fall in high ecclesiastical appointments of secular M.T.'s, Pope Gregory IX published the great 'Charter of the University', the bull *Parens scientiarum*.[32] This bull re-organized the university after the great strike of 1229-31, and marked a recognition of it as the 'city of knowledge' (*Cariath Sepher*). Thus, it seems probable that secular masters who obtained their degree prior to 1229 regarded it mostly as a stepstone to a career in the church, except some dedicated to study such as William of Auxerre.[33] Later, however, M.T.'s would be more inclined to see the usefulness of remaining to study, teach and determine the truth for the whole Christian world, in the light of *Parens scientiarum*. Possibly there was higher status in such a career than in becoming a bishop; there were, after all, many bishoprics, but few chairs. From the point of view of the masters, remaining at the university thus had distinct advantages.

A second point which is relevant to the decline in the number of ecclesiastical appointments of secular M.T.'s requires us to look at the men who controlled these appointments, the popes. Table 2 shows us the changes in the number of secular M.T.'s appointed by each pope, only the first appointment being considered and not subsequent advancements:

Table 2: Popes and their Appointments of M.T.'s to High Ecclesiastical Positions, 1198-1334

Pope		Seculars	Regulars
Innocent III	(1198–1216)	3	–
Honorius III	(1216–1228)	4	–
Gregory IX	(1227–1241)	7	0
Innocent IV	(1243–1254)	5	2
Alexander IV	(1254–1261)	0	1
Urban IV	(1261–1264)	1	1
Clement IV	(1265–1268)	1	1
Gregory X	(1271–1276)	0	2
Nicholas III	(1277–1280)	1	2
Martin IV	(1281–1285)	1	1
Honorius IV	(1285–1287)	0	0
Nicholas IV	(1288–1292)	0	2
Boniface VIII	(1294–1303)	3	9
Benedict XI	(1303–1304)	0	1
Clement V	(1305–1314)	0	4
John XXII	(1316–1334)	1	12

Source: *ibid.*

It can be seen that the sharp drop in the numbers of secular M.T.'s appointed does not occur in the 1230s — on the contrary, these are the peak years — but in the 1250s. This tallies with our former conclusions for there would on the average be a lag of some ten to fifteen years between a person's obtaining the M.T. and his being elevated to high church rank. Thus Gregory IX and Innocent IV appointed the M.T.'s of the 1220s, while the fall in appointments for the M.T.'s incepting in the 1230s can be ascribed to Alexander IV and his successors.

Personal reasons can partially account for this phenomenon. While Innocent IV appointed five secular M.T.'s to high ecclesiastical posts, his successor, Alexander IV, in his seven years in office did not elevate a single secular M.T., the worst record of any thirteenth century pope who reigned for over a year. The background is Alexander's sharp struggle with the secular masters over their relations with the regulars, whom he constantly favoured.[34] This policy was a sharp departure from those of his uncle Gregory IX and great-uncle Innocent III. But this cannot be the whole explanation, for why did Alexander's successors refrain from appointing secular M.T.'s from Paris to high church posts? Competition with the regulars, and popes favouring them, does not seem to have been a factor again until the time of Boniface VIII (see below). Four popes in the period 1254-1294 had studied at Paris: one, Innocent V (Peter of Tarentaise, pope in 1276) was a regular M.T., three others, Gregory X, John XXI and Honorius IV, M.A.'s who had also studied theology. It seems therefore that knowledge was still considered important for appointments, just as in the days of previous popes with university backgrounds such as Innocent III, Gregory IX and Innocent IV, who appointed many M.T.'s to high ecclesiastical positions.

On the whole therefore, the explanation for the change in the number of M.T.'s appointed by each pope does not lie in shifting personal preferences but in a change in the way the university was viewed by both M.T.'s and popes: from an institution preparing some men for high church careers, to one intended to preserve and further Christian knowledge. As a result, popes appointed fewer and fewer M.T.'s to high posts.

The third, and perhaps the most fundamental reason for the decline in appointments of secular M.T.'s has to do with a phenomenon already noticed by Glorieux: starting around 1230, there is a sharp decline in the quality of the work produced by those masters. The early secular M.T.'s included such names as Stephen Langton, St Edmund of Canterbury, William of Auxerre, John Blount, and William of Auvergne, each of whom has left us some significant writings. Of the secular masters who incepted after 1230, it is hard to find well known names — those which are, are famous for other reasons (Robert of Sorbon, William of St Amour, Stephen Tempier). One of the few exceptions is Henry of Ghent, M.T. 1275, who made a name for himself as a theologian and was the leader of the seculars of his day.

This decline is probably related to the decline in appointments. Which came first? It is natural to argue that talented men would be less inclined to embark upon the long and arduous quest for the M.T., if the chances of getting an ecclesiastical appointment were slimmer. This would hold for the later period, but not for those entering the course in the 1230s and 40s, a period when their own masters were frequently obtaining high posts in the church. Yet the decline seems evident from these years on. It would seem, therefore, that the decline in quality preceded the decline in appointments and partially caused it — perhaps even was its chief and most profound cause.

What is the explanation for the apparent fall in the quality of works by secular masters after 1230? It was not that nothing new could be said in theology — St Thomas is proof enough to the contrary. Nor could it have been that all the talent was drawn into the orders. It is true that the Franciscan and Dominican masters of the whole period include an impressive list of names, in fact almost all of the great theologians of the latter half of the century. Yet this could not have been the only reason. For not every talented young man would be ready to enter an order and submit to its discipline.

The reason for the decline must lie elsewhere. It resulted from the fact that many talents from *c*.1231 onward decided to remain in the faculty of Arts and declined to advance further into theological studies. It is possible to list several well known secular M.A.'s who taught at Paris after 1230 without ever reaching an M.T., or even entering the course: Roger Bacon, Siger of Brabant, Boethius of Dacia, Peter of Spain. Others, like Henry Bate of Malines, M.A. *c*.1274, returned only many years later (1301) to get a theological degree.[35]

The probable explanation for this change is also to be found in the policy of Gregory IX. From 1210 on, the teaching of Aristotle's books on natural philosophy and metaphysics was forbidden in the faculty of arts. As we try to show elsewhere, this was the result of the masters of theology wishing to keep these spheres of knowledge within their faculty. However, Pope Gregory, fearing that too much secular philosohy was "polluting" pure theology, in 1231 transferred the study of natural philosophy and metaphysics to the artists.[36] This was in line with the importance he attached to the Faculty of Theology at Paris as responsible for defining true doctrine for all of Christendom. The result was that the study of the arts became much more interesting and many talented young men chose to remain there rather than embark on a course of pure theology. The regular theologians, who were less tied to teaching, were also less affected; but there occured a noticeable decline in the quality of the seculars, which led to a decline in appointments as well. During the 1270s, the seculars attempted to strike back, leading to the great condemnation of 1277. This, however, is a matter for another study.[37]

Regular Masters' Careers, 1229-1320

The careers of secular masters differed from those of regular M.T.'s, Franciscans, Dominicans or others; the latters' was partly governed by considerations of their respective orders. The decision whether to

continue teaching or move to another endeavour was normally not
their own, but that of their superiors in the order, who had sent them
to study in the first place. Thus the significance of changes would
reflect outside policies and attitudes even more than for the seculars.

The first Dominican master at Paris was Roland of Cremona OP,
who became M.T. as a secular in 1229 before entering the order. The
Franciscan chair was established in 1231 by Alexander of Hales OFM
(M.T. *c.*1229), likewise an ex-secular master. Afterwards, chairs and
foundations at Paris were established for the Cistercians (1256),
Benedictines (1259), the monks of Val des Écoliers (1259) and of Mt
St Eloi (1274), Augustinians (1285) and Carmelites (1295). Table 3
gives a synopsis of the post regency careers of all regular M.T.'s. An
additional category includes regular M.T.'s who reached high
positions inside the order, i.e., provincial and master - (or minister) -
general. Most of the regulars who reached high ecclesiastical office
served first in such posts, e.g. Matthew of Aquasparta OFM, M.T.
1275, teaching till 1287, then minister-general till 1289, and cardinal
from 1288. But Jacques Fournier, a Cistercian, became pope
Benedict XII in 1334 without first serving in high ordinal posts.[38]

Table 3: Regular Masters' Careers, 1229–1320

Date of M.T.	University Career	Extra University	High Ordinal	High Eccles.	Unknown	Total
1221–30	3	0	0	1	0	4
1231–40	3	0	0	0	0	3
1241–50	6	0	0	2	2	10
1251–60	8	2	1	4	3	18
1261–70	6	0	0	3	1	10
1271–80	7	2	5	3	2	19
1281–90	7	1	5	5	1	19
1291–00	5	1	5	6	1	18
1301–10	8	3	12	7	5	35
1311–20	7	1	2	7	2	19
Total	60	10	30	38	17	155

Source: *ibid.*

A glance at the totals given in table 3 reveals various facts. The
relative number of known regular M.T.'s who stayed in teaching
posts is lower than that of the seculars, 60 of 155 (39 percent) as

against 65 of 131 (49 percent). This is significant, especially if we remember the following points: First, regulars had no economic worries while teaching, since they were supported by the foundation of the order, such as St Jacques for the Dominicans. Second, the number of regulars staying to teach includes members of smaller orders, such as the monks of Val des Écoliers and Mt St Eloi, who invariably established one master at Paris to teach for life. Moreover, the larger orders also were initially oriented towards teaching (see below), and many of their famous masters, such as St Thomas Aquinas OP and John Duns Scotus OFM, had teaching careers. Nevertheless, no less than 68 (44 percent) of all known regular masters reached high office either within the order or outside it. The number of known M.T.'s who did not succeed either in the university or outside is small (10), as is the number of 'unknown' careers (17).

While for the secular masters the trend was from high church to university careers, here we observe an opposite phenomenon. Until the 1270s, the proportion of regulars who were mostly teachers was relatively high and that of M.T.'s who had other careers correspondingly low. This was the result of a deliberate policy: young Dominicans and Franciscans were sent to Paris to study towards their M.T. and later teach, usually not in Paris but in various *studia* of the order. The career of Bernard of Trilia OP is typical: sent to Paris in 1260 as a young man, he later taught at Montpellier, Avignon, Bordeaux, Marseilles and Toulouse.[39] St Thomas Aquinas taught first in Paris, then at Rome and Naples, Duns at Paris and later at Oxford. Other regulars stayed in Paris: Gueric of St Quentin OP, M.T. 1233, taught there from 1233 to 1242, John of La Rochelle OFM from 1238 to his death in 1245.[40]

It appears that there was a period between 1251 and 1271 in which neither secular nor regular masters were appointed in high numbers to extra-university posts. This may explain the sharp clash between seculars and regulars during the 1250s:[41] the seculars were not getting extra-university appointments, while the orders were not interested in them; both desired chairs, the seculars as stepping stones to appointments as before 1250, the orders for their increased teaching needs. The resultant struggle did much to diminish the power of the seculars, who, as we have seen above, never regained their lost opportunities.

A change can be discerned in the 1270s, first in the number of inter-ordinal appointments which rose from none in the 1260s to five in the 80s and 90s and 12 (of 35) in 1301-10. This change indicates a shift in the attitude of the orders towards the university. The M.T. was no longer considered as preparatory mainly for a teaching career, but

also as a solid background for provincials and masters-general. Prior
to 1271 only one Franciscan master might have served as provincial
of France prior to his regency.[42] In the decade 1271-80, however,
three Dominicans and two Franciscans reached similar positions; in
the 1280s we have three in all and in addition two masters-general-
Stephen of Besançon OP, M.T. 1286, master-general 1292-94, and
Arlotto of Prato OFM, M.T. 1282, minister-general 1285-86.[43] This
change is presumably connected with the growing institutionalization of the orders. The first masters-general were more likely to be
charismatic personalities having no university education, with the
exception of St Bonaventure, M.T. 1253. The rising respect for
education, furthered by the stature of early teachers such as Sts
Albert the Great and Thomas Aquinas, may explain why provincials
and masters-generals were increasingly drawn from the ranks of the
regular M.T.'s.

High ecclesiastical appointments were determined outside the
orders and thus reflect their changing status in the eyes of the papacy.
Occasional appointments were made early, such as that of Hugh of St
Cher OP, M.T. 1230, later provincial, vicar-general, and finally
cardinal in 1244.[44] Nevertheless, the high tide of ecclesiastical
appointments for regular masters begins only with Boniface VIII,
who elevated no less than nine of them. Afterwards, appointments
follow regularly, their number being roughly proportionate to the
number of years the pope was in office: one for Benedict XI, who
reigned one year, four for Clement V, pope for nine years, and no less
than twelve for John XXII, in office for eighteen years (see Table 2
above). No regular masters ever declined a post offered them,
indicating that the policy of the orders favoured such influential
appointments of their members.

The beginning of this rise in appointments of regular masters may
be attributed to personal factors: while legate in France in 1290
Benedict Gaetani, later pope Boniface VIII, had a sharp clash with
the secular masters led by Henry of Ghent concerning the privileges
of the regulars, ending with his declaration that the pope 'would
prefer that the university be destroyed, rather than the privileges of
the regulars be lessened one whit'.[45] Benedict XI may also have
favoured the regulars, being himself a former master-general of the
Dominicans. Yet Clement V and John XXII were both French
lawyers and had no particular personal reason to appoint regular
M.T.'s, while Nicholas IV (1288-92), despite being previously
minister-general of the Franciscans, had not preferred them. The
change in the number of regular M.T.'s appointed to high posts from
Boniface VIII onward should therefore be explained otherwise. It is

partly a result of the previous change on the part of the orders: as we have noted, most high ecclesiastical appointees who were regular M.T.'s had previously held high ordinal positions, so that the more masters entered those positions, the better their chances were of rising further. However, the change is also probably the result of a conscious decision by the papacy to rely more on the international orders against the rising national monarchies.

Finally, we have to ask whether there was a link between the development of regular M.T.'s careers towards high ecclesiastical posts and the decline in appointments of secular masters to these same posts described above. On the face of it, there was no competition, for regulars began to be appointed long after the decline had started. Yet there probably was an indirect connection. From 1254 on the regulars occupied six out of twelve chairs. This reduced by two the number of chairs originally held by the seculars, and made it harder for them to get teaching posts, which could serve as the basis of a career. Further, and perhaps more importantly, appointments were at least partly based on talent, and much of the best talent from the 1250s on is to be found among the regulars — names like St Albert, St Bonaventure, St Thomas, John Pecham, Giles of Rome. All of these, except St Thomas, reached high ecclesiastical posts. There are no seculars of similar stature, perhaps until Oresme in the fourteenth century. This diversion of talent may contribute to explain the decline of appointments of seculars, which formed the background for the bitter quarrels between the two groups from the 1250s on.

To sum up:

During the first three decades of the university's organized existence in Paris, its secular M.T.'s were being appointed in relatively large numbers to high ecclesiastical posts. From 1231-40 onward, however, this trend rather abruptly ceases. The reasons are manifold and relate to several aspects of the university, the Church, and the Papacy. First, there was a decline in the number of secular M.T.'s wishing to be appointed, as indicated by several refusals of positions. This phenomenon resulted from a change in the attitude towards the university, from regarding it as an institution preparing men for careers in the Church, to one in which Christian learning is pursued for its own sake. This change is also reflected in the attitude of the popes, from Gregory IX's *Parens scientiarum* onward. While Alexander IV may have had personal motives for not appointing secular M.T.s to high ecclesiastical positions, subsequent popes saw the M.T. as a degree leading mainly to a university career for the advancement of sacred knowledge.

The decline in appointments of secular M.T.'s was also related to the entrance of the regulars into the university since 1229. The regulars were initially not in direct competition with the seculars for appointments, which they began to receive in large numbers only from 1280 on. This was a result of the orders' conception of the university mainly as an institution for preparing teachers for their respective *studia*. Nevertheless, there was indirect competition between seculars and regulars, since talented men were opting for the orders and were occupying the chairs serving as stepping stones for careers. In the 1250s appointments of seculars had almost stopped, while the orders displayed a lack of interest in such offices. This led both groups to vie for university chairs and to the sharp clashes of that decade. From the 1270s on, the orders increasingly relied on M.T.'s to fill the higher ordinal positions of provincial and master-general, indicating a change in their view of the university. The initial charismatic leadership was being replaced by trained scholars and administrators. Beginning with Boniface VIII, the popes also appointed regular M.T.'s to high ecclesiastical posts. This was a result both of these M.T.'s advancement within their orders, since regular M.T.'s usually had to reach high ordinal positions before attaining the rank of bishop, as well as of the popes' increasing reliance on the orders in face of the rising national monarchies.

The decline in secular appointments also resulted from a definite decline in the quality of work produced by the secular M.T.'s. This was probably a result of Gregory IX's redefinition of the sphere of theology, by which he excluded natural philosophy. Previously the M.T.'s had attempted by the condemnations of 1210 and 1215 to limit the M.A.'s to the preparatory subjects of the *trivium*. Gregory IX, however, transferred philosophy to the Faculty of Arts, in accordance with his view of the Faculty of Theology as guardian and propagator of Christian knowledge. As a result talented men preferred to remain in the faculty of Arts, which also gained an institutional preponderance. The secular theologians' work declined and was taken over by the regulars, who were not tied to Paris or to teaching.

Two major conclusions may be drawn from our investigation. The first concerns the changing nature of the university of Paris. It is likely that when pope and king united in the early thirteenth century to confer privileged status on the nascent university, they had mainly in mind the furtherance of a centre which would train administrators for both the papal and the royal services. This would have been in line with the University of Bologna's function of training canonists for the curia and romanists for the Emperor. However, the gradual institutionalization of the university changed the outlook of both masters and popes. Since the 1230s they began to consider it a centre defining and advancing the basis of Christian knowledge. This led to an increasing use of M.T.'s to rule on basic questions of dogma, such as the 'Eternal Evangel' in the 1240s or the poverty of Christ in the 1290s.[46] It gave the University of Paris a unique status in the Church which was lost only in the late fourteenth century.[47]

Our study also yields some conclusions concerning the status of M.T.'s. A person obtaining the degree of master of theology had reasonable career prospects: three quarters of known M.T.'s succeeded in finding lifelong posts as teachers or administators. About a quarter of all known Parisian M.T.'s reached high ecclesiastical positions. Of these, thirty-one became bishops, fourteen archbishops, twenty cardinals, and two popes. Six other popes had studied in Paris before entering upon their career, one of whom, Peter of Spain, was a famous Master of Arts. These promotions illustrate the high status which knowledge, and specifically theology, was accorded, so that its bearers were considered worthy to be appointed to the positions in the Church. Indeed, many were elevated straight from their chair to an archbishopric or cardinalate.[48] From the opposite point of view, a decline in the level of scholarship brought about a corresponding decline in appointments for secular M.T.'s. Such a high valuation of knowledge was natural in a period when medieval Europe's view of the world was being transformed by a wave of new information brought in by the translations from Arabic and Greek. There was a degree of reverence for knowledge as magic, as shown by the reputations of Michael Scot, Roger Bacon, and even St Albert the Great.[49]

It thus seems that the Faculty of Theology in the University of Paris served in the thirteenth century two important functions. It enjoyed high prestige which enabled it to define Christian doctrine for the whole of the Latin west. It also served as a training ground for a large proportion of the top administrators of the church. These two roles make it well deserving of further study.[50]

Department of History
Boston College
Chestnut Hill, MA 02167
U.S.A.

REFERENCES

*   I wish to thank Profesors Michael Shank of Harvard University and David Jacoby and Benjamin Z. Kedar of the Hebrew University of Jerusalem, as well as the late Dr Charles Schmitt of the Warburg Institute, who read drafts of this paper and offered many helpful suggestions.

1.   Cf. J. Overfield, 'Nobles and Paupers at German Universities to 1600', *Societas*, 4(1974), 175-210; H.-J. Brandt, 'Universität, Gesellschaft, Politik und Pfründen am Beispiel Konrad von Soltau', in J. Paquet and J. Ijsewijn, eds., *Universities in the Late Middle Ages* (Louvain, 1978), pp. 614-627.

2.   Cf. R. N. Swanson, *Universities, Academics and the Great Schism* (Cambridge, 1979); G. F. Lytle, 'Universities as Religious Authorities in the Later Middle Ages and Reformation' in Lytle, ed., *Reform and Authority in the Medieval and Reformation Church* (Washington, D.C., 1981), pp. 69-98; and the studies collected in J. Baldwin and R. Goldthwaite, eds., *Universities in Politics: Case Studies from the Late Middle Ages and Early Modern Period* (Baltimore, 1972); also Brandt, n. 1 above.

3.   E.g. A. B. Cobban, *The Medieval Universities* (London, 1975), ch. 9: 'The Universities and Society', pp. 218-234; F. M. Powicke, 'The Medieval University in Church and Society', in his *Ways of Medieval Life and Thought* (New York, 1971), pp. 198-212. Most studies focus on the impact of society on the university, not the other way round. There is no good modern study on the masters of theology at Paris as a whole; cf., however, B. Geyer, 'Facultas Theologica: eine bedeutungsgeschichtliche Untersuchung', *Zeitschrift für Kirchengeschichte*, 75(1964), 133-145; P. Glorieux, 'La faculté de théologie de Paris et ses principaux docteurs au XIIIe siècle', *Révue d'histoire de l'église de France*, 32 (1946), 241-246; and the monumental work of P. Feret, *La Faculté de Théologie de Paris, Moyen Age*, 4 vols. (Paris, 1894-1897). Other relevant studies are P. R. McKeon, 'The Status of the University of Paris as *Parens Scientiarum*', *Speculum*, 39(1964), 651-675; and L. Hall, *Der Anspruch der Philosophie und der Einspruch der Theologie im Streit der Fakultäten* (Munich, 1960). The major study of Gordon Leff, *Paris and Oxford Universities in the Thirteenth and Fourteenth Centuries, An Institutional and Intellectual Approach* (New York, 1975) makes, despite its title, almost no attempt to relate institutional to intellectual aspects. The exception is John W. Baldwin's article, 'Masters at Paris from 1179 to 1215: A Social Perspective' in *Renaissance and Renewal in the Twelfth Century*, ed. Robert L. Benson and Giles Constable (Cambridge, Mass., 1982), pp. 138-172, which deals in greater depth with some of the issues in this article over a shorter time span.

4.   H. Denifle and J. Chatelain, eds., *Chartularium Universitatis Parisiensis*, 4 vols., (Paris, 1889-1897), vol. 1, no. 20, pp. 78-79 (henceforth CUP).

5.   P. Glorieux, *Répertoire des Maîtres en Théologie de Paris au XIIIe siècle*, 2 vols. (Paris, 1933-1934) (henceforth GR with number of master discussed); additions by V. Doucet, *Archivum Franciscanum Historicum*, 27(1935), 531-564.

6.   GR, introduction, p. 3.

7.   GR 152, 156.

8.   GR, introduction, pp. 39-40.

9.   Leff, *Paris and Oxford*, p. 84.

10.   GR, chart (middle of vol. 1). Cf. also Baldwin, 'Masters', p. 148, on the likelihood that most M.T.'s are known.

11.   E.g. Raoul of Montdidier, M.T. 1248 (GR 152), may be the same person as

Raoul of Colebruge, M.T. between 1240 and 1249, who entered the Franciscans and taught at Oxford (GR 153).

12. GR 158.

13. GR 112.

14. GR 133.

15. GR, vol. 1, p. 23. It is possible that the number of chairs was later increased to twenty.

16. Cf. D. E. R. Watt, 'University Clerks and Rolls of Petition for Benefices', *Speculum*, 34(1959), 213-229.

17. GR 101.

18. GR 158.

19. GR 100, 101, 102.

20. GR 104.

21. GR 130, 132, 135.

22. GR 137, 140.

23. GR 140.

24. As stated above, the numbers in this column were probably greater in actuality.

25. GR 103.

26. GR 120.

27. GR 144.

28. Cf. Table 1 above.

29. GR 198.

30. GR 36.

31. GR 186.

32. CUP vol. 1, no. 79, pp. 136-137.

33. Cf. the judgement of Robert of Courçon: Eadem est obiectio de theologo, qui alia causa principali legit quam propter deum, qui, si intentionem ferat principaliter ad hoc quod promoveatur ad prelationem, mentalem committit simoniam. *Summa*, Ms. B. N. Lat. 14524, f. 37^v, cited in Baldwin, 'Masters', p. 153.

34. Leff, *Paris*, pp. 34-47.

35. GR 209.

36. CUP vol. 1, no. 79, pp. 136-139; cf. also his letter of 1228, ibid., no. 59, pp. 114-116.

37. R. S. Avi-Yonah, 'Transgressing the Limits: Theology and Arts at the University of Paris, 1210-1277', forthcoming.

38. GR 318, 370.

39. GR 41.

40. GR 4, 302.

41. On this cf. Leff, *Paris and Oxford*, pp. 34-47; M. M. Dufeil, *Guillaume de S. Amour et la polémique universitaire parisienne* (Paris, 1972).

42. William of Ardembourg, Provincial from 1257 to 1261, might have served as regent M.T. c.1266-67: GR 310.

43. GR 42, 323.

44. GR 2.

45. Cf. J. Miethke, 'Papst, Ortsbischof und Universität in der Pariser

Theologenprozesse des 13. Jahrhunderts', in A. Zimmermann, ed., *Die Auseinandersetzungen an der Pariser Universität im XIII. Jahrhundert* (*Miscellanea Medievalia*, 10) (New York- Berlin, 1976), pp. 52-94, esp. pp. 93-94.

46.   On this cf. Leff, *Paris and Oxford*, pp. 255-270.

47.   Cf. also J. Le Goff, 'Quelle conscience l'université médievale a-t-elle eue d'elle même', *Pour un autre moyen age* (Paris, 1977), pp. 181-197.

48.   Occasionally popes also appointed men who were famous for their learning but had not attended a university, e.g. Michael Scot, whom Honorius III attempted to make archbishop of Cashel. Cf. L. Minio Paluello, 'Michael Scot', in C. C. Gillispie, ed., *Dictionary of Scientific Biography* (New York, 1974), vol. 9, pp. 361-365.

49.   For further information on appointments of masters in the early period, cf. Baldwin, 'Masters', pp. 154-158.

50.   For an example of the amount of research which needs to be done on the Parisian Theologians cf. R. S. Avi-Yonah, *The Aristotelian Revolution: A Study of the Transformation of Medieval Cosmology, 1150-1250* (unpublished Ph.D. Diss., Harvard University, 1986).

UNIVERSITY MASTERS AND THOMAS BECKET: SERMONS PREACHED ON ST THOMAS OF CANTERBURY AT PARIS AND OXFORD IN THE THIRTEENTH AND FOURTEENTH CENTURIES [*]

Phyllis B. Roberts

In the years following his martyrdom in 1170, the cult of St Thomas of Canterbury spread rapidly across western Europe. So well known was the story of his life and murder that in the generations and centuries that followed, his cult flourished in all parts of Latin Christendom. The medieval Church, ever alert to a dramatic martyrdom, canonised Thomas of Canterbury less than three years after his death.[1]

The details of Thomas Becket's life, his friendship with King Henry II and his elevation from the role of royal chancellor to the archbishopric of Canterbury have become familiar to a variety of audiences. The drama of Thomas' life and martyrdom at the hands of King Henry's knights in the Cathedral Church at Canterbury on 29 December 1170 has attracted the attention of scholars, historians as well as playwrights. Although there were many points at issue between king and archbishop, a crucial one concerned the respective jurisdictions of church and state over clergy convicted of crimes. Becket as martyr came to symbolise an important issue in medieval political life: the relationship between the Church and the State and the ongoing question of ecclesiastical liberties in the face of a growing secular and lay consciousness in the society at large.

This article is part of a larger study of Latin sermons preached about St Thomas of Canterbury from *c.* 1220-1350. Most were designated for his feastday on 29 December, but there are also a number that were preached on 7 July, the Feast of the Translation of the Relics, which marked the occasion on 7 July 1220 when the relics of St Thomas the martyr were solemnly elevated at Canterbury Cathedral and installed in the new Trinity Chapel.[2] My aim is twofold: first, to determine the connections between the medieval Latin preaching tradition and the spread of the cult of Becket, and second, to examine the texts themselves for evidence of how the Becket of history, myth, and legend was perceived generations after his death and what the martyrdom meant in terms of the struggle between the spiritual and temporal authority in the high and late Middle Ages. I shall focus here on two texts that have a university setting[3] and illustrate how Becket and the martyrdom were interpreted at Paris by the Dominican John of St Giles in 1230 and at Oxford by the Chancellor Henry Harkeley in 1315. Moroever, these sermons illustrate the ways in which university masters saw in Becket a symbol of the Church's resistance to temporal authority, a defender of ecclesiastical liberties and an *exemplum* of the *bonus pastor* who was also defender of his flock.

My first text comes from a Paris cycle of university sermons for the academic year 1230-31 which may be found in MS Paris, Bibliothèque nationale lat. nouv. acqu. 338, ff. 84[r]-87[v].[4] The 84 sermons in the manuscript are arranged in a preaching cycle from 8 September 1230 to 29 August 1231. The respective dates of each sermon are further identified as either a Sunday or feastday. This is followed by the name of the preacher and/or his order, and, where the information is available, the names of particular churches where at least a dozen of these sermons were preached.[5] The sermons in this cycle are very likely résumés. Medieval preaching was usually very lengthy, but these texts could be read in about a quarter of an hour.[6]

The entry for Sunday 29 December on St Thomas the martyr is a sermon by the Dominican friar, John of St Giles.[7] The sermon was preached at the church of St Jacques where the Dominicans had established their convent in 1218.[8] Situated along the rue St Jacques, just within the walls of thirteenth-century Paris, this church was the customary place for the delivery of university sermons,[9] and so it was with our sermon of 29 December 1230 on the feastday of St Thomas of Canterbury.

The preacher was John of St Giles,[10] born near St Albans *c.* 1180. A celebrated physician to whom has also been attributed a work on medical prescriptions, John taught medicine at Paris and then at Montpellier until 1209 when he became doctor to King Philip Augustus of France. He then embarked upon his theological studies in Paris. Already a renowned preacher, he became regent master in theology by 1227. His entry into the Order of Preachers in 1230 gave the Dominicans a second official chair in the Faculty of Theology. Hastings Rashdall described this dramatic event:

> John of St Giles, a secular master, under whom Roland of Cremona had incepted in theology, was invited to preach *ad clerum* in the Dominican church. He preached on the beauty of voluntary poverty. In the midst of his discourse he stopped, and, that he might confirm his words by his own

example, descended from the pulpit, received the habit of the friars, and therein returned and finished his discourse.[11]

This event apparently occurred on 22 September 1230, the feastday of St Maurice, and the sermon on St Maurice in fact also appears in this same university cycle.[12] From 1233-35, John was in Toulouse as reader in theology and in 1235 returned to England at the invitation of Robert Grosseteste, bishop of Lincoln. John was last mentioned in 1258 and died in either 1259 or 1260.

John's sermon, although in résumé form, is, nonetheless, organised in accordance with the guidelines of the *ars predicandi*[13] which set forth the various divisions and subdivisions of the thematic sermon which so characterised university preaching of the thirteenth century. The preacher takes as his theme Lamentations 2.20: 'Shall priests and prophets die within the Temple of the Lord?' John goes on to point out that this biblical text is especially well suited to the blessed Thomas and to his audience which included scholars and others who serve the Church. Says John: 'It is clear that the blessed Thomas was slain in the sanctuary of the Lord, namely, in the church, as he sang before the altar. He was a priest, indeed an archbishop. Likewise, he was a prophet who predicted many things that afterwards happened'.[14] John continues to describe how Thomas died in four different ways in the sanctuary of the Lord. His first death was the change effected when he put aside his old self, the man of the court and king's chancellor, to become archbishop and to lead a new and religious life, thereby changed into another man. His second death was the martyrdom of compassion which he undertook and endured for the sake of those who accompanied him in exile as a consequence of his resistance against the king. His third death was the sacrifice of his own body, in his wearing of the hairshirt and his self-flagellations. His fourth death was the martyrdom of persecution which culminated in his being raised up from the earth as it is written in Zechariah (9.16): 'On that day the Lord will save them for they are the flock of his people; for like the jewels of a crown they shall shine on his land'.[15]

The preacher John of St Giles then likens Thomas to a hard and unyielding stone because he could be bent neither by gifts nor by threats. John then quotes Ecclesiasticus (32.7): 'A concert of music at a feast of wine is as a ruby set in gold' and compares the ruby and its various properties to St Thomas of Canterbury. Like a ruby which has health-giving and life-sustaining properties, Thomas defended the health and well-being of his flock, despite the persecution of certain legates and prelates who wrote harsh letters against him. The redness of the ruby is a vivid reminder of the blood of the martyr as he lay slain on the pavement of his church. The ruby likewise seems to be aflame, as was the blessed Thomas aflame with many virtues.[16]

This passage which compares Thomas to a ruby is of interest in that it may reflect something of John's medical background. Medieval medicine included a variety of folklorist beliefs that credited efficacious powers to precious stones and gems. Red stones like rubies were symbolic of blood and were believed to confer invulnerability from wounds. The ruby or carbuncle was often viewed as a symbol of Christ's sacrifice. The ruby's glowing hue further suggested an inextinguishable flame which burned within the stone. In a fourteenth-century treatise attributed to Sir John Mandeville, the ruby was held to afford peace and concord to its owner and to assure him protection from all dangers.[17]

Thus did John of St Giles interpret St Thomas of Canterbury to his university audience whom he continually advises to emulate Thomas' example since they are the priests, scholars, and teachers of the modern church who should in turn act as role models to others. 'Yet', warns John, 'the world has many false prophets who teach in order to acquire prebends and honours for themselves and who care more for the necessities of their present life than for the consideration of eternal life . . . Let them take heed of the lesson and example of the martyred Thomas who was above all the *bonus pastor*, the good shepherd of his flock'.[18]

This Paris sermon of 1230 takes a rather traditional approach to the issue of Becket's martyrdom and calls to mind the strong pro-Becket sympathies of Paris masters like Peter the Chanter, who, as Caesar of Heisterbach reported, praised Becket as a martyr who had died for the liberty of the Church.[19] The notable master of theology and biblical commentator, Stephen Langton, spent his student days in Paris with this group that was strongly pro-Becket. In his years of exile, from 1207 to 1213, the newly named archbishop of Canterbury found temporary refuge with the Cistercians at Pontigny who had welcomed Becket many years earlier. By the time of his return to England in 1213, Langton may well have been convinced that he was himself a successor to Becket in spirit as well as title. Langton's long struggle with King John and his stubborn efforts to achieve the freedom of the English church from royal interference are well in the tradition of Thomas Becket who had earlier declared his independence and that of the Church from John's father, Henry II. Langton preached on Becket at least twice in the year 1220, extolling him as saint, martyr and defender of church liberties.[20]

On one level, therefore, our thirteenth-century sermon rehearses many of the commonplaces about Becket as martyr and example to 'modern' clerics. These were already a firm part of the Paris tradition. Our sermon, however, should also be examined more closely for its authorship and its setting. We have taken note of the fact that the sermon was preached in 1230 by a Dominican, during a period of considerable dissension and disturbance in the university. The great dispersion of 1229-30 grew out of the town-gown riots of the carnival season of the previous year during which several students were wounded or killed. In the aftermath of the riots, many of the Paris masters suspended lectures and resolved to leave the capital for six years if no redress was made. They subsequently dispersed from Paris to other French schools as well as to Oxford. Eventually, King Louis IX and Pope Gregory IX came to the rescue of the university, but many of the masters and students did not return to Paris until the beginning of 1231.

Furthermore, the role of the friars in the university should be taken into account here, for by this period, they constituted an important part of university life. Apparently the friars remained rather aloof during the great dispersion of 1229-30. They continued to teach at Paris, thereby incurring the resentment of the secular masters. (This was to happen again, by the way, some twenty years later in 1253 when clashes between townsmen and scholars again took place.) The secular masters at Paris were also resentful of the privileges enjoyed by the mendicants who had their own independent schools and organisation free from the regulations and demands of the university. Yet they, the mendicants, like John of St Giles, held chairs and membership in the theological faculty. In addition to problems of jurisdiction were conflicts with the friars over their role in the secular church — hearing confessions, preaching, and performing a variety of pastoral and sacramental duties. The mendicants, for their part, had the full support of the papacy. Dominicans had come to Paris in 1217 and Franciscans, in 1219. With the dispersion, the friars who remained in Paris became directly involved in teaching. They opened their schools to secular students in theology and retained their chairs of theology even when the secular masters returned to Paris in 1231. Further exacerbated, therefore, were the feelings of the secular masters who felt threatened by the increasing numbers of mendicants and the privileges enjoyed by them.[21]

John of St Giles, in his preaching on St Thomas of Canterbury, reflects, therefore, the traditionalism of much of the preaching on the martyred archbishop in this period. The presence of his sermon in this particular Paris university sermon cycle (along with four other sermons that he preached in that year)[22] is indicative of the continuity of university preaching afforded by the mendicants who, though resented by secular masters, had to be reckoned with as an increasingly important part of the university scene. The role of the mendicants at Paris has its echo as well at Oxford where similar struggles involving Dominicans and secular masters also took place, furnishing some of the background of our next sermon text.

Nearly 100 years later, in 1315, Master Henry Harkeley, who was Chancellor of the University of Oxford, also preached a sermon about St Thomas of Canterbury.[23] The era was the reign of King Edward II and Walter Reynolds, archbishop of Canterbury. We know something about Harkeley from Emden and from various other Oxford sources, including an essay by the bishop of Chichester, E. W. Kemp, published in 1981 in *Essays Presented to R. W. Southern*.[24] Harkeley's *Questiones* were also the subject of a lengthy paper written in 1924 by Franz Pelster.[25] An MA by 1296 and doctor of theology by 1312, Harkeley was Chancellor of the university from 1312 until his death in Avignon in 1317. As Chancellor, he presided at the condemnation of certain theological statements as heretical in February, 1314[26] and was also involved in the litigation on university teaching rights from 1312 on, which pitted the Dominican friars against the Chancellor and masters of Oxford, an issue, by the way, in which the king interceded at various times with the pope and cardinals against Harkeley and the university in favor of the Dominicans.[27]

Harkeley's sermon, which may be found in MS Lambeth Pal. 61, ff. 143[ra]-147[v],[28] is a rather lengthy and rambling discourse on a variety of subjects. It takes as its main theme Lamentations 5.16: 'The crown is fallen from our head'. Harkeley immediately comments on the suitability of this theme to Becket. Like many other preachers, he seems to have been obsessed with the manner of Becket's death, in that the crown of his head was literally cut off and fell to the church pavement.[29]

An interesting feature of this particular sermon, however, is the lengthy discussion on the nature of martyrdom. Harkeley distinguishes between martyrs who have died for the sake of the faith (*pro fide*) and a martyr like Thomas who died for the sake of the liberty of the Church (*pro libertate ecclesie*). In his argument that Thomas' cause was even greater than that of one who died for the sake of the faith alone, Harkeley takes up the precedent of St Alphège's martyrdom which had become a subject of discussion between Archbishop Lanfranc and Anselm, then a monk in the monastery of Bec.[30] Some background, which our sermon, by the way, does not provide, will be useful here. Alphège, bishop and martyr was born in 954 and died in Greenwich in 1012. He was raised to the archbishopric of Canterbury at a time when England was being ravaged by the Danes. Canterbury was betrayed to the marauders and the archbishop was captured and carried off to Greenwich. A ransom was demanded for him which he would not allow to be paid. The Danes, in a drunken fury, set on Alphège, pelting him with bones, and although one of the Danes, Thorkell the Tall, tried to save him, the archbishop was killed by a blow on the head with an axe. Lanfranc consulted Anselm concerning Alphège's claim to the title of martyr. Anselm, on his visit to England in 1078, defended the claim, saying that even though Alphège did not die for any point of Christian belief, yet he died for Christian justice in refusing to plunder his people to obtain a ransom for himself. In this decision Lanfranc acquiesced.[31] Thus Harkeley takes this earlier example and applies it to the question of the martyrdom of St Thomas of Canterbury. Just as Alphège died for Christ's sake, so was this the reason for Thomas's martyrdom.[32]

Harkeley also takes the following passage (Mt. 23.35) as being fulfilled in the martyrdom of Becket: 'That upon you may come all the righteous blood shed upon the earth, from the blood of righteous Abel unto the blood of Zacharias, son of Barachias, whom ye slew between the temple and the altar'. Zacharias, he compares with Thomas, for as Zacharias owed his office as high priest to the king, so was Thomas royal chancellor who owed his office of archbishop to the king. Both were slain between the temple and the altar.[33]

Becket's persecution reminds Harkeley of the problems that faced the clergy of his own day. He says: 'If one examines the Clarendon statutes for which Thomas died, one would find that in our own time, there are more severe customs and practices which secular princes use [against us] and which do more injury than those which led to the Constitutions of Clarendon . . .[34] We are not lacking persecutors of ecclesiastical liberty, and indeed we should be afraid lest we have to sacrifice an Abel or a Zacharias'.[35]

Oppression of the Church and denial of her liberties were frequently charged against King Edward II and his supporters. This may well have been in Harkeley's mind as he made these comments. While the Ordinances of 1311, four years earlier, began with a statement that acknowledged the traditional liberties of the Church, the Ordinances also went on to detail the various abuses ascribed to the king and provisions to correct them. In January, 1316, a month after this sermon was preached, the clergy at the Lincoln Parliament put forward a number of questions relating to the limits of clerical and temporal jurisdictions. King and council reviewed their answers and, as amended, these statements were enrolled in the *Articuli cleri* of 1316, a series of clerical complaints that concerned the relations of Church and State in England and spoke to the rights and liberties of the Church in England.[36] This was an era of widespread discontent especially among the lower or non-episcopal clergy whose grievances of a political or financial nature were expressed in convocations of both Canterbury and York. There were objections to the taxes which both pope and king levied on the clergy. There were also objections to the 'form and substance of royal summonses of clergy to convocation and parliament'. The lower clergy of Canterbury province, for example, vigorously protested in 1314-16 and again in 1322-23 'over what they considered was the derogation of proper ecclesiastical liberty'.[37]

Yet Harkeley, in this sermon on St Thomas of Canterbury's feastday, recalls a happier day for the Church when he points out that the tradition of royal domination over episcopal elections was broken by Becket's resistance. 'Earlier on, in accordance with ancient custom', he says, 'the kings of England had granted vacant episcopacies to whomsoever they wished. Such elections generally took place in the king's presence'. 'In those times', Harkeley further observes, 'this was considered to be canonical and legitimate, but Thomas abrogated that custom when he resigned his office into the hands of the pope, and from then on the Roman Church was made *domina et magistra* of all others of this realm'.[38]

Historically, however, Harkeley's view was simplistic and had little relevance to the political reality of his own day. As W.A. Pantin has observed, the reign of Edward II was a turning point in the development of the provision of bishops, and in the course of the century, papal provision became the normal method of appointment to a bishopric. Pantin goes on to say:

> The general rule seems to have been provision by the pope, more or less at the king's nomination. The form of election by the chapter was still gone through, even though it was regularly superseded by a provision. It was not at first obvious that free election was a thing of the past . . . Thus on the whole, after the time of Edward II, papal provision had the effect of giving the king the bishops he wanted.[39]

There was, morever, no more vivid reminder for this audience of clergy at Oxford in 1315 of the power of royal intervention (with the assistance of the pope) in the affairs of the English church than the selection two years earlier, in 1313, of the king's favorite Walter Reynolds as archbishop of Canterbury. It must have been rather painful for these Oxford clergy to learn that the election of one of their own, the learned and virtuous Thomas Cobham, who had distinguished himself as a scholar-theologian at Oxford *c*. 1288-93, had been overruled by Pope Clement V who agreed to Reynold's selection.[40]

Dr J. Robert Wright's recently published study of the English church and crown from 1305 to 1334 has done much to revise our view of Reynolds whom the chroniclers hardly admired and whom the *Vita Edwardi Secundi*[41] describes as a mere clerk, scarcely literate, who had excelled in theatrical presentations, and through this obtained the king's favour. Wright astutely observes that the 'liberties of the church in England have to be interpreted for every age', and Reynolds was very much a man of his time, little given to the politics of independence and confrontation for the sake of high ecclesiastical principles.[42]

Thus this sermon preached on the feastday of St Thomas of Canterbury in 1315 at Oxford to a university audience raises issues that went beyond simply marking the occasion of Becket's martyrdom. Such an audience undoubtedly would have been responsive to Harkeley's finely drawn analysis of martyrdom and to the issues of royal persecution and restriction of church liberties which Becket's martyrdom so dramatically and nostalgically portrayed. Harkeley was an academic theologian whose interpretation of the Becket myth and legend was quite traditional. It contrasted the virtuous Church defending its liberties against the king who constantly encroached upon them. This sermon is also especially interesting because it took place in the midst of political squabbles concerning, as we have seen, the litigation involving the Dominicans and the university, the appointment of Reynolds as archbishop of Canterbury instead of Cobham, and other clerical grievances in which Harkeley and his university colleagues found themselves in opposition to the secular authority. This sermon, furthermore, also illustrates the caution with which historians must approach sermon materials. Harkeley has to be understood in the context of his setting and his own biases. In this case, for example, the historical record reveals that Harkeley, far from representing the mainstream of the thinking in the hierarchy of the English church, set forth a purist view that was far more congenial to the university setting in Oxford, and that Reynolds, notwithstanding the derogatory remarks of the chroniclers, represented an effort to reconcile the interests of Church and State, avoiding the kind of confrontation that Becket's martyrdom stood for. *Caveat lector sermonum!*

That Thomas, archbishop of Canterbury, was a subject of intense interest among the intellectuals of his own day has been admirably demonstrated by Beryl Smalley in her book, *The Becket Conflict and the Schools*. Pointing out that Becket drew both his inspiration and his arguments from the schools, Smalley wrote:

> After his murder scholars exploited the Becket story for all it was worth. Theologians had influenced him in his life; now his passion added a new page to the expanding Bible of the schools. St Thomas' deeds and martyrdom served two purposes, the narrow one of ecclesiastical freedom and clerical immunities, the wider one of evangelisation: his passion brought men close to Christ's.[43]

I submit that we have in these two university sermons examples of both these streams of thought. In the Oxford sermon of 1315, Becket's martyrdom became an *exemplum* for contemporary clergy who increasingly resisted the encroachments of the secular authority on ecclesiastical liberties. The Paris sermon of 1230, on the other hand, touches on the wider lesson of Thomas' role as *bonus pastor* who was an example in life of defender of his flock and in death of a martyr who died in the cause of the liberty of the Church. The time, place, and circumstances of these preachers may well have changed, but St Thomas of Canterbury remained a vivid and compelling symbol for these university masters of Paris and Oxford in the thirteenth and fourteenth centuries.

670 West End Avenue
New York, N.Y. 10025
U.S.A.

REFERENCES

*   A version of this article was originally presented at the Nineteenth International Congress on Medieval Studies, Western Michigan University, May 1984. This research was supported (in part) by a grant from the City University of New York PSC-CUNY Research Award Program. I should also like to acknowledge and thank the following institutions for providing me with photocopies and/or microfilms of manuscript texts: Hereford Cathedral Library, Lambeth Palace Library (London), Bibliothèque Nationale (Paris), and Institut de Recherches et d'Histoire des Textes (Paris). My thanks also to Professor Nancy Siraisi for her helpful bibliographical references.

1.   For the most significant primary sources on Thomas Becket, see J. C. Robertson (ed.), *Materials for the History of Thomas Becket, Archbishop of Canterbury*, Rolls Series, 6 vols. (London, 1875-85). Much of the modern secondary literature is surveyed by J. W. Alexander in 'The Becket Controversy in Recent Historiography', *Journal of British Studies* 9 (1970), pp. 1-26. D. Knowles' *Thomas Becket* (London, 1971) is an

excellent reexamination of the life and career of the martyred archbishop. See also the collection of essays edited by R. Foreville, *Thomas Becket: Actes du Colloque International de Sédières 19-24 Aout 1973* (Paris, 1975).

2.   R. Foreville's important study, *Le jubilé de Saint Thomas Becket du XIIIe siècle au XVe siècle 1220-1470: Étude et documents* (Paris, 1958), fits the jubilees of Becket's martyrdom into the religious and social events of the time. A number of articles published by R. Foreville on the cult of Becket (especially on the Continent) have been reprinted in *Thomas Becket dans la tradition historique et hagiographique* (London, Variorum Reprints 1981).

3.   Of the 155 Latin sermons on Thomas Becket that I have studied to date, 4 were preached at Oxford and 16 at the University of Paris.

4.   MS Paris, Bibliothèque nationale lat. nouv. acqu. 338 (previously MS 88, Cluny) is a thirteenth-century MS, parchment, 260 ff. Its contents are described in B. Hauréau, *Notices et extraits de quelques manuscrits latins de la Bibliothèque Nationale*, 6 vols. (Paris, 1890-93), vol. VI, pp. 196-260. Other copies of the text may be found in MS Lille, Bibl. mun. 107, ff. 141-42^v (thirteenth century, parchment, 173 ff.) and MS Paris, Bibliothèque nationale lat. 12418, ff. 106va-107rb (thirteenth century, parchment, 124 ff.). The latter MS is described in Hauréau, *op.cit.*, vol. II, pp. 83-4. The text of the sermon has been edited by M. M. Davy, *Les sermons universitaires parisiens de 1230-31* (Paris, 1931), pp. 281-87.

5.   See A. Callebaut, 'Le calendrier parisien des prédications universitaires de l'année scolaire 1230-1231', *Archivum franciscanum historicum* 26 (1933), 541-48. Cf. in the fourteenth-century calendar of the University of Paris the following entry: [December] 23 G X 'Note that from Christmas eve till the morrow of St Thomas, archbishop of Canterbury and martyr, there are no lectures in any faculty . . . 29 F iiii St Thomas, archbishop of Canterbury and martyr'. See L. Thorndike (tr.), *University Records and Life in the Middle Ages* (Columbia University Records of Civilisation, 1944, repr. Norton 1975), p. 188.

6.   See Davy, p. 21.

7.   The sermon is noticed in J. B. Schneyer, *Repertorium der lateinischen Sermones des Mittelalters für die Zeit von 1150-1350*, 9 vols. to date (Münster, 1969-80), vol. III, p. 720 and vol. VI, p. 14.

8.   The rubric in MS Paris, lat. 12418, f. 106va adds the information where the sermon was preached: *Sermo Magistri Johannis de Sancto Aegidio apud sanctum Jacobum in festo beati Thome martiris*. Cf. in MS Paris, lat. nouv. acqu. 338, f. 84^r: *Sermo fratris Johannis de Sancto Aegidio in festo Beati Thome*.

9.   G. Leff, *Paris and Oxford Universities in the Thirteenth and Fourteenth Centuries: An Institutional and Intellectual History* (New York, 1968), p. 167.

10.   On John of St Giles (also known as John of St Albans), see A. B. Emden, *A Biographical Register of the University of Oxford to A.D. 1500*, 3 vols. (Oxford, 1957-59), vol. III, p. 1626; P. Glorieux, 'Jean de Saint-Gilles', *Catholicisme* 6, 24 (Paris, 1964), pp. 567-68; P. Glorieux, *Répertoire des maîtres en théologie de Paris au XIIIe siècle, 2 vols. (Paris, 1933), vol. I, pp. 52-53; C. L. Kingsford, 'John of St Giles', D.N.B.*, vol. X, pp. 883-85. On medical studies at Paris and Montpellier, see D. Jacquart, *Le milieu médical en France du xiie au xve siècle* (Genève, 1981) and L. Dulieu, *La médecine à Montpellier*, t. 1, *Le Moyen Âge* (Avignon, 1975).

11.   H. Rashdall, *The Universities of Europe in the Middle Ages*, eds. F. M. Powicke and A. B. Emden, 2 vols. (Oxford, 1936), vol. I, pp. 372-73.

12.   See Callebaut, p. 543.

13.   For a survey on the organisation of the sermon and literature on the *ars*

predicandi, see P. B. Roberts, *Stephanus de Lingua-Tonante: Studies in the Sermons of Stephen Langton* (Toronto, 1968), pp. 75-79.

14.   'Si occiditur in sanctuario Domini sacerdos et propheta'. . . Uerbum istud beato Thoma competit, et uobis scolaribus et ministris ipsis . . . De beato enim Thoma planum est quod occisus est in sanctuario Domini scilicet in ecclesia, cantans coram quodam altari. Sacerdos fuit, quia archiepiscopus. Item propheta, quia multa predixit que postea acciderunt. MS Paris, lat. nouv. acqu. 338, ff. 84^r-84^v.

15.   Quasi dicat: hoc est mirum et notandum quod quatuor modis interfectus est beatus Thomas in sanctuario Domini: prima mors eius mistice fuit depositio ueteris hominis et inductio noui. Erat enim homo curialis, scilicet cancellarius regis, et factus archiepiscopus religiosam duxit uitam. Unde mutatus est in uirum alterum . . . Secunda mors eius fuit martirium compassionis quod ipse sustinuit pro suis qui cum eo coacti sunt ire in exilium, propter hoc quia regi resisterat in faciem . . . Tercia mors eius fuit uictimatio proprie carnis . . . De ipso enim legitur quod brac(c)as habuit de cilicio et in flumine dicebat horas suas et post uerberebat se uel faciebat uerberari. Quarta mors eius fuit martirium persecutionis que durauit per sex annos et unum diem et de eo, qui conciuis erat Dei, dicebatur quod proditor erat in terra. Hoc quarto martirio eleuatus est a terra, secundum quod de eo dicitur in Zacharia: 'Saluabit eos Dominus ut gregem populi sui, quia lapides sancti eleuantur de terra'. *Ibid.*, ff. 84^v-85^r.

16.   Iste lapis fuit, scilicet durus et inflexibilis, quia nec muneribus nec minis flecti potuit . . . De isto Thoma dicitur in Ecclesiastico: 'Gemma carbunculi in ornamento auri et comparatio musicorum in conuiuio uini' . . . Gemma carbunculi fuit propter tria, que habet carbunculus. Primum est quia ex interuentione eius sanatur, etiam aqua benedicta, pestis ouium, que ex aqua illa bibunt. Sic et beatus Thomas pesti resistit, defendendo gregem suum per aquam id est per tribulationem suam . . . Item aqua benedicta amara est, quia falsa, sic tribulatio quam passus est fuit amarissima, quia etiam a quibusdam legatis persecutus est, et etiam a prelatis persecutus, qui contra eum durissimas scribebant litteras . . . Secundum est quia carbunculus rubet. De beato autem Thoma, non est dubium quin rubuerit . . . Ad litteram occisus est, et rubicunda facta est ecclesia sanguine ipsius . . . Tercium est quia carbunculus flammescit; sic et beatus Thomas, mirabilis scilicet uirtutibus . . . *Ibid.*, ff. 85^r-85^v.

17.   On the properties of *carbunculus*, see Bartholomeus Anglicus, *De proprietate rerum*, Lib. XVI, cap. xxvi (Frankfurt, 1601), p. 729 and *S. Isidori Hispalensis Episcopi Etymologiarum Libri XX*, Lib. XVI, cap. xiv, Migne, *PL*, 82, 578-79. On the properties of stones and gems see J. M. Riddle, ed. *Marbode of Rennes' (1035-1123) De Lapidibus* in *Sudhoffs Archiv*, Beiheft 20 (Wiesbaden, 1977) and *Albertus Magnus Book of Minerals*, tr. D. Wyckoff (Oxford, 1967). See also Joan Evans, *Magical Jewels of the Middle Ages and the Renaissance particularly in England* (Oxford, 1922); William Jones, *History and Mystery of Precious Stones* (London, 1880; reissued 1968), p. 92; and George F. Kunz, *The Curious Lore of Precious Stones* (Philadelphia and London, 1913), pp. 33, 61, 101-103.

18.   Sed hodie mundus habet multos falsos prophetas qui docent ut prebendas et honores sibi acquirant, et ut presenti uite necessaria habeant, qui pocius de eterna uita cogitare deberent . . . MS Paris, lat. nouv. acqu. 338, f. 86r. Unde de ipso uere dicitur: 'Ego sum pastor bonus'. (Joh. 10. 11). *Ibid.*, f. 85^r.

19.   Caesarius of Heisterbach, *Dialogus Miraculorum*, viii, 69.

20.   For the texts of the sermons that Stephen Langton preached on Becket, see P. B. Roberts, ed. *Selected Sermons of Stephen Langton* (Toronto Medieval Latin Texts, 1980), pp. 55-94.

21.   See Leff, pp. 31-40.

22. The other four sermons in the cycle preached by John of St Giles were: September 22 F (1230) Dom. 17 p. Pent. S. Mauritii; November 17 F Dom. 25 p. Pent.; Ianuarius 12 E (1231) Dom.; Iunius 15 E (1231) Dom. 5 p. Pent. See Callebaut, *op. cit.*

23. The sermon is noticed in Schneyer, *Repertorium*, vol. II, p. 764.

24. See Emden, vol. II, pp. 874-75; *D.N.B.*, vol. VIII, p. 1274; P. Glorieux, La faculté des arts et ses maîtres au XIIIe siècle (Paris, 1971), pp. 183-84; E. W. Kemp, 'History and Action in the Sermons of a Medieval Archbishop', *The Writing of History in the Middle Ages: Essays Presented to R. W. Southern*, ed. R. H. C. Davis and J. W. Wallace-Hadrill (Oxford, 1981), pp. 349-65. (I am most grateful to Fr P. Osmund Lewry for calling my attention to this essay.)

25. F. Pelster, 'Heinrich von Harclay, Kanzler von Oxford, und seine Quästionen', *Miscellanea Francesco Ehrle*, 5 vols. (Rome, 1924), vol. I, pp. 307-56. See also Mark C. Henninger, 'Henry of Harclay's Questions on Divine Prescience and Predestination', *Franciscan Studies*, 40:18 for 1980 (1982), pp. 167-243.

26. For the text of those articles condemned at Oxford in 1314, see H. Anstey, ed. *Munimenta academica, or documents illustrative of academical life and studies at Oxford*, Rolls Series, 2 vols. (London, 1868), vol. I, pp. 100-02.

27. S. Gibson, ed. *Statuta antiqua universitatis Oxoniensis* (Oxford, 1931), p. xli.

28. MS Lambeth Pal. 61 (twelfth-fifteenth centuries, vellum, 148 ff.) is described in M. R. James and C. Jenkins, *A Descriptive Catalogue of the Manuscripts in the Library of Lambeth Palace*, Part I, nos. 1-97 (Cambridge, 1930), pp. 97-99. There is a note that the sermon was preached at Oxford in the year (1315) in which Piers Gaveston's remains were taken to Langley for burial. Since this took place on 2 January 1315, the likely date for the sermon's delivery would be 29 December 1314, the previous Sunday. On Piers Gaveston, see J. S. Hamilton, 'Piers Gaveston, earl of Cornwall 1307-1312', *Dissertation Abstracts International* A 43:6 (1982), 2054-55. The text of the sermon may also be found in MS Hereford Cath. Libr. P. 5. XII (thirteenth-fourteenth centuries, vellum, 115 ff.), ff. 99vb-107va, described by A. T. Bannister, *A Descriptive Catalogue of the Manuscripts in the Hereford Cathedral Library* (Hereford, 1927), pp. 157-58. There are excerpts of the text printed in H. Wharton, ed. *Anglia Sacra*, 2 vols. (London, 1691), vol. II, p. 524n and in W. D. Macray, 'Sermons for the festivals of St Thomas Becket, etc. Probably by Archbishop Stratford', *English Historical Review* 8 (1893), 85-91. Macray suggested that the period of the sermon was the reign of Edward III and the preacher, Archbishop John Stratford (1333-48). See also G. R. Owst, *Literature and Pulpit in Medieval England* (Oxford, 1961), pp. 126-32. There is general consensus, however, that the sermon was preached by Henry Harkeley, chancellor of the University of Oxford. E. W. Kemp concludes that the 'Hereford manuscript (contains) a sermon collection which has a strong association with Archbishop John Stratford . . . the Harkeley sermon stands out as something different from all the rest'. He further points out 'that Stratford was still at Oxford at the beginning of 1315 and could have heard Harkeley's sermon and obtained a copy of it. Whether this was the beginning of his interest in Thomas Becket is impossible to say'. Stratford did found in 1331, in association with his younger brother, Robert, a chantry of St Thomas the Martyr in Holy Trinity Church, Stratford-on-Avon, his birthplace. See Kemp, *op. cit.*, pp. 363-64. See also on the text R. Haines, 'Some Sermons at Hereford Attributed to Archbishop John Stratford', *Journal of Ecclesiastical History* 34:3 (1983), 425-37 which lists all the sermons in the Hereford MS.

29. 'Cecidit corona capitis nostri' . . . Ista uerba possunt applicari ad sanctum Thomam Cantuariensis cuius corona ad litteram cecidit amputata . . . MS Lambeth Pal. Libr. 61, f. 143ra.

30. Autem Lanifrancus iam existens archiepiscopus consulit Anselmum adhuc monachum in monasterio de Bekko degentem, de causa martirii sancti Elfegi quondam Cantuariensis archiepiscopi quem Dani interfecerunt dum terram Anglie depopularent hoc modo. Cum enim iste sanctus episcopus Elphegus nomine captus esset a Danis dederunt ei licenciam redimendi ob pecuniam. *Ibid.*, f. 144ra.

31. See A. E. McKilliam, *A Chronicle of the Archbishops of Canterbury* (London, 1913), p. 113.

32. Ita mortuus est Elphegus pro Christo . . . eadem omnino ratio est de Thoma. MS Lambeth Pal. Libr. 61, f. 144rb.

33. 'Ueniet super uos omnis sanguis iustus qui effusus est a sanguine Abel iusti usque ad sanguinem Zacharie filii Barachie quem occidistis inter templum et altare'. (Cf. Zechariah 1. 1 which identifies Zechariah as the son of Berechiah.) Consideremus conditiones istius Zacharie et conditiones Thome. Iste fuit summus sacerdos. Ita et Thomas saltem huius prouincie. Iste etiam Zacharias quia pater eius maximum beneficium contulerat regi Johas (i.e. Joash) quia per eum regnauit. (Cf. II Chronicles 24. 20-21 which identifies this Zechariah as the son of Jehoiada who, despite his father's kindnesses to the king, was slain 'in the court of the house of the Lord'.) Et certe Thomas dum esset in officio cancellarie propter summam circumspeccionem et prouidenciam in quibus non habuit parem egit strenuissime negocia regni in omni loco dominationis eius. *Ibid.*, f. 145vb.

34. Siquis enim inspiciat statuta edita apud Clarendonam pro quibus Thomas passus fuit, inueniet quod nostris temporibus sunt consuetudines multo deteriores quas exercent principes seculares et magis iniuriose quam fuerunt illa de Clarendona . . . *Ibid.*, f. 145rb.

35. Apud nos non deficiunt persecutores ecclesiastice libertatis et ideo timendum est nobis ne requiratur a nobis omnis sanguis iustus a sanguine Abel uel Albani iusti [i.e. Albani Sancti] usque ad sanguinem Zacharie i.e. Thome. *Ibid.*, f. 145vb.

36. J. Robert Wright, *The Church and the English Crown 1305-1334: a study based on the Register of Walter Reynolds* (Toronto, 1980), p. 188.

37. *Ibid.*, p. 186.

38. Nam tunc fuit consuetudo regum Anglie quod dabant episcopatus uacantes quibus uellent; et si fiebat electio fiebat in capella regis ipso rege presente cum aliis per eum uocatis et reputabatur tunc temporis talis ingressus satis canonicus et legitimus. Sed Thomas istam consuetudinem in humili resignatione quam fecit in manus pape decetero abrogauit . . . Ad hec omnia respondit legatus nomine Pandulphus quod illa consuetudo fuit abolita per sanctum Thomam Cantuariensis quando resignauit in manus pape totum suum . . . ex tempore facta est Romana Ecclesia omnium aliorum huius regni domina ac magistra . . . MS Lambeth Pal. Libr. 61, f. 147ra.

39. W. A. Pantin, *The English Church in the Fourteenth Century* (Notre Dame, Indiana, 1962), pp. 55, 57.

40. Dr Wright (pp. 271-72) observes that Thomas Cobham was 'in his scholarship and in his independence of the crown more in the stamp of Winchelsey'. Winchelsey, for his part, 'felt himself to be treading in the footsteps of Becket'.

41. N. Denholm-Young (ed.), *Vita Edwardi Secundi Monachi Cuiusdam Malmesberiensis* (London, 1957), p. 45.

42. Wright, pp. 271-72. Notice Reynolds' connections with the Becket legend: 'His best set of high mass vestments in red and gold was embroidered with Becket's life, he bequeathed two magnificent pontifical rings to the martyr's shrine at Canterbury, he owned a book about Becket, and the martyrdom was depicted on Reynolds' small

counterseal (as it had been on those of several of his predecessors) together with the legend *Ad Christum pro me sit semper passio Thome'*. *Ibid.*, p. 271.

43.   Beryl Smalley, *The Becket Conflict and the Schools: a study of intellectuals in politics in the twelfth century* (Oxford, 1973), p. 239.

LEARNING AND LIVINGS: UNIVERSITY STUDY AND CLERICAL CAREERS IN LATER MEDIEVAL ENGLAND

R. N. Swanson

In recent years, the graduates of the medieval English universities have received a great deal of attention. In many respects, perhaps, there has been too much concentration on this small fragment of England's population, based on elitist assumptions of their importance which have themselves dictated the nature of many of the questions posed about their place within the clerical career structure. The graduates have been studied for their own sake, tacitly ignoring the fact that they had to compete in a wider world, where they had to face, and if possible outface, competition. It is that competition which provides the main focus of this essay, attempting to view the position of the graduates within the clerical career structure from the perspectives of the patrons as potential benefactors, and of the other clergy as rivals for promotion. To that end, it is necessary to direct attention to three main areas: the basic motivation for attending university in the first place; the attitudes of patrons in their exercise of patronage; and finally the element of competition in the search for benefices, not just among graduates, but between those with university education and those without.

I

The relationship which developed between the universities and the church following the rise of the *studia* in the later twelfth century was always a complex one. Essentially the universities were ecclesiastical institutions: there was an ecclesiastical purpose to their educational programme, even if sometimes difficult to define. Their theologians claimed a determinative role in theological development; while as ecclesiastical bodies the universities sought (and achieved) independent representation at the general councils of the church in the fifteenth century. Their very creation emphasised their ecclesiastical status, at least by the later middle ages: whatever kings and emperors might hope, no university could properly exist without papal approbation. In England, the available evidence indicates, the members of Oxford and Cambridge remained almost exclusively clerics until the fifteenth century, although then a change set in with developing laicisation. If they progressed to holy orders, these university members would expect ecclesiastical careers, including receipt of benefices and other promotions. Indeed, because of the relative paucity of sources from the university end before the late fourteenth century, it is usually only because of their beneficed careers, and the appropriate records in church archives, that their graduate status or even their university can be identified. Whilst it is frequently possible to assign these graduates to either Oxford or Cambridge, there remain large numbers for whom no such certainty is possible. The end result is that the English universities were at best mere appendages of the church, at worst parasites on it, but undeniably institutions which could not exist independently of it.[1]

That this was so, that the universities and their members did live off the church, raises an immediate and important question. Precisely what were the relationships which developed between the four main components of the career of a graduate within the church: the university as an institution; the student or graduate as an individual; the benefice, as a source of funds to permit study, as well as a reward for it; and the patron, without whose involvement the benefice could not be obtained? Elucidation of the complex connections between these elements is vital in any attempt to determine the relationships between university study and clerical careers in pre-Reformation England, although the likelihood that all the influences will be adequately identified is extremely remote.

Before considering graduates' careers, one major question demands attention: why did people go to university at all? The question is as valid for the late medieval centuries as it is for the twentieth, and I suspect that the responses have changed little. For some, university study would represent the opportunity for individual intellectual development, the opportunity to enquire and find answers. Such students would be reflected in Chaucer's Oxford clerk, eking out a meagre existence on uncertain income, subsisting on a diet of charity and Aristotle, and thus satisfying his mental if not bodily hunger.[2] A second, and probably rarer, type would be the escapist, not so much avoiding work, as evading responsibility and discord. An instance of this is provided by a Berkshire letter from the turn of the thirteenth and fourteenth centuries, its writer seeking support for an application on behalf of a friend to the bishop of Bath and Wells. The friend, a rector of a chapel, was in conflict with his patron, who had adopted a threatening attitude towards him. The bishop was to be petitioned to grant the rector a licence for non-residence for study at the schools, with permission to farm his benefice, for at least twelve years![3] In this instance university study was intended merely to provide a safety valve for local conflicts, rather than being an end in itself.

But such cases — the committed student and the escapist — would probably account only for a minority of students; and the determined academic is likely to be found in the higher faculties (principally among the theologians), with their lengthier courses and greater intellectual demands. The majority of students were probably not motivated by such concerns. They went to university largely as an investment: education paid off. Whatever may have been the motives for the creation of the universities, there can be little doubting the immediately perceived financial benefits of a university education; and from the first days of their existence, there is clear evidence of a mercenary attitude to study, roundly condemned by self-conscious academics. Thus, in his *Metalogicon* John of Salisbury castigated those who, with a smattering of knowledge, considered themselves experts, and went on to rook their clients.[4] He returns to the attack in his *Policraticus*, deriding the abuse of philosophy which was the guiding light for his generation, and probably for many of their successors at the universities.[5] Later, Robert de Courson admitted that even theologians might be afflicted by mercenary considerations, that theology might be studied because it profited the pockets rather than the souls of its pursuers.[6]

Some of these criticisms ring rather hollow. John of Salisbury, for instance, is evidence of more than just distaste for this perversion of education. If anyone has to serve as a model for later careers of university graduates, I suspect it has to be him. If anyone proved the validity of his own strictures, it is this complainer against those who profited from their eduction. For his philosophy eventually brought its rewards. It earned him employment, first with archbishop Theobald of Canterbury, then at the papal court, and after that again with the archbishops of Canterbury. His secretarial activities earned him canonries, and finally made him the successful candidate for the see of Chartres.[7] Few in later centuries would parallel his career precisely, but there are some with remarkable similarities. Take, for example, Robert Hallum, in the late fourteenth century. After an initial spell at Oxford, and apparently alongside work for higher degrees, he was employed by successive archbishops of Canterbury as chancellor. This allowed for the accumulation of a succession of benefices, including an impressive array of prebends. After failing to obtain a bishopric, he moved to the papal curia, with perhaps three years working there. This culminated in his (ineffective) provision to the archbishopric of York, compensated for by effective appointment to the see of Salisbury in 1407. Hallum's career also included a period as Chancellor of Oxford University, and after his promotion involved attendance at the general councils at Pisa and Constance, some diplomatic work for Henry IV, and nomination to the cardinalate — which he was obliged to reject.[8] Although Hallum's experiences and those of John of Salisbury differ, the similarities are more significant. Many of those attending university probably aspired to follow their pattern, but their progression through the full scheme would have been being curtailed at one level or another, with them having to be content with their prebend, rectory, or whatever.

Even if reality intervened, the ideal remained. University study could be perceived as the route to a career. Those at university hoped, perhaps expected, to profit from their studies; when disappointed, as Thomas Gascoigne was in the fifteenth century, they might well turn cantankerous.[9] However, perceptions of reality might not reflect reality. Did university study necessarily guarantee a clerical career? And, if so, what type of career? Since we know of graduates because of their careers within the church, there is a danger of imposing a false causality. Yet the fact has to be faced that there were few careers for which a university education was actually necessary, even within the church. When chancellors of cathedral churches were theoretically responsible for maintaining the educational standards of their diocesan clergy, and from the surviving evidence seem actually to have arranged for some theological instruction at their churches, where did the universities fit in?[10] In any case, why should the learning be at the high level implied by its university origins, rather than mere grammatical instruction, which should have been obtainable locally? The educational needs of the parish clergy seem in fact to have been relatively basic, until at least the start of the sixteenth century, when reformers began to worry about such matters. For ordination, for example, the requirements may have been rather meagre. Ordinands were certainly examined, but beyond their fulfilment of the technical qualifications as to age, birth, and so on, and occasional vague references to the testing of 'scientia', sometimes found wanting, little is known.[11] However, the level demanded was probably not high, as local reputation was sufficient qualification for orders. The standard demanded was probably not much better (if better at all) when it came to the test for holding a benefice. A rather detailed statement of an examination before bishop Philip Repingdon of Lincoln in the early fifteenth century indicates the demands made of a would-be incumbent. In this case the candidate failed, because he could not read or construe (presumably, if this is comparable to other examinations, a reference to his abilities to deal with the missal), nor could he differentiate between substantive and adjective. This seems to indicate roughly the level of grammatical knowledge required. When it came to theology, the bishop asked him to define the articles of faith, which he could not do. At this point, he was rejected,[12] but it is possible that the theological examination could have been rather deeper, testing his knowledge of the Ten Commandments, the Seven Deadly Sins, the sacraments, and other matters — the basic rudiments of Christianity which formed the backbone of many of the injunctions to the clergy for the instruction of their parishioners throughout the period, and provided the material for many of the volumes giving advice to parish priests.[13] What seems clear is that the clergy were expected to know what they were talking about, but not necessarily to comprehend in any depth: their role was choreographic and expository, rather than elucidatory.

If this was the case, then the question returns: why go to university? If university education was perceived as paying dividends, then in what terms, and in what contexts? Benefices may have been seen as the end result, as the desserts of the student because he had studied; but benefices were also the end result of another process. They were not there just for the asking. Their receipt required the activity of an intermediary, the patron, and securing patronage was a critical stage in the path to a benefice for anyone, graduate or not. For the man with a university education, that might just provide the qualification which would make him an attractive proposition for the patron.

II

The problems of patronage relationships within the medieval church are considerable; those affecting graduates and university members are particularly complex in view of the varying demands and expectations of all parties, and the difficulties of the source material. The last qualification is especially important, because at certain levels it prevents any conclusions being drawn. Whilst it is legitimate to try to assess the role of graduates within the church, for the wider class of 'university educated' the position is more difficult: they are rarely identifiable, but they must surely have outnumbered the graduates if all are included, such as those going for only part of a course. From here on, there are two strands to the argument. On the one hand, it is possible to discuss graduates, and make real suggestions; on the other, there is the continual counterpoint of the educated non-graduates, who can be introduced at the level of generalisation, but not of statistics, and whose existence necessarily tempers anything said about the graduates.

The problems of graduate employment in later medieval England have been extensively aired since 1974, when G. F. Lytle suggested that Oxford graduates encountered a 'crisis of patronage' in the period 1330-1430. My own thoughts on the matter broadly support Lytle's hypothesis, although with a more restricted chronology, limiting the crisis to *c.* 1380 to *c.* 1430.[14] I would also prefer not to try to quantify the crisis, turning from concern with numbers being appointed to a discussion of the level of appointment in contrast to career expectations, making the crisis one of the mechanism of promotion rather than simply one of numbers — although numbers do come into it. Essentially, my argument is that during the fourteenth century a number of important supports to graduate clerical careers were removed, especially as they affected the gaining of the first benefice, and support for study at the university. Thus, on the one hand non-residence for study was affected by a reduction in episcopal generosity in granting the necessary licences (perhaps especially those in accordance with the papal constitution *Cum ex eo*, which was intended to facilitate lengthy periods away from a benefice at university), and also by a real reduction in the number of rectories throughout England by their appropriation to religious corporations, and possibly by the effects of changing economic conditions after the Black Death — when only rectories and sinecurist prebends could support non-residence and study over long distances. At the same time, the virtual abolition of papal provisions during the fourteenth century, and the extinction therewith of the only machinery allowing universities to petition the papacy directly for patronage for their members, removed a crucial prop which could have allowed individuals to break into the benefice market without needing to secure an individual patron.

Whilst this was happening, the possibilities for fulfilling career aspirations were changing. New patronage patterns were emerging, less institutionalised than those previously in existence. Economic changes were also altering the relative values of individual benefices, as well as making some so worthless that they had to be extinguished by merger. Increasing competition for benefices from members of the religious orders also reduced the scope for promotion of secular graduates. There were, at the same time, more vicarages, more chantries, which needed to be served, and a continuing demand for unbeneficed clergy. In comparison with the fourteenth century, I argue that in the fifteenth graduates would be increasingly found among these lower office holders, even as parochial chaplains.[15] Unfortunately, statistical proof is probably impossible. But the basic problem remains, and the remainder of this essay will indicate some of the difficulties of the research, and suggest various other considerations.

A major danger in any assessment of clerical career prospects, and perhaps a particular danger with the discussion of graduate careers, is to distort the perspective. Concentrating solely on university study and the students does introduce such a distortion, seeing a much wider issue solely in terms of their specific concerns. But there are other elements in the equations. Benefices had to be vacant before they could be filled — vacancy requiring death or resignation. Patrons also need some consideration, their demands and expectations of the successful candidate for their attention, their views on the nature and role of the benefice. Moreover, students and those with university experience were not the only benefice hunters; there were all the other clerics without posts, all equally anxious to secure benefices, and in competition with the graduates. All too often they are completely overlooked, but must be brought into the discussions.

Actually measuring the success of the university educated against 'the rest' (if there was such success), and then accounting for it, also raises problems. For a start, the university educated cannot all be assessed — the grouping is necessarily, but artifically, restricted to the graduates. But beyond that, just how is 'success' to be measured? In theory, there are several possibilities: simply counting appointments; modifying those figures to eliminate exchanges and pluralism to concentrate on first benefices; counting periods of actual occupancy; and others. Whatever the judgements, the sources will add their own complications, by the nature of their recording and survival. My own doubts about an overly statistical approach have already been expressed:[16] essentially, I do not think that the statistics will actually reveal much, will impose a comparability which may not exist, and will often fail to indicate with sufficient precision exactly what they reflect — it is all too easy to be beguiled by figures without appreciating what they really indicate, or perhaps more important, omit. So far, discussions have tended to concentrate on percentages of vacancies filled by graduates, ignoring the fluctuating position of the graduates as a proportion of potential candidates (i.e. the totality of the clergy), ignoring the factors affecting the nature of any vacancy, and ignoring the variety of influences which may have led the individual patron to make a specific appointment. So far, also, nuances concerning the types and values of benefices have been largely overlooked.

Given the need to take these other factors into account, a second major question arises with regard to university study and clerical careers: why should patrons have chosen the university-educated for appointment in preference to others? Obviously, from the church's theoretical viewpoint, there was the argument that their promotion would be of benefit to the institution — an argument which found its fruition in the exploitation of papal provisions to support graduates almost as of right.[17] But what about the interests of the patrons? What could the university-educated offer them and the benefices which they controlled — especially the benefices — which other clerics could not? The answer, for parochial purposes, must be very little. Although ecclesiastical institutions, the universities were not especially vocationally concerned — indeed, John of Salisbury's early strictures perhaps suggest an antipathy to vocational concerns which may have lasted throughout the middle ages. In the formal records for the regulation of university institutions in medieval England, there is little prior to the foundation of Lincoln College, Oxford, in the 1420s, and of Godshouse, Cambridge, in the 1440s to indicate an explicitly utilitarian view of university education. The main aim of the founder of Lincoln College, bishop Richard Fleming, was to encourage the study of theology, and thereby counter the spread of Lollardy — an ecclesiastical purpose for university study. Godshouse was less ambitious, being directed not at providing ecclesiastics, but schoolmasters, who need not have any precise parochial connections.[18] So, in assessing graduate careers, it is necessary to give some attention to the needs of the patrons. What would a patron actually want, other than someone to fill a gap? Control of appointments to benefices was an important element in local patronage and political control;[19] why should the job requirements of a graduate take precedence over such concerns? Benefices were a cheap way of rewarding loyal service; why should someone with university education be allowed to jump the queue simply because of his learning? When it comes to the specific usefulness of graduates, there is something of a difficulty. They might serve as bureaucrats for estate and household management; they could be employed as tutors; but there would be no need to appoint them to benefices simply because they were graduates. Grammar per se was not, at the levels reached at the university, a necessity for parochial cures. Given the relatively low level of theological expertise demanded of the parish clergy, where was the need for the questions and disputations of the later medieval university? For the majority of ecclesiastical benefices university graduates were, almost by definition, over-qualified. Granted, some courses would have career uses — canon lawyers for the church courts; civil lawyers for diplomacy; theologians for some positions within the church; but little more.[20] Many such careers could be fulfilled without, again, needing recourse to ecclesiastical benefices.

Neither patrons nor benefices specifically needed graduates; but graduates who aimed for an ecclesiastical career certainly needed both. (I am aware that I am here sliding over the question of the clerics' own perceptions of benefices, but that is rather outside the scope of the paper.) With the destruction of the system of papal provisions in the fourteenth century, a major safety-valve for graduate employment may have been removed.[21] Whilst individual graduates would have had specific links with patrons which would have secured their individual careers — via relatives, as a result of family contacts, because of employment in either church or state — the means whereby the unattached student or graduate could insinuate himself into the clerical career structure by exploiting his university status itself had now been extinguished, apart from the limited possibilities of exploiting a college's own advowsons. Now such a student needed to create such links himself, with all the difficulties that that entailed, and also had to be content with what he could secure rather than what he actually wanted. I suspect that many of those with university experience would have become for some time indistinguishable from the generality of the clergy. Thus, in the early decades of the fifteenth century, and probably beyond, they would have had to wait some years before securing a benefice, and then would have to be content with a vicarage or chantry rather than the rectories they might earlier have anticipated (although economic changes during the period had made some vicarages and chantries worth more than some rectories). With the removal of papal provisions, the graduates would need to create their own patronage connections, a change which requires further investigation of the machinery which might bring them to the attention of those with benefices to dispose of, and of the general arrangements whereby individuals acquired benefices. One outcome of such investigations might well be evidence of increasing lay involvement in patronising graduates, both within benefices under their immediate control, and through influence over (if not outright usurpation of) the patronage exercised by religious institutions.

Actually establishing any of these connections would be laborious.

Despite Emden's researches, massive gaps remain in our knowledge of the numbers of graduates (let alone non-graduates with university experience) among the clergy of medieval England. Much more prosopographical research is needed, which will allow the identification of as many of the educated clergy as possible, and permit some assessment of the importance of the timing of their education within the scope of their general careers. After all, every career includes a period when the individual concerned had no university education, just as it also contains a period when he had no benefice. What requires investigation is the point of cross-over between both strands of the complete career, and their inter-action.

   The possibility of the necessary research being successfully carried out in a sufficient number of cases is remote. Whilst the material could be computerised, I doubt if it could provide answers to all the questions. One major problem would be of identification of individuals in terms of overall careers — for example is the Master William Selby, found claiming the vicarage of Knaresborough in Yorkshire by papal provision in 1385, to be identified with the Master William Selby, an Oxford graduate of Salisbury diocese, who occurs at about this time, but whose recorded benefices are otherwise very much contentrated in the south of England?[22] Other problems are equally insuperable. Low status church posts are rarely mentioned in episcopal registers, although they do appear in visitation records and court material. Only chance preserves the names of stipendiary curates or failed candidates for posts. Whilst it is possible to trace the holders of formal benefices, the rectories, vicarages, chantries, and prebends whose transfer from incumbent to incumbent occupy so much space in episcopal registers, other job opportunities are much less frequently indicated. Episcopal administrators were unconcerned about the holders of household chaplaincies, only with the granting of licences for the chapels; they were anxious to ensure that non-resident incumbents acting under temporary licences made due provision for the services during their absences, but not with recording the names of those stand-ins. Nor are diocesan sources particularly useful for identifying the occupants of what can only be called informal chantries — chantries based on trusts, with the trustees hiring the priest at a salary, and without conveying any rights to the endowment other than distraint.[23] Identification of other low posts, such as choral vicarages within cathedral and major collegiate churches, is dependent on the survival of their own independent archives, which usually leave something to be desired. Yet graduates were to be found among these groups, perhaps as their first employment. Certainly the earl of Northumberland's household regulations in the early sixteenth century mention the possibility of employing graduates, at rates of pay above those of non-graduates, but below that allowed to the schoolmaster.[24]

Even if the names survive, there is the problem of identifying the graduates, and when they gained their degrees. Until the fifteenth century, it was usual only to identify as graduates those with MA status or above, although the omission of the title may not necessarily mean that no degree was held. There would always be a large number who, whilst not yet masters, were nevertheless BAs (and are increasingly identified as such during the fifteenth century), or who had some university experience without having taken their degree. It is these last two classes — especially the last — whose identification is most difficult, possible only from chance references, or the survival of university material from the fifteenth century onwards. Yet their existence, and untraceability, makes any consideration of the educational attainments of the clergy as a whole extremely precarious. Precise quantification of graduate occupancy of these lower positions within the ecclesiastical hierarchy is, therefore, impossible. Nevertheless, there is clear, in only occasional, evidence that they were holding them, even if in relative terms — that is, in comparison with the non-graduates - the numbers are fairly small. The returns of the clergy in the diocese of Lincoln in 1526, in response to the levy of a subsidy for the crown, thus show graduates occupying chantries, graduates as stipendiary chaplains, graduates as parochial curates — as well as graduate rectors and vicars. The minor posts were usually no better paid than those occupied by non- graduates, being generally worth between £5 and £7 p.a.[25] In such circumstances, education was not proving especially profitable. Just what the distribution of graduates in such posts throughout the country may have been is indeterminable: equivalent subsidy returns for other areas suggest a blacker picture, as with the records of the archdeaconry of Richmond in 1525-6, and the archdeaconry of Stafford in 1531, where no graduates are identified as such at all — although this absence may be a failing of the evidence rather than the clergy.[26] The subsidy evidence so far available is rather late and may in fact be from a period when some of the problems of graduate employment had been partially alleviated by one particular expedient, to be considered later. The non-recording of appointments to these preliminary positions, prior to receipt of endowed benefices, masks the creation of the initial links which might produce later patronage. Again, in assessing the success of the university educated in securing employment, greater concentration is needed on the creation and nature of the relationship between patron and protege, and on the mechanisms of patronage. The bland statements of most institution records, that X gained his post on the presentation of Y, may in fact conceal a more complex reality, especially when dealing with corporate patronage such as that of religious institutions. Thus, taking a specific instance, what is to be made of the case of Thomas Jacob, who received a chantry in Lichfield cathedral in the 1450s? His appointment was theoretically at the nomination of the dean and chapter of the cathedral; ostensibly therefore he was an agreed candidate. But the residentiaries had recently arranged a procedure to carve up the patronage of these chantries among themselves, so that each had his fair share of individual patronage in turn. Jacob therefore actually owed his position to his association with one member of the chapter. One record of his nomination notes that his patron was the dean, but this does not explain why he got the post. Two reasons are presented by other information. Firstly, that he was reasonably well educated, being a BA of Oxford. A further qualification would give him reason to hope for promotion from the dean — he was his kinsman, a fact possibly of greater significance in this case than the level of his education.[27] The partitioning of corporate patronage visible at Lichfield is matched elsewhere. At Lincoln, for example, the nomination to parish churches in the gift of the dean and chapter, and of choral vicarages in the cathedral, was shared among the residentiaries in order of seniority. A contrary trend appears in other cases, towards the monopolisation of supposedly corporate patronage by one individual, a charge levelled against George Grey, dean of Newarke college, Leicester, in 1518.[28]

Other aspects of patronage trends also require attention. The fifteenth century saw a general usurpation of patronage from religious institutions by the laity. Sometimes this was overt, as in Cheshire and Lancashire, where Sir John Stanley exploited both the complexities of the law and the connections of bastard feudalism to gain control over benefices at the expense of the monks of Nostell Priory and the nuns of Syon.[29] Usually the process was more subtle. The system of making grants of next presentation, the alienation of the patronage at the next vacancy of the church, became fairly common in the fifteenth century. Whilst benefices in lay patronage might be affected — the grant being itself an act of patronage — the transfers seem mostly to have affected benefices belonging to religious bodies. Episcopal registers often indicate that such a grant was being acted upon;[30] but do not reveal the nature of the connections between the acting patron and the individual being patronised. These could be varied, including a nomination restricted to candidates approved by a third party, or a nominal transfer of the patronage to the crown for purely legal purposes to meet a challenge from a rival (with the crown in fact nominating the candidate of the transferer).[31] More insidious would be the covert transfer only of the power to nominate to a benefice, which might well not surface in the episcopal registers. In such instances, the presentation would still be made officially by the owner of the advowson, but that patron would in fact be presenting another's candidate. Several indications of this use of nomination survive in Bishop Langton's Salisbury register, between 1485 and 1493, whilst transcripts of early sixteenth century deeds indicate it operating in benefices owned by the priory of Lewes.[32] All too often it might be assumed that there were connections between the presenter and the patronised, when in fact other links are involved. This is sometimes apparent in cases of disputed presentation, where in due course the patronage lapses to the diocesan bishop because the dispute made the vacancy last for more than six months — but the collating bishop in fact appoints the candidate of one of the disputing parties.[33]

Another means whereby patronage was effectively but unobtrusively usurped was with the exploitation of the religious houses by the crown and bishops to provide salaries for their adherents. Following set rules, the houses were required to provide pensions to nominated individuals until they could be presented to a suitable benefice. In such circumstances, the real patron was obviously the nominating king or bishop, but the apparent patron in the subsequent appointment to the benefice would be the religious house.[34] For university students, a further complication might arise if the nomination to the pension preceded or coincided with a period of study: the pensionary non-graduate dependent on one patron for his income might later appear as a graduate being presented to a benefice by someone else, with all the imponderables that introduces into the spectrum of career opportunities and patronage connections. Such a situation seems to occur with a graduate nominated to a rectory by the abbey of Bury St Edmunds in the early 1430s. In 1429 King Henry VI had demanded a pension until beneficed for one of his chapel clerks, Thomas Swallow — who is not qualified as a graduate in the demand. He is presumably to be identified with the Master Thomas Swallow whom the abbey nominated to Woolpit rectory, probably in 1431. The promotion in fact was ineffective, Swallow seemingly refusing the nomination because the benefice was not sufficiently profitable.[35]

Swallow's refusal indicates that, while the category of benefice to which an individual was nominated was obviously important in terms of status, for the recipients another major consideration would be its monetary value. Here, information is generally scarce before the sixteenth century. Until then, the only general valuation is provided by the Taxation of 1291, and there might be a considerable difference between values recorded then, and real value later on. However, value does appear to have been a working consideration in the fifteenth century, when a mechanism developed which, while on the one hand possibly releasing benefice income to support study without going through the rigmarole of receiving a formal licence for non-residence, would on the other have cut into the value of the benefice for its occupant, graduate or not.

During the fifteenth century, it became increasingly common for those resigning benefices of some value to act to retain a hold on some of the revenues as an annual pension. There might be hints of simony in such arrangements, but not always.[36] The abstraction of the pension from the income of the benefice legitimised a form of non-residence and pluralism which did not require a dispensation; it also clearly affected the value of the post to later incumbents. Where it was merely a matter of providing for old age, with rooms in the rectorial or vicarial manse, and an annual allowance, the long-term impact might not be significant.[37] However, some pensions did last many years — Alan Percy was allotted £8 from Giggleswick in Yorkshire in 1517, and sued for its continued payment in the 1550s. Successive incumbents would have had to take this deduction into account in intervening years.[38] If this system was as widespread as it appears to have been, then the release of the income might have made significant contributions to the maintenance costs of university students, particularly in the higher faculties, and especially if they derived from a collection of benefices. This effective creation of additional sinecures could also have contributed to a reduction in the pressures on graduate employment, if there were any. Here again, the Lincoln subsidy material of 1526 provides valuable evidence, with several benefices having to support graduates as pensioners, in addition to their graduate rectors and vicars.[39] This suggests a twofold impact: reduction in the pressure to find parochial employment to support study, and possibly a reduction in the overall expectations of the graduate grouping, who were now forced to accept that they would have to take benefices with pensions deducted, rather than receive the full income. This whole area still needs considerable research — usually we know only that the pension was granted, without knowing for how long it lasted, or the real value of the benefice from which it was deducted. It would be especially useful to know how such pensions fit into clerical career patterns: were some of their recipients using them to support their studies, returning to the benefice market later? One candidate for such a possibility is Master William de Chechester, who in 1509 resigned what appears to have been the family living of Arlington, in Exeter diocese. He received a pension of £4 a year from the benefice, until he obtained a replacement appointment. As he was closely connected with Oxford, where he had been principal of a succession of inns until only a couple of years before his resignation, he may have continued his studies using this income. In this case, as in most others, the period during which the pension was paid is not clear, but Chechester does not seem to have had to wait long for his replacement benefice.[40] An important consideration in the analysis of these pensions would be clarification of the processes whereby they were obtained in the first place. Whilst there was a feeling that bishops should allow pensions to elderly clerics, to prevent them from falling into total poverty after resignation, it is unlikely that such considerations operated with younger men. What machinery therefore operated for their patrons (or themselves) to persuade the bishops to authorise such arrangements?

III

There remains one other aspect of the patronage problem to be considered: the success-rate of the graduates in obtaining benefices in comparison with the rest of the clerical grouping. As already stated, too often the statistics are presented purely in terms of percentages of presentations, without taking account of the nature of the competition. Yet this competition is a vital element in the overall equation: graduates were only a fraction — a very small fraction — of the total clerical population in pre-Reformation England; any alteration in their rate of success in acquiring benefices in comparison with the non-graduate population may therefore indicate changing attitudes by the patrons towards university education, regardless of the changing patterns of benefice occupancy.

The size of Oxford and Cambridge in the later middle ages remains a matter of conjecture. Figures are few, their interpretation difficult. It seems not unreasonable, however, to assess the numbers of seculars at the universities at about 1500-2000 in the later fourteenth century, growing to c. 2500-3000 by the end of the fifteenth century.[41] Reliable evidence for the numbers completing the degree course is virtually non-existent for the pre-Reformation period, but what there is suggests that no more than a hundred (possibly less than fifty) new secular MAs were being produced by Oxford and Cambridge jointly in each year throughout the period. Placing these figures against the total number of benefices available is difficult; but if something like 9000 parochial benefices existed throughout the period 1350-1530, with beneficed careers averaging about 20 years, this should have meant that the provision of new MAs would be more than sufficient to fill vacancies, if graduates were to be deliberately chosen, and assuming that pluralism can be discounted.[42] On these admittedly vague figures there is no need to bring the sinecures and lesser positions into the picture: there should have been no major crisis of patronage, if the variables were as suggested, because there was no major surplus of graduates. Of course, this omits from the calculation those with university experience but without degrees, whose inclusion would make the position rather tighter, and might well push things over the brink. The calculation also omits the obvious, but as yet insufficiently-assessed, influence of pluralism, and the various changes which occurred within the structure of patronage and patterns of benefice holding in the fifteenth century. However, the basic arithmetic suggests no immediate reason for a crisis of patronage, and perhaps that the universities were making the whole thing up.

But were they? That there should have been enough benefices to go round does not mean that graduates actually got them. Whilst the figures might suggest a need to look elsewhere for some aspects of the crisis — to the prospects of non-graduates with university experience, for instance — much of the specific concern of the universities was for those with degrees. The proposals for reservations of benefices made at Canterbury convocations in the early fifteenth century refer only to those who were at least of BA status; there is no indication of any real concern with the non-graduate members of the university.[43] But even though the figures might argue against it in simplistic terms, the notion of a crisis of patronage can still be defended, a crisis of mechanisms perhaps more than numbers, although involving the latter as well. The universities were aware of the crisis, responding both with appeals for help, and with changes in career expectations of graduates within the church during the course of the fifteenth century.

However, the precise depths of the crisis remain uncertain. Moreover, it has to be approached in comparative terms, by testing the experience of the graduates against that of the rest of the clergy. Were graduates any worse off, in career terms, than their fellows? In fact, the position of the non-graduate seems to have been considerably worse than that of the graduates, but even so something of a paradox begins to emerge.

It would be impossible to produce a full-scale study of ordination patterns throughout England in the later middle ages; but such a study would be the only proper way of investigating rates of entry to the clerical profession. Only a few dioceses provide sufficient evidence to make anything beyond purely speculative comments; even fewer provide material to serve as a comparative base. The diocese of Lichfield and Coventry does, however, provide virtually complete evidence for ordinations from 1300 to the early 1500s.[44] Used together with partial evidence from elsewhere, general trends can be deduced.

The surviving Lichfield evidence indicates that, between 1300 and 1349, some 6000 priests were created within the diocese. In the next half-century, the number fell to about 4000 — dropping dramatically immediately after the Black Death, then recovering consistently from *c.* 1370 to a plateau in the 1390s. However, 1400-1449 sees a further drop, with priests numbering only some 2300, the lowest point for ordinations occurring in the 1430s. The next fifty years mark the start of a recovery, especially after 1480, when annual figures rise to those encountered last in the late fourteenth century, and even begin to reach pre-Black Death levels. Total ordinations in 1450-1499 approach 5000 priests. This growth is maintained in the final thirty-two years, although with signs of some levelling off. The number of priests ordained is about 5300 — which if maintained and extended over the full half-century would certainly be comparable to pre-plague levels.

The incomplete evidence from other dioceses confirms the three main thrusts of the Lichfield evidence: a high level of ordinations in the first half of the fourteenth century; a low point in the first half of the fifteenth (the precise dating varying between dioceses); and a major recovery in the later fifteenth century which was maintained through to the Reformation, although may have peaked by the late 1520s.[45] These trends provide the background against which to set alterations in the numbers of those with university education entering the clerical career system. In the absence of precise figures, only supposition is possible, but on presently available evidence the hypothesis seems fair. In the first half of the fourteenth century, benefice-seeking graduates were probably few; with the existence of dispensations invoking the papal constitution *Cum ex eo*, considerable numbers of students probably possessed benefices before embarking on study.[46] Certainly, benefice-seeking graduates would be a very small fragment of the total of new entrants to the clerical estate. Despite the collapse in numbers of ordinations later in the century, the numbers of benefice-seeking graduates may have remained fairly stable, or even increased. The decline in grants of dispensations for non-residence meant that more students entered university without holding benefices. At the same time, the university population may have been increasing, although evidence on this is extremely sketchy and not wholly convincing. It would be more logical to expect a fall, but whether this would parallel the drop in levels of ordinations is a matter for debate.[47] The combined effects of these changes would probably be that the proportion of benefice-seeking graduates among the overall intake to the clerical profession would increase; but so long as the universities could maintain some sort of pre-emptive claim to papal (and thereby monastic) patronage, there need be no crisis of careers. The first half of the fifteenth century does, however, indicate such a crisis, which may have begun towards the end of the fourteenth.[48] The situation is paradoxical: with the collapse of ordination figures generally, competition should have been much less serious. Just what was happening to numbers of benefice-seeking graduates is not clear. While membership of the universities may have been increasing, the onset of the laicisation of the graduate group may have compensated for this growth; endemic plague may also have taken its toll. Nevertheless, it seems likely that at the nadir of ordination levels, the proportion of graduates among those seeking benefices would have increased. With the need to make new arrangements for the promotion of graduates after the abolition of papal patronage it was at this point — when in theory the sheer pressure of numbers in terms of rivalry with the non-graduates should have been at its lowest — that the crisis of patronage appears to have bitten hardest. This can only be taken as a reflection of the concerns of patrons, who were choosing to appoint others to their benefices for their own reasons, or so the universities believed.

This odd situation at the start of the fifteenth century is apparently matched by another at the end of the period. Sheer pressure of numbers should then have increased competition for places. By this point, also, the proportion of benefice-seeking graduates among the clerical population was probably at a lowish point: despite the considerable percentage increase in numbers present at the universities, it would not compensate for the numerical increase in the numbers of ordinands.[49] The laicisation of the graduate class, still in progress, would further have reduced the figures. If, during the intervening years of the fifteenth century, clerical graduates had accustomed themselves to lower career expectations,[50] then any crisis of patronage should have been largely resolved. At precisely this point, however, the position of the graduates among the beneficed seems to have improved. The figures so far available are crude, and to some extent uninformative, being based solely on counts of presentations without making allowances for pluralism, exchanges, and so on. Even so, they do suggest that patrons were increasingly appointing the university educated to benefices in their gift, although the motives for the change — appreciation of university education, or self-interest — remain largely unfathomable.[51] Thus, just when in sheer competitive terms the position of graduates should have been at its worst, or approaching it, in fact it seems to have been improving. Reasons for this remain to be found, and the hypothesis needs more stringent testing, but some speculation is allowable. The change does suggest an alteration in the demands being made of the benefice and the priest, possibly a realisation that the overall quality of the clergy needed improvement, and that the university-educated were therefore suitable appointees. There is some supporting evidence for such a view, in the pronouncements on the need for education made by William Melton at York and John Colet in London.[52] But much more research is needed into just who the patrons of the graduates were, and why they were patronising them.

* * *

Much of the content of this paper is obviously speculative, a series of hypotheses which require detailed testing. But it does seem that there was in the later middle ages an awareness of changes occurring in the relationship between university study and career patterns within the church, which included a major crisis of patronage and its apparent subsequent resolution. However, we still lack any accurate identification of the forces which resulted in the learned obtaining livings in pre-Reformation England. To allow that identification, we need to resolve the basic questions, to look beyond the graduates to the wider ecclesiastical structure. We still need to know why individuals made the deliberate decision to go to university, and the factors which governed the length of their stay and the level they reached within the degree system. We still need investigation of the concerns of patrons, and to determine why they chose particular individuals for promotion, perhaps especially whether they consciously distinguished between those with university education and those without. And, in considering those in receipt of patronage, we need more detailed assessments of patterns of clerical recruitment, and the extent to which those in possession of a degree or a university education were thereby guaranteed greater likelihood of promotion (if they were) — and whether that situation did change over time as superficial examination suggests that it did. Only when we have answers to these questions will we be in a position to make anything other than speculative judgements on the nature of the relationship between university study and clerical careers in later medieval England.

School of History
The University of Birmingham
P.O. Box 363
Birmingham B15 2TT

REFERENCES

1.   For the religious authority of the universities, see G. F. Lytle, 'Universities as religious authorities in the late middle ages and Reformation', in *Reform and authority in the medieval and Reformation church*, ed. G. F. Lytle (Washington, D. C. , 1981), pp. 69-97. For the members of Oxford and Cambridge, see T. H. Aston, 'Oxford's medieval alumni', *Past and present*, no. 74 (February, 1977), pp. 3-40; T. H. Aston, G. D. Duncan, and T. A. R. Evans, 'The medieval alumni of the University of Cambridge', *Past and present*, no. 86 (February, 1980), pp. 9-86; A. B. Emden, *A biographical register of the University of Cambridge to 1500* (Cambridge, 1963); A. B. Emden, *A biographical register of the University of Oxford to A. D. 1500* (3 vols. , Oxford, 1957-9) — with supplements in *Bodleian Library Record*, 6 (1957-61), pp. 668-88, 7 (1962-7), pp. 149-64; A. B. Emden, *A biographical register of the University of Oxford, A. D. 1501 to 1540* (Oxford, 1974). On the parasitic nature of universities, R. N. Swanson, 'Universities, graduates, and benefices in later medieval England', *Past and present*, no. 106 (February, 1985), pp. 29-30.

2.   F. N. Robinson, *The complete works of Geoffrey Chaucer* (2nd. ed., Oxford, 1957), p. 20.

3.   R. M. T. Hill, 'A Berkshire letter book', *Berkshire archaeological journal*, 41 (1937), p. 19.

4.   D. D. McGarry, *The Metalogicon of John of Salisbury: a twelfth-century defense of the verbal and logical arts of the trivium* (Gloucester, Mass., 1971), pp. 15-20.

5.   See the translation of these comments in J. B. Pike, *Frivolities of courtiers and footprints of philosophers* (Minneapolis and London, 1938), p. 275.

6.   J. W. Baldwin, 'Masters at Paris from 1179 to 1215: a social perspective', in *Renaissance and renewal in the twelfth century*, ed. R. L. Benson and G. Constable (Oxford, 1982), p. 153 and n. 67.

7.   C. C. J. Webb, *John of Salisbury* (London, 1932), pp. 1-21, 102-25.

8.   Emden, *Oxford to 1500*, ii, pp. 854-5; J. M. Horn, *The register of Robert Hallum, bishop of Salisbury, 1407-17*, Canterbury and York Society, 72 (1982), pp. ix-xi.

9.   J. E. T. Rogers, *Loci e libro veritatum* (Oxford, 1881), *passim*.

10.   K. Edwards, *The English secular cathedrals in the middle ages* (2nd ed., Manchester, 1967), pp. 197-204.

11.   P. Heath, *The English parish clergy on the eve of the Reformation* (London and Toronto, 1969), pp. 16-18; for reference to *scientia* see e.g. Cambridge University Library, Ely Diocesan Records, F5/32, f. 14^v.

12.   For the examination, Cambridge University Library, MS. Add. 7802, f. 110^r; for other examinations, and the reference to the missal, H. Jewel, 'English bishops as educational benefactors in the later fifteenth century', in *The church, politics, and patronage in the fifteenth century*, ed. R. B. Dobson (Gloucester, 1984), p. 148.

13.   W. Pantin, *The English church in the fourteenth century* (Cambridge, 1953), pp. 192-4, 217.

14.   Swanson, 'Universities, graduates, and benefices', pp. 29-61, with the list of earlier contributions to the debate at p. 28, nn. 2-3. See also now on Oxford careers, J. Dunbabin, 'Careers and vocations', in *The history of the University of Oxford, vol. I: The early Oxford schools*, ed. J. I. Catto (Oxford, 1984), pp. 565-605.

15.   Swanson, 'Universities, graduates, and benefices', pp. 55-7.

16.   Swanson, 'Universities, graduates, and benefices', pp. 45-8.

17.   Swanson, 'Universities, graduates, and benefices', pp. 42-3.

18.   On Lincoln College, V. Green, *The commonwealth of Lincoln College, 1427-1977* (Oxford, 1979), p. 6; on Godshouse, H. Rackham, *Early statutes of Christ's College, Cambridge, with the statutes of the prior foundation of God's house* (Cambridge, 1927), pp. 2-3.

19.   P. Hosker, 'The Stanleys of Lathom and ecclesiastical patronage in the north-west of England during the fifteenth century', *Northern history*, 18 (1982), pp. 214-27.

20.   Dunbabin, 'Careers and vocations', pp. 573-7.

21.   For papal provisions in England in the later middle ages, see W. E. Lunt, *Financial relations of the papacy with England, 1327-1534*, Publications of the mediaeval academy of America, 74 (Cambridge, Mass., 1962), pp. 325-56, 381-408, 418-28, 430-2, 441-2.

22.   York, Borthwick institute of historical research, CP. E. 143; Emden, *Oxford to 1500*, iii, p. 1665.

23.   For methods of informal foundations, A. Kreider, *English chantries: the road to dissolution*, Harvard historical studies, 97 (Cambridge, Mass., and London, 1979), pp. 73, 76-80.

24.   T. Percy, *The regulations and establishment of the household of Henry Algernon Percy, the fifth earl of Northumberland* (2nd ed., London, 1905), pp. 47, 311: graduates received 5 marks, non-graduates 40s., and the schoolmaster 100s.

25.   H. Salter, *A subsidy collected in the diocese of Lincoln in 1526*, Oxford historical society, 63 (1913): chantry priests at pp. iii, 67, 84, 125, 135, 149, 162, 261, 266; curates at pp. 20, 26, 101, 148, 171, 190, 204, 209, 251, 254, 257-8; stipendiaries at pp. 60, 153, 177, 198, 208, 210-11.

26.   Heath, *English parish clergy*, p. 82. Non-ecclesiastical sources may also present problems. A brief comparison of the returns of the Lincoln subsidy (n. 26 above) with the Buckinghamshire muster roll of 1522 (A. C. Chibnall, *The certificates of musters for Buckinghamshire in 1522* (London, 1973)) suggests that the latter is inappropriate for tracing graduates, for example. Although graduates were identified in 1526, the muster rarely notes them as such. Thus, John Crosse has no degree in the muster, but is named master in the subsidy (Chibnall, *Certificates*, p. 316; Salter, *Subsidy*, p. 231), while at Ivinghoe the M. Thomas Wodmane located there in 1526 is probably identical with the Thomas Wodmancye named as vicar in the muster, with no degree, but probably to be identified with one of that name who was BCnL of Cambridge in 1520-1 (Salter,

Subsidy, p. 230; Chibnall, *Certificates*, p. 157; J. Venn and J. A. Venn, *Alumni Cantabrigienses*, Part 1 (4 vols., Cambridge, 1922-7), iv., p. 459).

27.   Cambridge University Library, MS. Mm. I. 48, pp. 15-16, supplementing Emden, *Oxford to 1500*, ii, p. 1011.

28.   M. Bowker, *The secular clergy in the diocese of Lincoln, 1495-1520*, Cambridge studies in medieval life and thought, 2nd series, 13 (Cambridge, 1968), pp. 171, 175.

29.   Hosker, 'Stanleys of Lathom', pp. 218-23.

30.   For use of such grants, see D. P. Wright, *The register of Thomas Langton, bishop of Salisbury, 1485-93*, Canterbury and York society, 74 (1985), nos. 78, 106, 110, 120, 159 (a grant for life), 180, 207, 292-3, 364, 407.

31.   See e.g. R. Horrox and P. W. Hammond, *British Museum, Harleian Manuscript 433* (4 vols., Upminster and London, 1979-83), i, p. 61, ii, pp. 198-201.

32.   Wright, *Register of Langton*, nos. 156, 226, 319, 461; York, Borthwick institute of historical research, Cav. Bk. 1, ff. 42^v-43^r, 49^r.

33.   See, e.g., the case of the appointment of John Sergent to Milton Damarel in 1385, as set out in F. C. Hingeston-Randolph, *The register of Edmund Stafford, (A. D. 1395-1419); an index and abstract of its contents* (London and Exeter, 1886), p. 256. The earlier statement of his institution is less revealing, laconically recording only that collation devolved to the bishop by lapse: F. C. Hingeston-Randolph, *The register of Thomas de Brantyngham, bishop of Exeter (A.D. 1370-1394)* (2 vols., London and Exeter, 1901-6), i, p. 92. Probably several other instances where the bishop collated by lapse hide similar compromises over patronage.

34.   G. O. Sayles, *Select cases in the court of King's Bench under Richard II, Henry IV, and Henry V*, Selden society publications, 88 (London, 1971), p. 186; Heath, *English parish clergy*, p. 28; R. N. Swanson, *A calendar of the register of Richard Scrope, archbishop of York, 1398-1405*, Borthwick texts and calendars: records of the northern province, 8, 11 (2 vols., York, 1981-5), i, nos. 116, 281, 367, 665.

35.   London, British Library, MS. Add. 14848, ff. 41^v, 313^v-314^r: the person there named to replace Swallow at Woolpit was admitted in August 1431, which suggests the date of his nomination and refusal (Emden, *Cambridge*, pp. 451-2).

36.   Cambridge University Library, MS. Add. 7802, f. 36^r.

37.   Cambridge University Library, MS. Add. 7802, ff. 36^v-37^r. Lichfield, Lichfield Joint Record Office, B/A/1/8, ff. 29^v-30^r, secures the large pension of £10, but as rooms are mentioned suggests continued residence.

38.   York, Borthwick institute of historical research, CP. G. 82.

39.   Salter, *Subsidy*, pp. xii, 4, 19, 30, 66, 74, 79, 83-4, 97, 102, 157, 172, 180, 187-8, 221-2, 243, 250, 253, 256-7, 261, 263, 275.

40.   Exeter, Devon record office, Reg. Oldham, f. 41^v (I am grateful to Dr J. A. F. Thomson for the loan of a microfilm of this register); see also Emden, *Oxford to 1500*, i, p. 414.

41.   These figures are modifications of those given in Aston, 'Oxford's alumni', pp. 6-7, and Aston, Duncan, and Evans, 'Alumni of Cambridge', pp. 11-27.

42.   For numbers of rectories and vicarages see Swanson, 'Universities, graduates, and benefices', p. 36 and nn. 34-5. The length of beneficed career is admittedly conjectural, but from work I have done in other contexts on clerical careers seems about right. For Cambridge material on graduations, see S. M. Leathes, *Grace Book A, containing the proctors' accounts and other records of the university of Cambridge for the years 1454-1488*, Luard memorial series, 1 (Cambridge, 1897); M. Bateson, *Grace Book B, part I, containing the accounts of the proctors of the university of Cambridge,*

1488-1511, Luard memorial series, 2 (Cambridge, 1903), with degrees from 1501-11 tabulated at p. xxiv; M. Bateson, *Grace Book B, part II, containing the accounts of the proctors of the university of Cambridge, 1511-1544*, Luard memorial series, 3 (Cambridge, 1905), with degrees tabulated at pp. vi-vii. For Oxford graduations see W. A. Pantin and W. T. Mitchell, *The register of congregation, 1448-1463*, Oxford historical society, n. s. 22 (1972, for 1969-70), with comments on graduation evidence at pp. xiv-xv, xx-xxii; J. M. Fletcher, 'The faculty of arts', in *The history of the university of Oxford, volume III: the collegiate university*, ed. J. McConica (Oxford, 1986), p. 162.

43.   These proposals and attendant discussions are summarised in *The register of Henry Chichele, archbishop of Canterbury, 1414-1443*, vol. 1, ed. E. F. Jacob, Canterbury and York society, 45 (1943), pp. clii-clviii.

44.   What follows is based on a study of the ordination lists contained in the bishops' registers, in print or deposited at the Lichfield Joint Record Office: see D. M. Smith, *A guide to bishops' registers of England and Wales; a survey from the middle ages to the abolition of episcopacy in 1646* (London, 1981), pp. 54-63.

45.   For additional studies on ordinations see J. A. H. Moran, 'Clerical recruitment in the diocese of York, 1340-1530: data and commentary', *Journal of ecclesiastical history*, 34 (1983), pp. 19-54; R. K. Rose, 'Priests and patrons in the fourteenth-century diocese of Carlisle', *Studies in church history*, 16 (1979), pp. 201-10, 217; R. L. Storey, 'Recruitment of English clergy in the period of the conciliar movement', *Annuarium historiae conciliorum*, 7 (1975), pp. 290-313.

46.   Swanson, 'Universities, graduates, and benefices', pp. 32-3.

47.   W. J. Courtenay, 'The effects of the Black Death on English higher education', *Speculum*, 55 (1980), pp. 704-5, suggests an increase in Oxford's membership in the later fourteenth century, but I am unconvinced of the validity of his approach. For some comment on the earlier size of the university, *ibid.*, p. 700, n. 12. For a slightly different interpretation of the trends, Dunbabin, 'Careers and vocations', pp. 570-2.

48.   Swanson, 'Universities, graduates, and benefices', pp. 29, 51-2, 61.

49.   The proportion of benefice-seeking graduates would also be reduced if the patrons were promoting candidates prior to study. However, the unsubstantiated assertion that 'Of those 1200 students at Oxford in the fifteenth century, about 900' were supported by benefice-income, with the recipients as non-resident incumbents, seems to me a major distortion of the position (F. J. Pegues, 'Philanthropy and the universities in France and England in the later middle ages', in *The economic and material frame of the mediaeval university*, ed. A. L. Gabriel, Texts and studies in the history of mediaeval education, 15 (Notre Dame, Indiana, 1977), p. 76).

50.   Swanson, 'Universities, graduates, and benefices', pp. 55-8.

51.   Bowker, *Secular clergy*, pp. 44-5, 78-9; Heath, *English parish clergy*, p. 81.

52.   Heath, *English parish clergy*, pp. 70-3.

THE UNIVERSITY OF HEIDELBERG IN THE EARLY MODERN PERIOD: ASPECTS OF ITS HISTORY AS A CONTRIBUTION TO ITS SEXCENTENARY

Notker Hammerstein

With all its peculiarities and individuality, it would be nevertheless surprising if Heidelberg University had not shared in the more general development of German and European universities.[1] The early modern period, as it is usually labelled, was the era of the 'Holy Roman Empire of the German Nation', when the individual states were in fact responsible for all university and related educational institutions. Nevertheless each institution was not so isolated that it was not, even in the post-Reformation period, also an integral part of the whole Empire.[2] For this reason they were not beyond the influence of general political developments, although the extent of such influence naturally varied from place to place. In general however it is still possible to fit the individual cases into a general scheme of development; something which is necessary to avoid the usual dangers of over-enthusiastic centennial publications, namely that the role of outside influences is neglected through an obsession with the institution itself.

Without getting involved in somewhat peripheral discussions on the chronological or historical classification of the 'early modern' period, I would like to point out that the use of this classification is not without its problems in the case of Heidelberg, where current fashionable classifications overlap. Hautz had already given the first volume of his fundamental interpretation the title *The Scholastic Era; from 1386 to 1556*.[3] Most later works followed more or less closely this classification,[4] which had its advantages. However it appears that this customary classification has been abandoned in the most recent work known to me, where the period in question — after a chapter 'Foundation and Development' — has simply been called 'Golden Age and Decline; the sixteenth to the eighteenth Centuries', without going into the issue.[5] Nor do I wish to do so here, for the aim of this article is to deal primarily with the history of Heidelberg University itself, and not necessarily with its relationship to general university history within the Empire. Nevertheless I feel that this cannot be ignored for the early modern period.[6]

As is well known, humanism everywhere energetically opposed the late scholastic university curriculum. The need for a reform of university and educational institutional life in general was increasingly recognised in the last half of the fifteenth century and not least in Heidelberg. This movement did not occur everywhere at the same time or with the same aims, but was united in opposition to the scholastic *Quisquilien*, the 'ivory tower' of academe and the barbaric Latin to be found there. Unlike in Italy, this was the reason why humanists flocked to the universities within the Empire, for outside them and a few courts and some of the larger imperial cities, there was little place for public appearance and discussion, without which freedom humanism could not thrive.[7]

This desire for reform, which was not limited to the universities or to scholarship, reached its strongest most influential, and innovative, form with the Reformation itself. This meant an end to the optimistic, worldly beginnings of humanism, at least where they had already taken root. Above all the Reformation was a blow to the universities. Since 1470 the number of students had been continually increasing, the high point being reached when 2000 students presented themselves for matriculation in 1515. There was a dramatic decrease in numbers after 1520,[8] and the lowest number of matriculating students, 600, was reached in 1530. Numbers only revived with great difficulty, reaching the former level as late as *c*.1550, and thereafter continually increasing.

There were many ways in which the Reformation helped to bring about this decline. Not the least of these was the way in which the value of study was questioned in Luther's original dislike of the institutions 'that had supported the Papacy' in 'increasing Sin and Error', where 'the blind pagan Aristotle alone ruled, more important than Christ', as Luther wrote in 1520 in his appeal *An den christlichen Adel deutscher Nation*.[9] However Luther's experience of fanatics and Anabaptists convinced him of the importance and benefits of scholarly Christian education even in those areas that most readily accepted his teaching. This conviction was reinforced by the persistent arguments of Melanchthon.[10] Henceforth the Reformation and important aspects of humanism were to be allies, resulting in the formula *Sapiens et eloquens pietas*.

It was not only the 'New' Church which increasingly encouraged study, but also the 'Old', and the fast developing early modern state.[11] Princes, and generally speaking even more their learned advisers, valued and desired suitable education. All, whether Protestant or Catholic, encouraged universities and schools. It had long been a characteristic of German univerities that they were in general founded on the initiative of the ruling prince. Only occasionally did a city government found an institute of higher education — indeed in the early modern period this was only the case in Strasbourg and Altdorf.[12] Correspondingly it became important for all the electorates and principalities within the Empire to have their own university, whereas this was forbidden to lesser rulers such as the Imperial Counts. So it was that the important Calvinist Academy at Herborn lacked university status, having no Imperial privilege, and was limited in its ability to grant degrees.[13]

It became particularly important to have available qualified, capable and educated divines, lawyers, physicians, teachers and officials,[13a] all of the right confession, both for the sake of the 'consolidation' (as it is generally termed) of the territory and as a result of the growth of confessional tension. As part of this development it was natural to have such people drawn to the university under territorial control, or at least to the university of an 'ally'. This resulted in an unusually high number of universities at this time — even for Europe. It was also unusual that these were practically the only places within the Empire where intellectual life and freedom were able to flourish, an unusual position for an early modern European university to be in.[14] For this reason the univerities were extraordinarily important for German intellectual and scholarly development at this time, and have been correspondingly respected for their central role in early modern German history.

There was an enormous increase in student numbers, up to 4700 in the year 1620, and this can be explained not only by the increasing role of law in general life, but also increasing polemical 'confessionalisation'.[15]

On the Roman Catholic side this can be seen in the appearance of the Jesuit Order in the late sixteenth century. Since 1570 there had indeed been a general flourishing of universities within the Empire that corresponded to this increase in numbers. Admittedly the Thirty Years War meant a substantial fall in numbers with, in 1640, a mere 2000 students matriculating. Nevertheless this was not such a crippling blow to intellectual life in general as earlier historians liked to claim. The suffering of the universities of the Empire was varied, determined by local conditions and the fortunes of war. Some such as Königsberg or Rostock were almost undisturbed, indeed they flourished. Such was also the case with Salzburg; troops never subdued the Archepiscopal Capital and it became a Benedictine refuge for all baroque non-Jesuit learning.[16]

Moreover if one turns away from areas affected by the war one can see the evidence of many important new scholarly enterprises, all full of promise. They were greatly stimulated by the rebuilding of scholarly relations with Western Europe, above all with the Netherlands, as by the need for a new model for learning. In Helmstedt, or Jena, or in Frankfurt on the Oder, the 'successor' to Heidelberg, this led to a sort of early or pre-Enlightenment. The preeminence of theology was weakened, to be replaced by Law as the new basis for knowledge, the new 'Queen of the Sciences'. Henceforth the arts disciplines — the 'Philosophy Faculty' as it had been called since the late sixteenth century — was subordinate to the 'Law Faculty'. So the University ideal of the German Enlightenment reached its classic stage with the foundation of Halle in 1693 and Göttingen in 1734.[17]

Admittedly even this ideal, as a result of somewhat over-subtle and prejudiced exploitation, became a damaging influence on learning and within the universities by the second half of the eighteenth century, with the result that in some places the traditional university came to seem irrelevant. Partly through their own efforts — a sort of metamorphosis — and partly through the challenge of the French Revolution and the Napoleonic wars, a new model came to the fore. This new strong and succesful ideal, of Humboldt's, replaced the old when first realised in Berlin.[18]

This in rough outline is how the development of the university in early modern Germany may be described, and we must put our time-honoured university within this framework. Humanists, seeking to carry through their reforms, came to Heidelberg too — and extraordinarily early. By 1450 the military ascent of the Palatinate was over, and the Court was open to southern ideals and novelties.[19] Under the Elector Philipp and his Chancellor Johann von Dalberg, Heidelberg became one of the most elegant courts, the most generous patron of humanists, in the Empire, at least equal to that of the Emperor Maximilian. Connected to the university were Peter Luder, Rudolf Agricola, a brother of Reuchlin, Wimpfeling, Trithemius and of course Konrad Celtis.[20] It is usually argued that this extraordinary Heidelberg humanism was a creation of the court — the result of the intervention of the ruling prince, and that it certainly could not have been due to the university, sunk in a staleness not least resulting from the *Wegestreit*. Nevertheless this explanation does not really get to the heart of the matter — for just about everywhere humanists had to thank princely protection for their university positions.

Princely intervention was as much, if not more, supported by the court learned counsellors (most of whom had at least for a time studied in Italy) as by the professors of law or medicine.[20a] This trend was opposed by the universities not only out of ancient prejudice, incomprehension and narrow-mindedness, but out of concern for their privileges and liberties. They were in the end most concerned, as corporations, not to have their rights infringed. That was — and is — ever a constant motive of every institution and was to be exactly the same under Friedrich III as it had been earlier. So it was that in 1498 the University refused to accept Dionys Reuchlin as teacher of Greek before he had 'been examined and disputed for his magisterium'.[21] Of course such an excuse easily hid animosities to be found among 'career humanists', who could be almost unbearable, distastefully self-satisfied figures. On the other hand they also transmitted, in however limited a way, a taste for the classical languages, *belles lettres*, history and practical pedagogics. Humanism was not able to change the basis of the scholastic curriculum, and indeed did not want to, because it had not developed as a systematic scientific discipline, but instead as one based on the languages and literature. The aim of humanism was to improve scholasticism, with changes both in its methodology and in its practice, so that it would awake a feeling for the beauty and civilising effects of linguistic, historical learning. Above all it was to promote *bonae litterae*. Practical results would only be apparent over a long period of time, and the opportunity to put the theory to practice was in Heidelberg all too soon destroyed. The death of Dalberg in 1503 and even more the effects of the war of succession with Bavaria, dealt the Palatinate blows, which by 1505 had put the state well back, and from which it would take a long time to recover.[22]

The University stagnated, till at least it became increasingly aware of its degeneracy, if only because of the extent to which the late scolastic curriculum was so obviously over-due for reform. The attempt to attract Erasmus, for example, was one way in which it tried to remedy the situation, an attempt that failed due to the attitude of the Elector, or more likely thanks to his empty treasury.[23] This was also the situation that led to some of the most respected men of the university turning their backs on it, men such as Oecolampad, Hermann von dem Busche, Simon Grynaeus, Sebastian Munster and Jacob Micyllus, all of whom nevertheless were able to work there for a few years.

Attempts at a broad-based reform in the early 1520s, following the advice of Jacob Sturm or Wimpfeling, nevertheless led to a mere superficial improvement rather than a real rejuvenation.[25] Little real progress was made towards a love of *bonae litterae*, the use of humanist textbooks and the reduction of 'verbosa disputationes . . .

de quidditatibus essenciis et ceteris infinitis ', those scholastics with which it was impossible to convert either Jews or Mohammedans, as Wimpfeling observed.[26] Nor was it possible to improve the study of law; as Jacob Spiegel suggested, 'Italici doctores magis curarunt quam fructum auditorium'.[27] The Elector Ludwig (1508-1544) being unimaginative and in financial difficulties was both unable and unwilling to help. Even if financial affairs were better organised under his successor Friedrich II (1544-1556), attempts at reform remained largely vain.[28]

Nevertheless opportunity was at that time taken to end the traditional rivalry between the different individual student houses, which had often led to open riot within the city, by combining them all into one College organisation[29] Yet such dangerous bad habits, which certainly dated back to the *Wegestreit*, were to be heard of again later in a statute of Otto Heinrich commenting that

> the young students and pupils are encouraged and pressed by the heads of their halls to promise to keep and hold sectarian and heretical ways, before they are of an age to judge these things for themselves, as a result of which later on a great deal of dispute and division has arisen.[30]

Such a merger would not only avoid these problems but would lead to a more economical use of resources, even if new, particularly disciplinary, problems would be created by the concentration of such numbers into one organisation. We need not follow these matters further, just as there is also no need to detail the many government or university ordinances against bathing in the Neckar,[31] the profusion of barbarous initiation ceremonies (*Depositionen*),[32] for more cleanliness in the city or against the use of the river as a general tip. Such ordinances were continually repeated until well into the seventeenth century, and were not unique to Heidelberg. Everyday life is certainly revealed in an entertaining way, when we read these instructions not only to 'all Guilds' but also to university institutions, that

> no inhabitant who desires to breed pigs in the city, should allow them to roam the streets, drive them into the Neckar, nor wash or feed them outside his house.[33]

In other words the Elector, as this early modern policey of 1558 ran, had 'a fatherly care for the health and happiness of the inhabitants'.[34]

Returning to the reforms of Friedrich II we see signs of the advance of humanism in the foundation of grammar schools and a chair for mathematics and ethics.[35] It was increasingly clear that professors, councillors and indeed the whole Palatinate inclined more to the 'new' than the 'old' faith. With married professors the university lost its priestly character and became more colourful. The cautious, indeed irresolute, religious policy of these two princes, hardly surprising after the debacle at the beginning of the century, forced the university to remain equally inconspicuous on the vital confessional front.[36] Even Luther's own disputation in the Arts Faculty in 1518 had no great effect.[37] Outwardly Heidelberg appeared unchanged in its devotion to the 'old' faith, however much the majority now supported the 'new'.

So it was that a lasting reform and a clear allegiance to the evangelical faith could only be announced under Otto Heinrich (1556-1559). The Elector made clear his devotion to the Arts and to learning,[38] with the statutes that were to remain fundamental to the University until 1786,[39] and enabled it to compete with the leading Academies of the Empire. Heidelberg, moulded to the humanist ideal and committed to the evangelical faith, was at last able to flourish as it should. The theologians were firmly committed to a faith that was young, and not yet defined with any great precision. The Law Faculty was committed to the *jus civile*, just as members of the Faculty of Medicine were enjoined to possess a practical knowledge of their discipline (a particularly modern aspect of Erastus' revision of the statutes), the Arts Faculty, as the largest and most influential, was ordered to pursue the humanist ideal, so that peace and unity would reign, orderly methods of teaching and learning be inculcated, and the previous divisions of the *Wegestreit* into *realium* and *nominalium* be avoided 'which practice led more to useless squabbles than to a rightful and true knowledge'.[40] These reform ideas were now in line with topical needs, recognising

> the necessity of planting and nurturing Christian teaching, the fine arts and virtue, and the establishment of a well-based Christian study

which

> would be of great use and a blessing for the carrying out of both secular and relious government, so that lack of such people and instruments or tools which God gives provides should not cause both to decline and fall.[41]

The influence of these basic statutes could not be assured without changes in personnel. Here also the role of Otto Heinrich was fruitful, especially since the customary university salaries could now be promised, attracting an excellent teaching body from elsewhere.[42] Even if it was not possible to engage Melanchthon himself, who had given his seal of approval to these reforms, it was possible to attract others of his rank. Franciscus Balduinus, a French Huguenot, and Christopher Eheim, the future Court Chancellor, were gained for the Law Faculty; as Erastus and Lotichius were gained for the Medical Faculty (although both were active in many other areas, as was not unusual at that time); and Xylander for the Arts Faculty.

The Italian Petrus Vermigli, the Huguenot Boquin and Tielemann Heshusius were engaged by the Theology Faculty, the latter a fanatical Lutheran, a sign that Otto Heinrich was as yet more interested in other matters than the final form of Protestantism in his territories. It appeared that a form of Melanchthonian Protestantism was to prevail.[43] Hardly was this so, when there occured an enormous dispute between Melanchthonians and more orthodox Lutherans, something that I do not wish to go into here. It is enough to remember that this was an age excited by, for us, an almost inconceivable preoccupation with doctrinal matters. Doctrinal differences, particularly within the new churches, broke out into open warfare in the second half of the sixteenth century, to the extent that very often the original opponent — the Roman Catholic Church — was forgotten.[44]

Friedrich III (1559-1576) carried on the University reforms that Otto Heinrich had begun. It was his religious convictions, which eventually lead him to Calvinism, that placed such high value on education and a proper upbringing.[45] A Reformed Christian had, after all, to know what it was he believed and why; only then could he be a responsible member of the church community, for it was on this level that all important decisions were taken.[46] The distinction between ministers and laity, which had already returned to Lutheranism, was in this way avoided.

That these convictions were demonstrated in the Second Reformation more in theory than in practice, did not alter the fact that they had a great effect upon education and stood the university in good stead. The university was able to attract comparatively large numbers of 'foreigners', because the simple demand for educated ministers, teachers and Professors could not be met. Friedrich III, politically threatened by Spain and spiritually threatened by those upholders of the Catholic Church, the Jesuits, always considered the interests of the whole Protestant Church. He found Calvinism the most effective and determined form of Protestantism that could face these dangers. From the very beginning it had a more international, less limited, view of the religious struggle, unlike the Lutheran preocccupations with the Empire, the Emperor, and the Estates. The Reformed were forced to be more 'political', more decisive, more specific in their aims and negotiations, because they were in a minority, and because they were the more threatened, being at the very centre of religious tension, not only within the Empire. This was what distinguished the Second Reformation, which was a movement towards Calvinism, within the Empire as a whole.[47] There was to be a systematic and comprehensive reformation of all things in both public and private life, not simply a reform of doctrine as with the earlier Reformation. Life was to be watched over, it was to be well ordered and was to be morally improving. Schools and universities would have a decisive role to play in creating such an attitude to life.

It only became clear after 1560 whether and in what way the Palatinate was to become Reformed. The Elector increasingly leaned towards the Swiss doctrine, influenced by arguments with his Protestant cousins and events in the *Reichstag*.[48] This tendency could be followed in the religious colloquies and disputations arranged between Lutherans and Palatines. The appointment of the theologians Tremellio, Olevian, Ursinus and Zanchi, showed that the Palatinate would be following a form of Protestantism closer to Calvin than to the middle-German version. The new order was finally confirmed in 1563 with the creation of the Heidelberg Catechism by Olevian and Ursinus, which was to be a fundamental document of international Calvinism.[49]

This is not the place to evaluate the doctrinal implications of this important religio-political document, but it did give Heidelberg University a different doctrinal position to that of any other German university. Not surprisingly this situation lead to more and even sharper polemical exchanges, whilst all those of a Reformed persuasion were strongly drawn to Heidelberg. However it must be pointed out that the difference between Lutheran and Calvinist at this time did not affect a common attachment to dogma and dislike of tolerance, which at any rate was a concept alien to all confessions, something very clearly shown in the execution of Silvanus.[50] It seemed obvious everywhere, and not least in the Palatinate with such Calvinists as Olevian and the Electoral Councillor Eheim, that only a strongly held and austere religion would please God.[51]

In such a situation it is understandable that there was argument as to the preeminence of the secular or the religious powers within the state. At first the Elector was most influenced by the group of ecclesiastical intransigents around Olevian. Erastus and supporters of a division of church and state, and indeed of the superior claims of the state, only triumphed after serious opposition and dubious machinations, support from the Zurich Church being of little help. They believed, as did all supporters of Zurich and Melanchthon, that secular authority was the 'pius magistratus', and thus responsible for ecclesiastical and secular life. Only thus could the unity of the state, the common weal, progress and the obedience of the subject be guaranteed. Flexibility and the ability to adapt to change was valued, not always blindly following dogma in an age where the world was continually changing and life progressed. Events in France or in the Netherlands were taken to support this view.[52] A strong Christian conviction, yet an open mind on matters of doctrine appeared more successful and appropriate than a churchmanship based on an orthodoxy comparable to that of the Papacy[53] such as Olevian championed. The more moderate Upper German view of the supremacy of the secular power, not only guaranteed a certain freedom for state servants, councillors and nobility, but also the survival of a diverse humanism in the university and Privy Council. The university became especially attractive to many intellectuals of the time, and bright students, devoted to *bonae litterae*, of noble as of bourgeois origin, flocked there to create a *res publica litterata* embracing all ranks of society.[54] They came from Hungary, Silesia, Bohemia, the Protestant parts of Austria, from Poland, Italy, France and north-east Europe.

The University of Heidelberg guaranteed the existence not only of a sort of intellectual clearing house that was of more than territorial significance, but also a Mecca for all intellectual opposition to Spain and to Rome, the real opponent.[55] The Jesuits, with their undeniable success in schools and universities, were seen as the major challenge, with the military might of Spain as an added threat. They for their part perceived in the Reformed a particularly dangerous and intransigent. Already, by 1563, P. Canisius was writing to another Jesuit: 'Calvinism is on the march, oh woe! and on a wide front — it is breaking into Germany from France'.[56] For this reason the Reformed were more decisive, conscious, active and aware than the Lutherans, who felt themselves protected in the Peace of Augsburg. For them the fomula put into words in 1600 applied: 'Omnis mutatio cum in politicis tum maxime in theologicis est periculosa'.[57] How differently a Heidelberg Councillor expressed himself in a letter which he wrote in 1585 to François Hotman, referring to the situation of the Huguenots and Henri IV, saying

> You will be hit first, but then it shall be our turn. For the Roman Cerberus and its executioner make little distinction between your Church and ours, as they also make little distinction between Lutherans and Calvinists.[58]

The Reformed accused the Jesuits, and above all Cardinal Bellarmin, who were not political innocents, of the most evil acts, in their attempt to destroy all non-Catholics. Georg Erasmus Tschernembl, the leader of the opposition among the Protestant Estates in Austria was of the opinion in 1600 that 'One should consider different ways to exterminate the scheming Jesuits, that the Devil may take them'.[59] The main interests and subjects of study for the students at Heidelberg were in the arts disciplines — a humanist/Reformed theology containing exegesis of Old and New Testaments and the humanist methodology of Melanchthon's *loci communes*. At that time there were many active in literature, the best known in Germany being Schede, Melissus, Opitz and Zincgref. They moved within a relatively free, open and intelligent court society,[60] united in a love of antiquity and in the use of the famous and splendid library presided over by Janus Gruter.[61] One of the leading Calvinists put it in these words: 'Ibi floreat litterae ubi est vera ecclesia'.[62] In this way the beginnings of a poetry that was German, and not solely Latin came to Heidelberg and gave new significance to the native language as a way of avoiding the Latin of international Catholicism. I would like to leave open the question of whether this was perhaps a too early flowering of the German national literature, as has been recently asserted.[63] However it is certainly true that many of the foreign students, and many native ones too, had more interest in the late humanism that flourished in Heidelberg, than in questions of religion. Valentin Loscher, one of the greatest orthodox Lutherans had aptly recognised this phenomenon in the early eighteenth century: 'The inclination to Zwinglianism of the followers of literature has been obvious since 1540'. He named this *Indifferentism*.[64] In fact it was a *pietas litterata* quite in the manner of Erasmus which influenced court and university under Friedrich III and even more under his successors from Johann Casimir to Friedrich V.

Even so there was in this period the attempt to re-introduce Lutheranism, and in an extreme orthodox form, that took place in the seven-year reign of Ludwig VI (1575-1583). This was the time when the wishes expressed in 1559 by Ludwig's grandfather, the fanatical Lutheran Duke Johann Friedrich of Saxony, were put into effect; 'that almighty God should grant us grace to restore the Christian religion in the state and do away with the Devil's brood',[65] this time referring to the Reformed. Thereupon many Reformed Professors moved to the *Casimirianum* in Neustadt, where a sort of semi-University[66] was set up in the lands remaining to Johann Casimir. Here a refuge was offered for Reformed professors and students, above all to study theology and other arts disciplines. When Ludwig in 1583 attempted to commit the professors that remained in Heidelberg to the orthodox Lutheran Formula of Concord, the last of the 'independent' or Reformed staff left the University. Nevertheless Ludwig's attempt to re-introduce Lutheranism on a permanent basis, failed not least because the new Lutheran scholars who were prepared to swear allegiance to the Formula of Concord adopted a most intransigent attitude under the Regency of Johann Casimir (1583-1592). Thus the original idea of setting up two Academies, one Calvinist and one Evangelical, on an equal basis became impossible. Even though during the exile in Neustadt several scholars died or moved elsewhere, including Ursinus, Olevian and Hugo Donellus. This did not hinder the new Golden Age of Heidelberg, described above, once again coming under Calvinist leadership. The extraordinary blossoming of the University between 1580 and 1620 under Reformed leadership and under the influence of the Heidelberg Catechism, has often lead to its being named the 'third Geneva' by later historians. Heidelberg was acclaimed as the Geneva of the North, as the third institution at the service of international Calvinism, after Geneva itself and after Leiden, which was founded in 1575 and was in a similar Golden Age. It is my opinion that this is not an entirely appropriate description, as it only hints at a real understanding of the university.

Following the advice of his leading councillors, Otto-Heinrich had introduced a Melanchthonian, Upper German form of Protestantism in his lands. This initial stage of Philippism, combined with a form taken over from Zurich and from Strasbourg,[67] prepared and influenced the eventual development towards Calvinism. The Counts of Erbach,[68] Erastus and even Eheim could be arbitrarily named as representative of this movement. Events such as the consolidation of Lutheranism, the persecution of Philippist crypto-Calvinists and the destruction of Sturm's Strasbourg ideal pushed the Palatinate towards developing its own university ideal, to be open and international, committed to a Christian form of humanism on the lines set down by Erasmus and Melanchthon. This, in the eyes of the supporters of the Formula of Concord, led to Mohammedanism,[69] the ultimate condemnation then imaginable. Yet the Melanchthonian position was considerably different to that of Geneva, as Friedrich III showed in his attempt to keep his distance from the Geneva of Beza, something common to all German Reformed institutions. Court and university were moulded by the late humanistic irenical attitude of many professors and councillors, in effect pursuing a form of religion for the scholarly elite.

The priority of political, especially international, interests over the more immediate ones of the Church was assured by the way in which the 'Second Reformation' had been introduced and controlled by the ruling prince and his closest advisors, something again very diferent from the Genevan pattern of reformation. It also meant a greater emphasis on the practical aspects of Christian life than on doctrine, which for them, as already noted, was capable of development. This too helps explain the attraction of this form of Protestantism to many scholars.[70] Hieronymus Zanchi, while being one of the most influential professors of theology in Heidelberg, reveals this tendency in his autobiographical references to a situation not yet benumbed by dogma:

'Ut Lutheranus non sum nec esse volo — sic etiam Zwinglianum aut Calvinianum vel quovis alio sectario nomine ne quis appetet me esse pernego Christianus igitur sum, non sectarius.'

Perhaps it was this open-mindedness that goes some way towards explaining the somewhat inexplicable opposition of many of the Reformed professors to Petrus Ramus holding a university position. Friedrich III's attempt to appoint Ramus to the chair for *Philosophia practica* in 1569, at which time he was already active in the university despite student protests, failed due to strong opposition, not least that of Erastus and Ursinus. In Heidelberg Ramus was accused of insufficient knowledge of Aristotle, the very basis of all learning — despite the fact that Ramus himself was to become an authority for those educational institutions that were only a little later to be Reformed. His views were considered too individualistic, too narrow and insufficiently accessible, and certanly also too new! Obviously it was the St Bartolomew's Night Massacre, in which Ramus also died, that brought about a change of opinion amongst the Reformed. In Herborn it went to the extent of having his 'Method' recommended in the very statutes of the Academy. The banning of Ramus' works in Lutheran universities towards the end of the century was partly a consequence of this new Reformed appreciation of him, which came rather too late for Heidelberg.

Lastly one must point out that, although the Heidelberg Catechism was conceived in Heidelberg, it did not make the university into the most important theological centre either for eastern nor indeed for western Calvinism. This was far more the role of tiny Herborn, the copybook Calvinist academy of the late sixteenth and early seventeenth centuries, which never achieved university status.[71] Moreover a little more water must be added to the beautiful

Heidelberg wine with the observation that the justly famous Golden Age of Heidelberg at this time was by no means unique. It was above all a Golden Age in confessional terms. For at that time there was a noted expansion in learning and in universities throughout the Empire, just as there was also a decisive increase in new scholarly enterprises and in attendance at educational institutions. One can note a 'Golden Age' similar to that at Heidelberg, taking place at Tübingen, Helmstedt, Ingolstadt, Dillingen, Jena and later at Giessen, to name only a few universities. Certainly that should not detract from the brilliance of Heidelberg and the role that it played for Calvinist scholars in Europe, but merely make us aware that this development was a general one.[72]

The collapse of the state, of the dynasty, and of the university, with Tilly's conquest of the city in 1622 at the beginning of the Thirty Years War, was dramatic and painful. I hardly need to describe the political events that led to the rash adventure of the Winter King, and yet as I see it, it has an interesting connection with this Golden Age of the court and university. It is worthy of note that in not one of the Calvinist Academies of the Empire,[73] and thus not in Heidelberg, had there developed a school of political and legal thought.

In Heidelberg, unlike in the Netherlands, Scotland and to a certain extent France, the lawyers and exponents of *philosophia practica* avoided involvement in theoretical thinking about the state and public law. Theories of resistance based on the ideas of the Monarchomachs, or on the rights of Estates, or even on Neo-Stoicism, had little obvious influence. Here were no circles of political thinkers such as the 'politiques' in France, or the German 'Reichspublicisten' of Giessen, Marburg and Jena.[74] Heidelberg was instead the proud home of Humanistic Jurisprudence, the work of famous French jurists from Baudoin through Donellus to Gothofredus, even including Marquard Freher. This discipline, or 'mos Gallicus', had more historical or antiquarian interests than practical. Of course the Huguenot Professors at Heidelberg, many fleeing from the St Bartholomew's Night Massacre like Donellus, knew litle of imperial law and had only passing knowledge of imperial affairs at all. It is noticeable that although the Faculty attempted to engage Matthaeus Wesenbeck, it came to nothing, due to his demands for: '400 thaler, housing, wine, bread, beer and wood as necessary'. So they recommended Hugo Donellus for the post, 'who is now in or near Basel, because of the murders in France'.[75]

Gothofredus on the other hand would only come to Heidelberg 'if the Elector would promise to support his new edition of the corpus iuris with commentary which he had been preparing for a long time and with great effort'.[76] This is in no way meant to deny the important achievements of these men, but it is just meant to point out (and here we must be careful in our expression) the lack of any close relationship of many at the university, even at court itself, to outside events and considerations of practical politics. The jurists instead conformed exactly to the ideals of the Arts and Theological Faculties, which were by far the most important ones for the Calvinists,[77] and the ones which possessed international significance. All were firmly committed to the humanist tradition.

Not for nothing were history and rhetoric around 1600 a preserve of the Calvinists. Heidelberg already had an excellent tradition in the teaching of history, which was taught in conjunction with poetry or ethics by those such as Micyllus, Pithopeus and Xylander. However, it only reached its Golden Age with the short term appointment of Johann Jakob Grynaeus, who was brought from Basle as professor of theology in the 1580s, and thereafter under the influence of Janus Gruter. The 'literati' — and these included the court — felt moved to have historical celebrations 'lusts und recreationis causa' as Johann Casimir, the Regent, claimed. They valued history because of its relationship with rhetoric and poetry, and not because of any legal relevance. Apart from the antiquarian end literary interest in history and *philosophia practica*, there was little that would lead either — nor even jurisprudence — towards the development of a political theory, capable of a practical definition of the situation and duties of man. Instead there was at best a general and correspondingly vague and idealised inclination on the part of the educated classes — including the Estates — towards resistance to the Habsburgs and the Roman Catholic Church. A tyrannical opponent who attempted to use absolutist means to suppress its enemies in religion and politics, was thus made the justification for resistance throughout the Empire and indeed made it necessary.

Such theories of resistance stood in stark contrast to both the reality and the theory of domestic policy in the Palatinate, where there were certainly no ideas of joint responsibility with Estates that were themselves not totally Calvinist. The undoubted reality was the unlimited right of the prince and his councillors to govern and defend the Palatinate and its religion. The ideas of the right to resist, the right to a say in government, like communal forms of ecclesiastical government, ceased to exist after the victory of the 'Erastian' party. In practice the subject was under the rule of a straight-forward early absolutist state. Yet in its foreign policy the Palatinate expressed just such justifications for resistance, and it failed to solve the problems consequent upon this inconsistency, nor was any attempt made to resolve the resulting tensions. No public law/political theory was developed adequate to the complexities of the Holy Roman Empire, nor was any attempt made to do so. It was perhaps this very lack of any practical political theory that helped lead to the disaster that followed the adventurous policies of the Palatinate. At the very least it could be said that the court lacked any advice that might have been available from the university, that could convincingly have drawn attention to the dangers of such a foreign policy.

The fate of the university was decided for a long time by the conquest of the city by Tilly; at first a modest existence was still permitted, even if the university was forced to become a Roman Catholic institution, but before long it was totally closed down. As soon as re-opened, however, it still suffered the effects of constant and damaging changes of regime. This was the time of the 'barbarous' loss of the greater part of the Bibliotheca Palatina to the Vatican. In fact this act probably saved the Library from destruction, in the devastation of the city by fire at the hands of Louis XIV's troops. Moreover it was the destruction of the university at Heidelberg that allowed for the development of Frankfurt on the Oder as a brilliant alternative. Similar educational opportunities were offered to students there, now unable to study at Heidelberg, albeit in a univeiʒity that was but half Calvinist.[78] Even such subjects as Neo-Stoical politics, the *jus publicum*, natural law and even rhetoric, all of which had been neglected at Heidelberg, were now offered at the Viadrina in Frankfurt. The Dutch model, of the supremacy of legal and practical studies, something that came from close relations with the Netherlands, took root at Frankfurt on the Oder, which in turn became the source of important attempts to spread Enlightenment ideals.[79] However we must turn from such things back to a Heidelberg permanently damaged by the war.

In effect there was no university. After the Peace of Westphalia, Karl Ludwig (1649-1680)[80] had also to concern himself with the reconstruction of the Landesschule (state school), which was reopened in 1652 and attracted students from afar. The Elector made very clear his desire to recreate the university on sound, modern lines and this involved the engagement of Samuel Pufendorf, albeit in the Arts Faculty and not in the Law Faculty as he had wished. So it was that the first chair of natural and international law founded within the Empire, indeed one of the first anywhere, was to be founded within the Philosophy Faculty and this without any real justification. This was the case also in other universities, even Lund whither Pufendorf later moved.[81] For these subjects were still new and appeared to satisfy the general requirements of subjects such as

Ethica and *Philosophia Practica*, but not those connected with the chair of jurisprudence itself, concerned solely with the *Corpus Juris*. Pufendorf was thus upset about particularly *his* lower status, being a member of a lower faculty, and not primarily about the classification of his subject. It was one of his successors, the extraordinarily successful scholar Heinrich Cocceji,[82] who managed to change the status of his subject in 1677, but by his time the new legal subjects that he taught, such as *jus publicum* or natural law had since become acceptable.

The recovery of the university hoped for by the Elector was however not yet complete. In 1672 he emphasised that

> it is the case with nearly all sciences and arts that much which is contained in our old university statutes is no longer apropriate, therefore our studies are not like those at some other high schools in and outside the Empire, where young people study with pleasure and profit.[83]

Therefore the statutes had to be changed. It was two years after Pufendorf had left the university and the year before Karl Ludwig in vain attempted to engage Spinoza, that the Elector adapted the old statutes to contemporary needs and ideas. In doing this he proceeded altogether very cautiously, he did not hurry any changes through and behaved with moderation concerning novelties. It seemed that two theologians would suffice, and only they had to be Calvinist. In other faculties this would not be a condition of appointment, which would be made on merit alone.[84] Greater permissiveness in behaviour and dress was planned and courtly manners were declared desirable.[85] The theologians were encouraged to be more tolerant[86] and were admonished

> that any desire for secular power to be yielded under the cloak of the church should be kept within limits, as should be the patronage at their disposal.[87]

Those in the Law Faculty were to be paid the same as those in the Theology Faculty, and would carry more weight, handling *jus publicum* as a new subject alongside *ius feudale* and *processus iudicarius*, all to be held as important as the *jus civile*, although they were 'encouraged not to criticise the *statum praesentem*'.[88] Moreover the law faculty was to be available for consultation on demand by the high courts and was also to ensure that all law students were to be educated in the humanities (*artibus humanioribus*) such as languages, history and *philosophia morali et civilis*.[89] Those in the Arts and Medical Faculties were to keep their old — small — salaries, and strangely received no new statutes.

Nevertheless the new statutes do reveal the thoroughly modern motives of the Elector and his councillors in the re-foundation of the university. For instance, some of the professors engaged after the re-opening of the university were respected and of international significance — such as Johann Heinrich Hottinger, Jakob Freinsheim, Johann Leuenschloss and Jacob Sylvester Danckelmann. However after the re-writing of the statutes this could only still be said of the Law Faculty, with professors like Johann Wolfgang Textor, Johann Friedrich Boeckelmann and the above-mentioned Cocceji.[90]

At this time of course such dramatic re-organisations were not only to be found in Heidelberg, but in many universities and throughout the world of learning. Attendance suffered in almost all institutions, as it was found necessary to break the theological domination in this hesitant preparation for the 'enlightened' university ideal. Only towards the end of the seventeenth century was there a noticeable increase in attendance and revival amongst the universities, not however in Heidelberg. The situation of the Palatinate at this time could almost be described as worse than during the Thirty Years War, and certainly the affects were to last longer. Under the Elector Karl, afer 1680, there was little court interest in scholarship and then followed the War of Palatine Succession from 1688 with the occupation and destruction of Heidelberg in 1689 and 1693, and finally there was the succcession of the Roman Catholic Pfalz-Neuburg line in 1690. The university as planned by Karl Ludwig practically ceased to exist, thanks to the economic ruin and financial problems of the Palatine, the destruction of most of the buildings in the fire of 1693, and the consequent flight of the few remaining professors at first to Frankfurt on the Main and thereafter (1698-1700) to Weinheim.

It is noteworthy that there was not one member of the Law or Medical Faculties among those who had remained until then. The last blow was the Elector's decision to reside in Mannheim from 1720, the loss of the traditional close contact with the court had a permanent adverse affect on the reputation of both university and court.

The problems of a predominately Calvinist land with a Roman Catholic ruler, did not take long to show themselves in the 'Pfälzer Religionsstreit' of 1719, which concerned not only the Palatinate but the whole Empire. It is thus obvious how difficult it was, even in the early eighteenth century, to escape the influence of theology in public life, and how ineffective were ordinances on religious toleration, indeed how toleration remained more an ideal than practice.[91] Arguments had already begun in the reign of Johann Wilhelm; the man responsible for the 'Ryswick Clause' in the Peace of Nymwegen, one should note. Certainly it should be admitted that Johann Wilhelm lived mainly in Düsseldorf, far from the Palaltinate, and paid very little attention to the state of affairs in his new territories, being totally absorbed in his role as a bold and busy negotiator in all European and Imperial matters.[92] It was his feel for a baroque patronage of the arts, that secured his financial support for the university and its library, and that encouraged the movement towards a more open, less Calvinistically dominated, institution. His close confidant and advisor Agostino Steffani introduced the Jesuits to Heidelberg in 1706 and was responsible for their activities and their keen support and eager use of the Baroque in their propaganda.

The arrangement made by the last Reformed Elector, in the 'Hallische Rezess' of 1685, was in effect abrogated by the *Religionsdeklaration* of 1705, when the Roman Catholics were given the upper hand in all university affairs. Henceforth the theological faculty was no longer the Reformed one that had been guaranteed at Schwaebish Hall. There were five Roman Catholics as opposed to a mere two Calvinists and their work was supposed to be co-ordinated by two Deans. The Roman Catholic influence in all other faculties was also continually increasing. By 1748 there were merely four Calvinist professors and one Lutheran fencing master but twenty-four Roman Catholic professors. As a rule the Calvinist theologians came from employment in the city parishes. It logically followed that the university never escaped disruption due to petty professorial disputes and the inability to come to common decisions. Student numbers that had increased under Karl Ludwig — at a time when many from abroad also studied at the university — soon fell rapidly.[93] The university was soon providing a practical and provincal education for those from the Palatinate who were preparing themselves for Church or Civil Service careers.

Of course the Elector Karl Philipp was also a convinced supporter of the Roman Catholic Church, but above all he believed that it was the prince who knew what was the best for his subjects, it was the *prince*'s job to rule for his subjects.[94] He attempted to ensure that all the non-Calvinist confessions in the Palatinate received the toleration that had been promised them since the Peace of Westphalia, and that naturally meant a particularly energetic support for his own religion, which eventually led to a head-on collision with the Calvinist Church

Council in 1719, in the above-mentioneed *Pfälzer Religionsstreit*. The more significant question hidden behind such conflicting confessional claims was to what extent the power of the Prince within his own lands was absolute. The Elector, in keeping with the general consensus of the times, insisted on absolute power.The Calvinist Church Council, having been used since the time of Karl Ludwig to having its own way in all religious — and that often meant political — matters, was not going to give up without a fight, no matter how antiquated and extravagant its claims were for the eighteenth century. The quarrel eventually became one of imperial significance and decided the Elector against Heidelberg as his residence.

So once again the university was affected, and by losing its role and not finding a new one it could no longer be considered a serious institution and was neglected. Of course in its own modest way it continued to exist. Certainly within modest bounds it continued to serve as the provincial institute for higher learning. But the university had revealed its feebleness and lack of collective will, by the way in which it was unable to decide to support either the prince or the Calvinist party. Besides, at that time, the consensus of the non-theological professors began to buckle under the strain. Under these circumstances, if ever a professor were to distinguish himself and reveal himself useful beyond the limited scope of Heidelberg, he would be drawn away to court either as a councillor or as a personal doctor. This practice became even more frequent in the second half of the eighteenth century.

Despite magnificent spectacles of Baroque rhetoric and music the attempt of Johann Wilhelm (1690-1716), of his advisor Agostino Steffani, and of his successor Carl Philipp (1716-1742), to bring the land and university back into the Roman Catholic fold was not totally successful. An attempt to carry out the instruction and education of a land — especially of a land so Calvinist and puritannical — along the lines of the Counter Reformation was bound to fail, the more so at a time when scholarship and society was prevailingly secular. For with time the Jesuits had lost much of their previous superiority in the world of learning, together with their brilliant aptitude for polemics, and could no longer be considered such a danger to the Protestants. Many, even Roman Catholic princes within the Empire came to consider the Jesuits as an obstacle to the building and development of a modern university and state, persisting as they did in the attitudes of the early seventeenth century.[95] The Jesuits did not teach, or were not allowed to teach most legal and medical matter, the two areas of greatest interest in the eighteenth century. This meant that the Jesuits lost much of their influence, and that the teachers of Law and Medicine were of no significance in Heidelberg.

The will or ability to modernise the University from within was totally lacking, it could only come from the Elector and court. Since there was no political necessity for such a reform, as the Electors felt no desire to rely upon such a useless institution, no attempt was made to bring Heidelberg into line with other universities. Any such attempt was anyway prevented by the financial difficulties of the government, the result of ambitious but hardly successful domestic and imperial policies.

Even with the succession of the worldly Carl Theodor (1742-1799) who was an energetic lover of the arts, the situation of the university hardly improved.[96] Despite new disciplines and a new series of statutes (not very different from the old)[97] the university did not flourish. The university indeed spent its time honestly vegetating away while the Court paid more attention to music and theatre and things such as the foundation of an Academy for Natural Curiosities.[98] So it was that unlike many German universities, Heidelberg remained virtually unaffected by attempts to follow the example of Halle and Göttingen, a movement that affected even many Romam Catholic states.[99] Such reforms as there were, were especially noticeable in the Law Faculty. Once again from the mid-eighteenth century, there were lectures on *ius publicum, ius feudale, ius Germanicum* and *ius patrium* alongside *historia Imperialis* and practice in the highest imperial courts.[100] However these rather arbitrary reorganisations had little lasting effect, since there were no professors capable of delivering the lectures, and none of the necessary ancillary subjects were taught within the Arts and Theology Faculties.

A university in such a position, without the all-important interest of the prince, was hardly likely to be able to cope with its own dire position and near dissolution. Neither the new endowments of 1782, nor the 1784 extension of the University with the foundation of the new sort of 'Kameral-Hoch-Schule' along the lines of that in Kaiserslautern were able to help the situation. This latter was a Political Economy Academy with three professors to lecture on the Cameralists, on natural and international law, on economic policy and practical science, whilst attached to the Arts Faculty. It brought no lasting influx of students and no new blood. Certainly, there were celebrations for the Quatercentenary of the university, but nevertheless it remained a local institution of no wider significance. The university, that had been paid little enough attention by the Elector when he resided at Mannheim, suffered even more neglect when he moved to Munich in 1778. It looked as though Heidelberg University would have to share the fate of several others, and be closed down. The reasons why this did not happen is beyond the scope of this article.

Must one judge the colourful fate of the University of Heidelberg as exceptional, as standing outside the general development of universities within the Empire? At first sight it appears so, even if only by the description of Heidelberg as a third Geneva, an analogy to the 'third Rome' that is not totally convincing.[101] Certainly at the time of Heidelberg's Calvinist Golden Age it was the only full Calvinist university within the Empire. and with four faculties and rights of graduation. This was only possible because the university at that time was already an old institution with existing full university status. All other similar institutions for Calvinists within the Empire — most of which acted as Gymnasia Illustra — were unable to achieve this status, being excluded as Calvinists from such protection under the Peace of Augsburg. This was the effective difference between Heidelberg and other institutions and this was rather a superficial than a basic distinction, one that does not allow any talk of a 'special role'. Certainly not when one considers that Heidelberg University was not especially distinguished in comparison with the others. For practically every university of the Empire, looked at closely enough, reveals characteristic peculiarities and for the most part totally arbitrary deviations from the norm.

What rather more distinguishes the University of Heidelberg was that it should twice have enjoyed such a Golden Age of learning and each time thereafter have suffered a sudden decline. Of course the same can be said of other universities — Wittenberg, Rostock, Freiburg and Dillingen to mention but a few. What this showed, something that was particularly clear in Heidelberg, was how closely the fate of a German university was determined by the politics of its prince, indeed to a great extent how dependant it was. The court — the prince and his councillors — was always the decisive factor in its intellectual condition. The court's interests, tastes and aims in the end moulded and limited those of the university. Part of this influence was, of course, that of religion and of the Church, but only in so far as this too was represented at court. This characteristic is especialy easily recognisable in the Palatinate, where there were so many changes, not only of different lines within the ruling dynasty, but also of the dynasty itself. Basic changes in policy were connected to such disruptions, and where leading to Calvinism, these changes were a significant boon to the university, whereas with Roman Catholicism the reverse was the case.This could be explained by the basic lack of interest shown by a broadly baroque court in the limited, tedious and puritannical affairs of the university. Thus the disastrous way in which the university was affected by purely political disturbances, such as those following on either the rashness of an Elector like Friedrich V or the unforseeable problems encountered by Karl Ludwig, hardly needs further explanation. They were the results of a certain political instability in the Palatinate, where the capabilities and strengths of the state were continually over-stretched in completely unrealistic attempts to play at Great Power status.

Similar consequences followed upon the similar policies pursued by the Wittelsbach cousins of Bavaria, as can be seen in the fate of the City and University of Ingolstadt, although at least it escaped reduction to a heap of smoking rubble. It is no surprise then that Heidelberg could never be accounted a leading university of the Empire, even in the early modern period. The only exception to this would be for the decades around 1600, but then these were exceptional years for many universities.

Historisches Seminar der Johann-Wolfgang-Goethe-Universität
6000 Frankfurt am Main 11
Postfach 11 19 32, Senckenberganlage 31
Federal Republic of Germany

REFERENCES

1.   On German universities in the early modern period see F. Paulsen, *Geschichte des gelehrten Unterrichts*, 2 vols. (Leipzig, 1921 and Berlin, 1960); O. Scheel (ed.), *Das akademische Deutschland* (Berlin, 1930), vol. 1; H. Rössler and G. Franz (eds.) *Universität und Gelehrtenstand 1400-1800* (deutsche Führungsschichten in der Neuzeit 4), Limburg 1970; P. Baumgart and N. Hammerstein (eds.) *Beiträge zu Problemen der Universtätsgründungen der frühen Neuzeit* (Wolfenbütteler Forschungen 4) (Nendeln 1978); *Town and Gown: the University in search of its origins*, *CRE-Information* 62 (Geneva 1983).

2.   See the article 'Reich' in *Geschichtliche Grundbegriffe. Histor. Lexikon zur politisch-sozialen Sprache in Deutschland V* (Stuttgart, 1984).

3.   Johann Friedrich Hautz, *Geschichte der Universität Heidelberg*, 2 vols. (Mannheim, 1862); Gerhard Ritter draws one of the best outlines of the University's history in Scheel (see note 1). Also very helpful is the G. Hinz (ed.), *Ruperto-Carola Sonderband; Aus der Geschichte der Universität Heidelberg und ihrer Fakultäten* (Heidelberg 1961). These works have been much used throughout this article; hereafter I will not cite them on every occasion.

4.   This is the case with the above-mentioned *Sonderband* as also in H. Weisert, *Geschichte der Universität Heidelberg* (Heidelberg, 1983).

5.   P. Classen, E. Wolgast, *Kleine Geschichte der Universität Heidelberg* (Berlin-Heidelberg- New York, 1983). Vol. I of the six-volume *Festschrift Semper Apertus*. *Sechshundert Jahre Ruprecht- Karls- Universität Heidelberg 1386-1986* Berlin/ Heidelberg/ New York/ Tokyo 1985): *Mittelalter und Frühe Neuzeit 1386-1803* appeared too late to be used thoroughly in this paper.

6.   N. Hammerstein, 'Zur Geschichte und Bedeutung der Universitäten im Heiligen Römischen Reich Deutscher Nation', *Historische Zeitschrift* 241 (1985) pp. 287ff.

7.   On Humanism see P. Joachimsen, *Gesammelte Aufsätze*, especially vol. 1 (Aalen, 1970); also A. Buck, 'Humanismus und Wissenschaft' in Buck, *Die humanistische Tradition in der Romania* (Bad Homburg-Berlin-Zurich, 1968) pp. 133ff.; Buck, 'Der Wissenschaftsbegriff des Renaissance-Humanismus' in Buck, *Studia humanitatis* (Wiesbaden, 1981) pp. 193ff.; Hammerstein 'Humanismus und Universitäten' in *Die Rezeption der Antike*, (Wolfenbütteler Abhandlung zur Renaissanceforschung, vol. 1) (Hamburg, 1978) pp. 23ff.

8.   The figures are based on those of F. Eulenburg, *Die Frequenz der deutschen Universitäten von ihrer Gründung bis zur Gegenwart* (Leipzig, 1904); see also L. W. Spitz, 'The Impact of the Reformation on the Universities' in Leif Grane (ed.), *University and Reformation* (Leiden, 1981) pp. 9ff.

9.   Martin Luther, *Ausgewälte Schriften* ed. by H. Bornkamm and G. Ebeling, vol. 1, 2nd. edition (Frankfurt am Main, Insel-Verlag, 1983) pp. 32ff.

10.   See also Hammerstein, 'Bildungsgeschichtliche Traditionszusammenhänge zwischen Mittelalter und Neuzeit' in *Der Uebergang zur Neuzeit und die Wirkung von Traditionen* (Göttingen, 1978) pp. 32ff.

11.   See relevant contributions to K. G. A. Jeserich et al (eds.), *Deutsche Verwaltungsgeschichte* (Stuttgart, 1983), vol. 1.

12.   For more on these cases see A. Schindling, *Humanistische Hochschule und freie Reichsstadt* (Wiesbaden, 1977); Schindling, 'Strassburg und Altdorf' in Baumgarten and Hammerstein (eds.), as in note 1.

13.   G. Menk, *Die Hohe Schule zu Herborn in ihrer Frühzeit* (Wiesbaden, 1981).

13a. See also Hammerstein, 'Universitäten — Territorialstaaten — Gelehrte Räte', in R. Schnür (ed.), *Die Rolle der Juristen bei der Entstehung des modernen Staates* (Berlin, 1986), pp. 687ff.

14.   See my work cited in note 6.

15.   E. W. Zeeden, 'Grundlage und Wege der Konfessionsbildung in Deutschland im Zeitalter der Glaubenskämpfe' in his *Konfessionsbildung* (Stuttgart, 1985) pp. 67ff.

16.   See my forthcoming contribution in: H. Holzhey (ed.), *Überwegs Handbuch der Philosophie, Das 17 Jahrhundert* (Basel-Zurich, 1988).

17.   Hammerstein, *Jus und Historie* (Göttingen, 1972).

18.   U. Muhlack, 'Die Universität im Zeichen von Neuhumanismus und Idealismus' in Baumgarten and Hammerstein (see note 1).

19.   Among other works used for Palatine history have been L. Häuser, *Geschichte der Rheinischen Pfalz nach ihren politischen, kirchlichen und literarischen Verhältnissen*, 2 vols. (Heidelberg, 1845 and reprint Speyer, 1978); also W. Volker in M. Spindler (ed.), *Handbuch der bayerischen Geschichte* III vol. 2 (Munich, 1971) pp. 1289ff.

20.   For the sake of simplicity I refer to works previously cited, even for these particular questions.

20a. See my work cited in note 13a and also W. Kühlmann and J. Telle, 'Humanismus und Medizin an der Universität Heidelberg im 16. Jahrhundert', in *Semper Apertus* I, pp. 255ff.

21.   E. Winkelmann, *Urkundenbuch der Universität Heidelberg*, vols. (Heidelberg, 1886) vol. 2, p. 63.

22.   Spindler, *Handbuch*, see above, note 19.

23.   See the petition to the Elector cited in Hautz, vol. 1 p. 369, where the Arts Faculty decided amongst other things that the University 'quae olim inter totius Germaniae Academias omnium fuerat florentissima, hodie flaccescentem et marcidam atque propediem interituram audimus predicari . . . '.

24.   Apart from Hautz see *Neue Deutsche Biographie* (incomplete), henceforth cited as NDB, and the *Ruperto Carola Sonderband* (see note 3).

25.   Winckelmann, vol. 1 pp. 214ff.

26.   Winckelmann, vol. 1 pp. 216f.

27.   Winkelmann, vol. 1 p. 219; even Spiegel naturally recommended: 'ante omnia querendi sunt, qui profiteantur linguas, Graecam inprimis . . . '.

28.   Hautz, vol. 1 pp. 413ff.

29.   Hautz, vol. 1 pp. 432ff: also Wolgast, 'Die kurpfälzische Universität 1386-1803', in *Semper Apertus* I, pp. 1ff.

30.   A. Thorbecke, *Statuten und Reformation der Universität Heidelberg im 16. — 18. Jahrhundert* (Leipzig, 1891), p. 92: 'die iungen angeende studenten und schuler (seien) von ihren burssen und derselben verwaltern dohin gehalten und getrungen worden, das dieselben zuvor und ehe dann sie zu rechtem verstand und alter komen, haben solche secten und wege der iren zu volnfuiren und halten sich versprechen muessen, dardurch nachmalss vil uneinigkeit und zwitracht . . . entstanden'.

31.   'Preterea magna maturitate et serio conquestum est nobis, certos ex vobis in Neccaro ad supremum molendinum illustrissimi principis nostri lavari seu balneare, discurrentes ibidem in aggere ex lapidibus collecto et duabus setibus circumsepto, vulgariter of dem werr, labides, deiiciendo, sepem utrinque frangendo et tumulum aque coequando ut aqua versus molendinum ducta rotas molares minus movere seu vertere queat'. (Winkelmann, vol. 1 p 209, no. 155). 'Audimus quosdam ex scholastico caetu tam esse etiam inverecundos, ut in flumine Neccari natantes foede lasciviant honestae matronae virgines aliique honore afficiendi'. (Winkelmann, vol. 1, p. 260, no. 186 — June 1551).

32.   It is worth noting that, during the Golden Age of the university at the turn of the century, Johann Casimir, certainly acting under the influence of the many foreign students and with the agreement of the university, decided to suspend the custom of *Deposition* at least in the case of 'the older foreign students' (Winkelmann, vol. 2 p. 153). This was unusual at that time; usually concessions were only made to the nobility regarding the severity and duration of their *Deposition*.

33.   The order was that; 'kein Inwoner allhie, der schwein begere zu ziehen, dieselbigen uff der gassen umbher lass spacieren, dieselben auch nit mer in den neckar treibe, auch nit fuer der thuer uff der gassen wasche oder zu essen gebe'.

34.   As quoted in Hautz, vol. 2, pp. 13ff.: (the Elector cared for) 'die gesondheit und gluecklich wolfahrt der Inwoner in vetterlich Fuersorge . . . '.

35.   From the point of view of the university and higher education, they included teaching at the *Gymnasium*, and at the Sapiens-college, so that Ursinus, who definitely preferred teaching at the College, in effect abandoned the university. The Sapiens-College was the Calvinist equivalent of a Roman Catholic seminary.

36.   This was naturally the case for the whole territory, since fear of the powerful Emperor was unavoidable.

37.   H. Scheible, 'Die Universität Heidelberg und Luthers Disputation' in *Zeitschrift*

130   *History of Universities*

für Geschichte des Oberrheins, 131, 1983, pp. 309ff; K. H. zur Mühlen, 'Die Heidelberger Disputation Martin Luthers vom 26. April 1518. Programm und Wirkung', in *Semper Apertus* I, pp. 188ff.

38.   See also G. Poensgen (ed.), *Sonderband Ott-Heinrich*, der Rupero-Carola, 1956.

39.   Thorbecke, pp. 2ff.

40.   Thorbecke, pp. 91f.

41.   Thorbecke, vol. 3: (The reform ideas recognised) '. . . wie zu pflantzung und erhaltunge christlicher lehre, auch gutter kuenste und tugenden hochnoettig ist, christliche wolangerichte gemeine studia . . . zu unterhalten . . . (which) zu verwaltung der kirchenempter und weltlicher regierung heilsamlich und mit grossem nutz zu gebrauchen, damit auss mangel solcher leute und instrumente oder werckzeug, die gott gibt, nicht beiden zu erbarmlichem abfall und ettwo gantzer verwustung gerathe'. See also H. Bornkamm, 'Die Reformation der Kirche und der Universität durch Ott-Heinrich' in *Ruperto-Carola* Jahrgang 8, nr. 20, 1956 pp. 25ff.

42.   For these events and personalities see the above-mentioned works on the History of the University, rich in infomation, see also K. Bauer, *Aus der grossen Zeit der theologischen Fakultät zu Heidelberg* (Lahr/Baden, 1938).

43.   Most of the Electoral Councillors came from Upper German cities and were thus committed to the form of Reformation and society that had developed there, closer to Zwingli than to the more central German Lutherans. Because these cities, after the Schmalkaldic War, were forced by the Emperor to join the Lutherans, it was these councillors who, as described by V. Press, attempted to save these ideals by transferring their ground of action to the Palatinate. To this extent Philippism and the Swiss influence had prepared the way from the very beginning for the 'second Reformation'. See V. Press, *Calvinismus und Territorialstaat* (Kieler Historische Studien, 7), (Stuttgart, 1970).

44.   See Zeeden, as in note 15.

45.   The basic work is still A. Kluckhohn, *Friedrich der Fromme, Kurfürst von der Pfalz, der Schützer der reformierten Kirche 1559-1576* (Nordlingen, 1879); see also B. Vogler, 'Die Rolle der Pfalzischen Kurfürsten in den franzosischen Religionskriegen (1559-1592)' in *Blätter fur Pfälzer Kirchengeschichte und religiöse Volkskunde*, 1970/71, vol. 1, *Festgabe für Th. Schaller* (Grünstadt, 1970/71)

46.   K. Holl, *Johannes Calvin* (Berlin, 1909).

47.   Amongst other works, see H. Schilling, *Konfessionskonflikt und Staatsbildung. Eine Fallstudie über das Verhältnis von religiösem und sozialem Wandel der frühen Neuzeit am Beispiel der Grafschaft Lippe* (Gütersloh, 1981); E. Münch, *Zucht und Ordnung. Reformierte Kirchenverfassung im 16. und 17. Jahrhundert* (Stuttgart, 1978).

48.   W. Hollweg, *Der Augsburger Reichstag von 1556 und seine Bedeutung für die Entstehung der Reformierten Kirchen und ihres Bekenntnisses* (Beiträge zur Geschichte und Lehre der Reformierten Kirche XVII) (Neukirchen, 1964); J. F. Gerhard Göters, in: E. Sehling (ed.), *Die evangelische Kirchenordnung des 16. Jahrhunderts*, vol. 14, Kurpfalz (Tübingen, 1969) pp. 34ff.

49.   Göters, pp. 40ff.; G. A. Benrath, 'Die Eigenart der Pfälzischen Reformation und die Vorgeschichte des Heidelberger Katechismus' and O. Weber, 'Analytische Theologie. Zum geschichtlichen Standort des Heidelberger Katechismus', both in *Heidelberger Jahrbücher* VII (Berlin-Gottingen-Heidelberg, 1963) pp. 13ff. and pp. 33ff.; G. A. Benrath, 'Zacharias Ursinus (1534-1583)' in *Blätter für die Pfälzer Kirchengeschichte und religiöse Volkskunde*, Jahrgang 37/38, *Festgabe für Th. Schaller* (Grünstadt, 1971), pp. 202ff.

50. On Silvanus see also, apart from Hauser, the article by J. F. G. Göters, 'Arianismus' in *Pfälzische Kirchenlexikon*, 1962, pp. 107ff.

51. In this area see R. Wesel-Roth, *Thomas Erastus. Ein Beitrag zur Geschichte der reformierten Kirche zur Lehre von der Staatssouveränität* (Veroff. d. Ver. f. Kirchengesch. d. Landeskirche Badens XV) (Lahr/Baden, without date, actually 1954), especially pp. 45ff.

52. Ludwig von Wittgenstein, the Palatine Councillor, expressed himself in a letter on the conditions of 1575 in a way that would have been unthinkable for Lutherans at that time. 'Denique tam etsi armis religionem propagare non decet, tyrannorum tamen crudelitatem repellere, verumque Dei cultum, cum aliter fieri non potest, non minus quam res et corpora bello conservare licebit: inferre ob religionem non licet'. Quoted from Wesel-Roth, p. 135, note 140.

53. Wesel-Roth, p. 57.

54. Hammerstein, 'Schule, Hochschule und res publica litteraria', in *Wolfenbütteler Barockforschungen* ed. by C. Neumeister and C. Wiedemann (Wiesbaden, 1987).

55. We can see how this was treated as a general European problem in a number of ways: in all Palatine foreign policy after Friedrich III; in the education of their princes at Huguenot academies; in relations with James I and with the Dutch rebels; in the attempt to pursue a policy of co-operation on religious and political grounds with the House of Nassau, with the *Wetterauer Grafenverein* and with Anhalt as with the protestant estates of Bohemia and Austria. D. Tossanus wrote along these lines to Beza in 1599: 'Hispani, qui Acheronta movere et toti Germaniae minas intentare non dubitabant . . .', quoted from F. W. Cuno, *Daniel Tossanus der Aeltere* (Amsterdam, 1898), vol. 2, pp. 46f. It was characteristic then that the French ambassador should write of Johann Casimir 'Non querit religionem, sed regionem', quoted from B. Vogler, p. 238. I will not bother to cite here the many possible references, but will simply draw attention to the article by G. Menk, 'Die politische Kultur in den Wetterauer Grafschaften am Ende des 16. und zu Anfang des 17. Jahrhunderts' in *Hess. Jhb. f. Landesgechichte* 39. 1984 pp. 67ff.

56. 'Der Calvinismus marschiert, oh Schmerz! auf breiter Front; aus Frankreich bricht er in Deutschland ein'. Quoted from Hollweg, pp. 2f.

57. Quoted from Schilling, p. 249.

58. 'Euch gilt zuerst der Schlag, dann aber uns. Denn der roemische Cerberus und seine Henker machen zwischen Euren und unseren Kirchen, auch ob sie lutherisch oder calvinistisch sind, keinen Unterschied'. Quoted from Cuno, *Tossanus* vol. 1, p. 184.

59. 'Man soll auf wege gedenken . . . die schelmischen Jesuiter zu vertilgen, dass sie der teufel holt'. Quoted from H. Sturmberger, *Georg Erasmus Tschernembl, Religion, Libertät und Widerstand* (Graz-Köln, 1953), p. 111.

60. Apart from works mentioned in note 54, the best modern articles are by K. Garber, 'Martin Opitz' and 'Gibt es eine bürgerliche Literatur in Deutschland im 17. Jahrhundert?', respectively in H. Steinhagen and B. von Wiese (eds.), *Deutsche Dichter des 17. Jahrhunderts* (Berlin, 1985), pp. 116ff. and *Germ.-Rom. Monatsschrift*, Neue Folge 31, 1981, pp. 462ff.

61. He too was a typical figure of these years at Heidelberg; see G. Smend, *Janus Gruter, sein Leben und Wirken* (Bonn, 1939).

62. This was Pezel, who was amongst others an influential figure in the *Bremen Gymnasium illustre*, quoted after J. Moltmann, *Christoph Pezel und der Calvinismus in Bremen* (Bremen, 1958), p. 85.

63. This is especially the position of Garber (see note 61).

64.   'Die Inklination der Literatorum zur Zwinglischen Meinung hat sich schon seit 1540 geaüssert', quoted after Moltmann, p. 85.

65.   (Duke Johann Friedrich hoped): 'es wert der allemechtige got genad verleihen, das man die kristelich religion im land wider aufrichte und des teufels geschmais wider hinweg due'. A. Kluckhohn, *Briefe Friedrichs d. Frommen*, vol. 1, 1868, p. 40.

66.   P. Moraw and Th. Karst, 'Die Universität Heidelberg und Neustadt an der Haardt (*Veröff. z. Gesch. von Stadt und Kreis Neustadt an der Weinstrasse* III) (Speyer, 1963).

67.   On this in general see Schindling.

68.   Hollweg, pp. 15ff.; V. Press 'Die Grafen von Erbach und die Anfänge des reformierten Bekenntnisses in Deutschland' in *Aus Geschichte und ihren Hilfswissenschaften, Festschrift W. Heinemeyer* (Marburg, 1979) pp. 653ff.

69.   This was Jacob Andreae's opinion; see Cuno, *Tossanus*.

70.   See in general here also Schilling (note 47) and Wesel-Roth (note 52).

71.   The best study is now that of Menk (note 13).

72.   See notes and bibliography in following works by Hammerstein; *Rolle und Bedeutung* (note 6); 'Universitäten des Heiligen Römischen Reichs Deutscher Nation als Ort der Philosophie des Barock' in *Studia Leibnitiana* XVIII, 1981, pp. 242ff.; 'Universitätsgeschichte im Heiligen Römischen Reich Deutscher Nation am Ende der Renaissance' in *Das Ende der Renaissance: Europaische Kultur im 16. Jahrhundert*, Wolfenbütteler Renaissanceforschungen, 1987.

73.   Althusius of course can be named as an exception to the general rule. Nevertheless his influence within the Empire remained minimal, certainly not as great as his influence generally within West Europe.

74.   Hammerstein, 'Jus publicum Romano-Gemanicorum' in *Diritto e Potere nella Storia Europea* (Atti del Quarto Congresso internazionale della Società Italiana del Diritto) (Florence, 1982) pp. 717ff.

75.   Winkelmann, vol. 2 , no. 1175, dated October 1572; see the letters in the article by H. Hautz, 'Die Juristen-Facultät der Universität Heidelberg unter der Regierung des Kurfürsten Friedrich III von der Pfalz', in *Akad. Monatsschrift* IV (Heidelberg, 1852) pp. 377ff.

76.   Winkelmann, vol. 2, no. 1437, dated September 1599.

77.   Through experience of Sturm's academic experiment, already by 1541 Calvin had decided that: 'Le degré plus prochain au ministère et plus conjoinct au gouvernement de l'eglise est la lecture de théologie dont il sera bon qu'il y en ait au Vieil at Noveau Testament. Mais pource qu'on ne peult proufiter en telles leçons que premièrement on ne soit instruict aux langues et sciences humaines'. Beza put forward the ideals of the Genevan Academy as the goal: 'le moyen d'estre nourris en la vraye piété et ès bonnes sciences'. Quoted from R. Stauffer 'Le calvinismus et les Universités' in *Bulletin, Société de l'Histoire du Protestantisme français* CXXVI (Paris, 1980) pp. 27ff., the two extracts here on p. 29 and p. 33.

78.   G. Haase and G. Winkler, *Die Oder-Universität Frankfurt. Beiträge zu ihrer Geschichte* (Weimar, 1983); Hammerstein article in preparation (see note 16).

79.   Hammerstein, *Jus und Historie.*

80.   See J. Fuchs in NDB 11 (Berlin, 1977) and V. Sellin, *Die Finanzpolitik Karl Ludwigs von der Pfalz* (Stuttgart, 1978).

81.   See K. A. Modéer (ed.), *Samuel von Pufendorf 1632-1982* (Lund, 1986); H. Denzer, *Moralphilosophie und Naturrecht bei Samuel Pufendorf* (Munich, 1972).

82.   On Cocceji, see Hammerstein, *Jus und Historie.*

83. (Karl Ludwig emphasised that): 'dieweil . . . jetziger zeit fast mit allen wissenschaften und kuensten es dergestellt, wie bekannt beschaffen, das viel, so in vorigen unserer universitaet statutis enthalten, anietzo nicht mehr staathaben kann, dahero die studia nicht, wie auff einigen andern hohen schulen in und ausserhalb des reichs, mit auffnahm lust und nutzen der studierenden jugendt alhier koennen fortgesetzt werden . . . '. Thornbecke, p. 249.

84. Thorbecke, p. 251, quotes the new statutes to the effect that, as far as the other three faculties were concerned, the main aim was to get the best possible staff for the university, who should do their duty as set down in the following statutum generale, not limited to famous Calvinist professors, but open to all qualified to teach, as necessity dictated.

85. Thorbecke, p. 253.

86. Thorbecke, p. 284, section 54.

87. (They were admonished) 'im uebrigen sonderlich dahin (zu) sehen, dass die unter dem geistlichen nahmen bedeckte weltliche regiersucht bey denen theologis in gebuehrenden schranken gehalten, auch die in anstaendige moderation foviret werden moege'. Quoted Thorbecke, p. 286, section 64.

88. Thorbecke, p. 287, section 66.

89. Thorbecke, p. 288.

90. On these figures see the bibliographies in the *Sonderband der Ruperto-Carola* and in the article by G. A. Benrath, 'Heidelberger Vorlesungsverzeichnisse aus den Jahren 1655, 1658-1662 und 1685' in the *Heidelberger Jahrbuch* V (Berlin-Gottingen-Heidelberg, 1961) pp. 85ff.

91. It is not necessary to go into this quarrel here; a quarrel which has been much discussed and which has kept its religious-political character even into this century. The shortest and most convincing account is now to be found in H. Schmidt, *Kurfürst Karl Philipp von der Pfalz als Reichsfürst* (Mannheim, 1963), especially pp. 114ff.

92. See M. Braubach in NDB 10 (Berlin, 1974) pp. 516ff.

93. So much so that *c*.1728 one of the law professors proposed that it was no longer worth his while to lecture on a subject to as few as two or three students. See Winkelmann, vol. 2, p. 251 no. 2029.

94. See also H. Schmidt in NDB 11, pp. 250ff.

95. Hammerstein, *Aufklärung und katholisches Reich* (Berlin, 1977).

96. On Carl Theodor see P. Fuchs in NDB 12, pp. 252ff.; L. Hammermayer, 'Das Ende des alten Bayern' in M. Spindler (ed.), *Handbuch der bayerischen Geschichte*, vol. 2 (Munich, 1966), pp. 985ff., pp. 1007ff. and pp. 1044ff.

97. Cf. Thorbecke.

98. P. Fuchs, 'Wissenschaftspflege in der Pfalz unter Kurfürst Carl Theodor' in *Pfalzer Heimat* 17, 1966, pp. 19ff.; W. Wegener, *Kurfürst Karl Theodor aus der Pfalz als Kunstsammler* (Mannheim, 1960); J. Voss, *Universität, Geschichtswissenschaft und Diplomatie im Zeitalter der Aufklärung: Johann Daniel Schöpflin (1694-1771)* (Munich, 1979), pp. 204ff.

99. See Hammerstein, *Aufklärung und katholisches Reich*.

100. H. Weisert, *Geschichte der Universität Heidelberg* (Heidelberg, 1983), pp. 61ff.

101. This is the idea of the real Rome being that of the Emperors and Popes, the second Rome being Byzantium, and the third Rome being Moscow or various cities or dynasties within the Orthodox Church. See also Ricerca d'Ateneo 'Aspetti Storico-Religiose Giuridici dell'Idea di Roma' in *Atti dei seminarie Da Roma alla Terza Roma* (Rome, 1984).

MATRICULATION AGES IN SIXTEENTH-CENTURY WITTENBERG

Owen and Miriam Gingerich

(This note was discussed with Charles Schmitt in Wolfenbüttel in December, 1985, and now is dedicated to his memory.)

In connection with research on the sixteenth-century astronomer Paul Wittich, who matriculated at Leipzig in 1563 and at Wittenberg in 1566, the question arose about the expected age of a student at the time of his initial matriculation. Although no birth year is known for Wittich, R. S. Westman suggested that the recorded matriculation dates offer at least a way of establishing a probable year of birth.

By chance we discovered in the Herzog August Bibliothek in Wolfenbüttel a set of manuscript horoscopes entitled 'Farrago thematum genethlialogicorun collecta per A[ugust] R[itter] G[orlicensis] L[?] Witebergae' (Astron 35.2), and among the numerous persons included, we could match 29 names (and home towns) with students found in C. E. Foerstemann's *Album Academiae Vitebergensis* (Leipzig, 1841-1905). Thus the farrago of horoscopes provides birthdays and therefore matriculation ages for a cross section of 29 students in mid-sixteenth-century Wittenberg. The sample is large enough to see that the typical age at matriculation was 17. Three of the slightly older students had matriculated earlier at Leipzig, Rostock, or Frankfurt an der Oder, and if we take this into account, the median age of first matriculation was 17, and half the students were 16, 17, or 18 at the time of matriculation.

For comparsion purposes we recorded 30 ages of sixteenth-century students at Oxford from Joseph Foster's *Alumni Oxoniensis* (Oxford, 1891) (arbitrarily selecting names beginning with C), and here again we found a median age of 17, with two-thirds of the students matriculating at ages 16, 17, or 18. A further larger sample from seventeenth-century Oxford gave exactly the same result, with a noticeable tendency for the ages to be more sharply defined in this narrow age bracket toward the end of the seventeenth century.

We give below the list of Wittenberg students in our sample. Note

Birthdates from a manuscript at the Herzog August Bibliothek, Wolfenbüttel, Astron 35.2, 'Farrago thematum genethlialogicorun collecta per A[ugust] R[itter] G[orlicensis] L[?] Witebergae'.

NAME	BIRTHDATE	WITTENBERG MATRICULATION	AGE
Caspar Cruciger	1504 Jan 1	April 1523	19
Paul Eber (Kitzingen}	1511 Nov 7	Summer 1532	20
Erasmus Reinhold	1511 Oct 21	Winter 1530-31	19
Joachim Rheticus	1514 Feb 15	Summer 1532	18
Georgius Fabricius (Chemnitensis)	1516 Apr 22	Winter 1536-37	20
Matthias Flacius Ilyricus	1519 Mar 3	May 1534	15
Valentine Ritter Sr (Gorlitz)	1522 Feb 9	June 1540	18
Victorin Strigelius	1524 Dec 26	October 1542	17
Caspar Peucer	1525 Jan 5	March 1543	18
Georgius Cracovius (Pommern)	1525 Apr 11	May 1542	17
Justin Jonas (Wittenberg)	1525 Dec 2	Winter 1530-31	6!
Matthias Stoy	1526 [Mar 25]	Nov 1543	17
Petrus Lotichius Secundus	1528 Nov 1	May 1546	17
Johannes Garcaeus (Wittenberg)	1530 Dec 13	April 1546	15
Paulus Crellius (Islebensis)	1531 Feb 5	Nov 1548	17
Joachim Maistorus (Gorlitz)	1532 Oct 31	July 26, 1558	25
[matriculated at Leipzig summer 1548, age 15]			
Nicolaus Selneccerus (Nuremberg)	1532 Dec 6	April 1550	17
Simon Siderus (Wittenberg)	1538 Feb 10	July 1555	17
Bartholemaeus Scultetus (Gorlitz)	1540 Mar 13	Sept 1557	17
Caspar Strubius (Wittenberg)	1547 Jan 2	July 1558	11
Valentine Ritter Jr (Gorlitz)	1551 Jun 1	April 1578	26
Marcus Lorleberg (Hameln)	1554 Oct 28	May 1575	20
Laurentius Finckeltaus (Lips)	1555 Dec 17	March 1579	23
Henricus Nortmeyer	1557 Jun 5	August 1580	23
(Hildeshemensis) [matriculated at Rostock spring 1578, age 20]			
Adamus Richter (Gorlitz)	1558 May 19	Oct 1580	22
[matriculated at Frankfurt a.d. Oder spring 1574, age 16]			
Georgius Rhonn (Gorlitz)	1559 Mar 25	April 1578	19
August Ritter (Gorlitz)	1559 Aug 28	May 1577	17
Petrus Beier	1563 Oct 2	Sept 1589	25
Petrus Ritter (Gorlitz)	1571 Jun 13	April 1589	17

that the inclusion of many of August Ritter's friends or relatives from Gorlitz helps balance out any distortions that might be present in a list consisting entirely of famous men. We believe that Justin Jonas of Wittenberg really did matriculate at age 6, but as he was the son of the rector, this may well fall in the category of a stunt rather than indicating that the lad was precocious. In general all the quite young students were from the town of Wittenberg, so they undoubtedly had close parental supervision, and we can speculate that they may not have been university students in the normal sense.

If Paul Wittich of Wroclaw matriculated in Leipzig at the median age, he would have been born in 1546 and would have the same age as his illustrious contemporary, Tycho Brahe (who matriculated at Leipzig in 1562 at a somewhat youthful 15).

Harvard-Smithsonian Center for Astrophysics and Cambridge, Massachusetts

COMMENTARY

John M. Fletcher

The age at which students at the medieval and renaissance universities began their studies has been for many years a subject of much controversy. Clearly, any answer to this problem must colour our view of the nature of the universities themselves: if students could enter at a very early age, it is hardly possible to have much respect for the academic content of courses offered. If more mature entrants only were accepted, then, in contrast, we must anticipate a programme of studies of some difficulty.

Space does not permit here a full discussion of recent research, but it would perhaps be useful to summarise some of the questions that have been raised and hint at possible solutions offered. The traditional and popular view is that students entered the early universities at a much younger age than is now the case. This impression was strengthened by evidence of some college students being hardly able to read, of the resort to corporal punishment by the authorities, of careful statutory regulation of the manner of life of such students who seemed to be regarded as unable to organise and control their domestic and financial affairs. The survival of so many such references from many parts of Europe indicates the existence at the universities of a substantial population of mere boys.

On the other hand, recent scholars have drawn attention to more scattered but equally significant details that indicate that the university student was expected to be a young man rather than just a boy: the requirement that a student should normally take oaths that he fully understood and that were legally binding, the references to ages before which students could not take degrees, the mention of married students and their children in some privileges, and the powerful indication in the statutes of some grammar schools that they expected to retain their pupils until around the age of sixteen before anticipating their departure for a university. Moreover, many modern writers have expressed doubts about the ability of boys to cope with so complicated a course as was normally required for the arts degrees.

The clear contradiction presented by the surviving evidence can only be resolved if the structure of the early universities and the nature of matriculation itself is understood. Frequently the universities exercised control over all aspects of education in their locality, licensing not only the masters of the university but also the teachers of the public grammar schools. In such cases, the school masters and their charges were then classed as 'suppositi', that is as full members of the university. It was, indeed, advantageous for such individuals to place formally their name on the university rolls as this action brought important benefits: exemption from the jurisdiction of the town courts, freedom from certain tolls and taxes and other valuable privileges. It is not surprising that town authorities frequently complained that the matriculation records contained the names of those who were not genuine students — the so called 'pretensi studentes'. Another group appearing in such records, especially in the early year of a new university's existence, was that composed of those celebrities who wished to honour the university by placing their names in its matriculation lists, or who were themselves honoured in this way by the university.

These three elements, the boys of the grammar schools, those who insinuated their names into the university lists with dubious legality and those who enrolled to honour the university without any intention of undertaking any courses there, could not be regarded as students in the modern, more restricted sense of the word. However, to contemporaries, they were certainly all full members of the university. It is amongst such elements that students both younger and older than those pursuing the normal courses offered by the university could be found. No doubt the six year old who matriculated at Wittenberg belonged to one of these categories. He was probably a school boy and, as the son of the rector, could have been honoured by the university with inclusion in its matriculation records.

If these reservations are kept in mind, it is possible to reconcile most of the apparent contradictions presented by the records. Unfortunately, however, it is not easy to obtain definite proof of the dates of birth of many of those students entering their names on the matricualtion lists. It is here that the Gingerichs have performed a valuable service to academic historians. Their conclusion, that, apart from such unusual entries as we have discussed above, students of the early universities did not differ greatly in their age at entry from their modern counterparts, is further useful evidence in discrediting the older, popular view that would people the early universities with a student body of irresponsible and immature boys.

Department of Modern Languages
University of Aston
Birmingham B4 7ET

Book Reviews

Stephen C. Ferruolo, *The Origins of the University: the Schools of Paris and their Critics 1100-1215*. Stanford University Press, 1985. xii + 380 pp.

This is a significant book on the origins of the university in Paris. Ferruolo's avowed aim is to show that the formation of the first 'universities of masters and scholars in Paris resulted not so much from the pragmatic need of scholars to band together to secure their interests against an external adversary, as from the prevailing influence within the schools of certain exalted educational principles and values' (p. 5). These values can be assessed by surveying the criticims of the schools both from within and from without. He divides the critics into four classes: the leaders of the new monastic and religious orders, the satirists, the humanists, and the moralists.

Under the first heading the author shows that those belonging to monastic foundations viewed the scholar as a threat to the Church and began closing their schools to students who were not members of their order. Thus the monastic school of St Victor, far from being an early 'college' for the University of Paris, turns out to be a rival establishment which became increasingly isolated as the secular schools developed. The contrast between life in the cloister and life in the school was emphasised. The aim in the former was a life based on contemplation; secular scholars attained only the level of reason, which bred arrogance. Adam of Perseigne can set seven spiritual disciplines in place of the seven liberal arts of the secular scholar. The approach to study was different in the schools and the monasteries. Godfrey of St Victor can claim that he abandoned the schools because of their 'unnourishing disputations over the profound mysteries of the divinity' and retired to St Victor in order to 'reflect on subjects more accesible to human understanding, such as Creation, the Fall and Redemption' (p. 42). Not until 1218, when the Dominicans established their own house of studies in Paris was it possible again to be a member of a religious order and to study and teach others outside the cloister.

The satirists, humanists and moralists are, most often, products of the schools, and advocate reform rather than rejection. Ferruolo rehearses the complaints, concerning the lack of respect given to learning, the poverty of the scholar and the influence of money, found in satirists such as Walter of Chatillon, Peter the Painter, Hugh Primas, John of Hauteville and Nigel Wireker. In general these complaints seem to be against a society which does not appreciate scholarship rather than against the schools themselves. Incidentally, Ferruolo misses the pun in Peter the Painter's poem *De Domno Vobiscum* (p. 104)[1] between *arismeticam* (a common medieval spelling for 'arithmetic') and *erismeticam*, a term 'our ancestors made up to describe the study of simony', whose first element is from the word used for a bronze coin.

The humanists, on the other hand, criticise the schools for acquiescing too much to the demands of society, and teaching people how to make money in lucrative professions, rather than promoting pure scholarship, based on knowledge of the Classics. The principal representative of this view is, of course, John of Salisbury, but Ferruolo also brings onto the scene Peter of Blois and Gerald of Wales.

The largest amount of space is devoted to the criticism of the moralists, or preachers. The place of preaching in the early history of the University is discussed. All masters of theology had a duty to preach, and many sermons were specifically addressed *ad scholares*. The subject-matter of these sermons is rather predictable, including the right attitude towards study, the qualities of the good teacher, and the dangers of idle curiosity, vanity and simony. The attitude towards the liberal arts in these sermons is ambivalent, but the scientific disciplines of the quadrivium, and medicine, are regarded with suspicion.

Ferruolo rounds off his work by reassessing the beginnings of the University of Paris, tracing the nature and the effect of the successive royal and ecclesiastical statutes by which the University's corporate status was established.

This book covers a wide range of material, of which some parts have been used more thoroughly and handled with a firmer grasp than others. Ferruolo has delved particularly deeply into the sermon-literature of the period and provides a valuable summary of its tone and contents. If anything, he has neglected the intellectual products of the schools themselves, which he could have used as indicators of the educational principles and values upheld there. He writes more as a social historian than as an intellectual historian, and, as such, follows closely in the footsteps of John Baldwin,[2] whom he acknowledges.

Charles Burnett
The Warburg Institute
Woburn Square, London WC1H 0AB

1. If he had used the new edition of the poems by L. Van Acker in *Corpus Christianorum Continuatio Mediaevalis*, 25 (Turnhout, 1972) he might have been saved from some small errors, such as *fuit* for *fugit* (line 5 of the quotation), and *affecti* for *effecti* (line 13).

2.   J. W. Baldwin, 'Masters at Paris, 1179-1215', in R. L. Benson, G. Constable and C. D. Lanham, *Renaissance and Renewal in the Twelfth Century* (Oxford, 1982).

Zénon Kaluza & Paul Vignaux (eds.), *Preuves et Raisons à l'Université de Paris. Logique, Ontologie et Théologie au XIVe Siècle. Actes de la Table Ronde internationale organisée par le Laboratoire associé au C.N.R.S. no. 152 du 5 au 7 novembre 1981. Études de Philosophie Médiévale, Hors Série.* Paris: Librarie Philosophique J. Vrin, 1984. 310 pp.

Universities have always been talk shops, but in different ways at different times and places. The title of the volume under review catches a lot of the flavour of the fourteenth-century University of Paris, particularly as regards its Theological Faculty. There was strong concern with logical argument, with what could be proved by natural reason, and with what was the proper relation between reason, revelation and authority at large. The sources make clear that tremendous excitement was generated, but for us it takes a great effort of historical imagination (and of erudition) to enter at all fully into the passions involved. The present volume is a valuable aid for this effort. It comprises sixteen substantive essays (nine from France, four from Italy, and one each from the United Kingdom, the United States, Denmark, and Poland), together with a summing-up by Paul Vignaux. By its nature the volume does not present a balanced synoptic picture of fourteenth century Parisian intellectual life as a whole; its strength lies rather in its particular insights and pieces of information.

Several of the essays are concerned either centrally or marginally with traditions deriving from seminal thinkers: Aquinas, Scotus, Buridan, and, above all, Ockham. The last of these made a particularly noisy impact on Paris, but a masterly essay by William J. Courtenay shows how important it is to attend to the nuances and chronology of the disputes and to distinguish between Ockham and Ockhamists. Ockham's *fortuna* also reminds us that thought was subject to other constraints than those of logic alone. It was, for instance, required of candidates for inception in Arts in the Anglo-German nation that, 'You shall swear that you will observe the statutes made by the Faculty of Arts against the scientia Okamica, nor sustain in any way whatsoever the said scientia and similar ones . . . ' (p. 51). References to administrative authority could also occur in the context of the much discussed question of whether God could deceive: 'In this university it is not held that God could deceive' (p. 198). Two essays in the volume are devoted to medieval treatments of this difficult problem, and here as elsewhere we meet with the frequently used distinction between God's absolute power and his ordained power. This distinction can be misunderstood. As Ockham said, a statement asserting that God can do something by his absolute power but not by his ordained power could quite naturally be read as saying that there were two types of power in God, by one of which he could do that thing, but not by the other. This is the false sense. Instead such a statement should be interpreted loosely (*improprie*). Taken thus it asserts that by his absolute power God can do that thing (because it does not imply a contradiction), but he has ordained that he never will in fact do it. In this as in other ways

Ockham is at a distance from the narrow literalists who were condemned in 1340, and who, as Courtenay points out, were later confused with Ockhamists.

Despite the condemnations and prohibitions, one of the most striking features of fourteenth-century thought is the relative lack of constraint on reasoning, which could wander hither and thither with little control beyond the articles of faith and the occasional statute. But this freedom had its price: if one could prove almost anything, or least show it to be probable or possible, then the very power of reason demonstrates its ultimate impotence, and this book reinforces the view that sees the fourteenth century as being pre-eminently a time of criticism and scepticism. This comes out in several places, and not least in a paper by Max Lejbowicz on Nicole Oresme and divinatory logic. It was a common humanistic trait to attack the supposed sterility of scholasticism. An essay by Cesare Vasoli examines the flow of humanistic currents into France, especially via the papal court at Avignon. It is perhaps significant that Oresme was associated both with the College of Navarre and the royal court, two particularly receptive centres for humanism.

This book contains many titbits: here I have only been able to point at some of them, and not even at all of the choicer ones.

A. George Molland
Department of History and Philosophy of Science
King's College
Aberdeen AB9 2UB

Studi e memorie per la storia dell'Università di Bologna. Nuova Serie, vol. 4. Bologna: Presso l'Istituto per la storia dell' Università, 1984. 186 pp.

This *strumento di ricerca* provides an historical guide to the archives of ten Bolognese colleges, i.e. endowed residences for students attending the University of Bologna.

Gian Paolo Brizzi, who organised the volume, begins with an historical introduction to the twenty-one Bolognese colleges beginning with the Collegio Avignonese founded in 1257. Modelled on the novice houses established by religious orders in university towns, student residences evolved into teaching faculties in northern European universities. They were generally limited to residential roles in Bologna and other Italian university towns and were less numerous, because communal governments, which financed and directed Italian universities, did not want teaching dispersed. In addition, the Italian colleges to a limited extent competed with the *paedagogium*, the home *cum* small boarding school of popular professors. Nevertheless, Bolognese colleges played significant roles. A benefactor endowed a college to provide lodging and board in Bologna for a small number (8, 18, 24, sometimes more) of poor students from the benefactor's homeland who studied at Bologna. Complaints about rapacious Bolognese landlords spurred the founding of colleges. Students might be as young as twelve, but most were older; they spent five years or more in the college. Although Brizzi does not mention it, the founding of colleges in the thirteenth and fourteenth centuries might be seen as part of a general concern by Italians in towns lacking a university to provide such training. For example, Lucca and other communes gave subsidies to local youths attending university in distant towns.

The fourteenth century saw six new colleges established in Bologna, the fifteenth century only one. Six more followed in the second half of the sixteenth century and another seven in the seventeenth century. The new colleges of the *Cinque-* and *Seicento* more often required boarders to take minor orders and/or to be members of the nobility or professional classes. Brizzi also argues that the new colleges exhibited more petty regulations. Perhaps this is true, but regulatory minutiae had always surrounded Italian education. One of the most interesting new colleges was the Collegio Ungaro-Illirico founded in 1553. Modelled on the Collegium Germanicum in Rome, it trained church leaders of these two linguistic groups for two centuries and more. Brizzi correctly points out that these new colleges, like the Jesuit academies on which he wrote an excellent book, *La formazione della classe dirigente nel Sei-Settecento* (Bologna, 1976), wished to train an exclusive governing class. This is obviously true, but hardly a new departure: universities did this long before and long after the Counter Reformation. The colleges gradually declined in the second half of the *Settecento*, and some suffered suppression in the 1780s and the 1790s when 'enlightened' monarchs forbade their subjects to study beyond the boundaries of the state.

In the bulk of the book Brizzi and his colleagues Laura Ricci and Claudia Salterini provide historical summaries and detailed guides to the extant archival materials for ten colleges (Ancarano, Ferrero, Ungaro-Illirico, Poeti, Panolini, Montalto, Sinibaldi, Palantieri, Jacobs, Comelli). They searched far beyond Bologna. For example, most documention for the Collegio Ancarano is found in Naples, the records of the Collegio Ungaro-Illirico in Zagabria, Croatia. They add bibliographies. A number of colour illustrations offer pictures of charters and collegial costumes with their *maniche lunghe*. Brizzi and his colleagues have prepared an excellent package of useful information for scholars to exploit.

Paul Grendler
Department of History
University of Toronto
Toronto M5S 1A1, Canada

Jan Pinborg (ed.), *Universitas Studii Haffnensis. Stiftelsesdokumenter og Statutter 1479* Copenhagen: University of Copenhagen, 1979. 147 pp.

As is fitting to honour the fifth century of its foundation, the university of Copenhagen has chosen to produce this attractive new edition of its foundation documents. Here we are given the Papal Bull of 1475, the various letters from Danish rulers and ecclesiastics concerning the establishment of the university, the earliest university statutes with later additions and related documents, and the statutes of the faculty of law. The Papal Bull and the university statutes are printed in facsimile. The Latin text is accompanied by translations into Danish and English and the useful introduction and notes are again in both languages; the English translation is by Brian Patrick McGuire.

All the documents presented here have been available for some time to academic historians, but ease of access to them is certainly assisted by this compact and useful presentation. Copenhagen relied heavily on the university of Cologne for both its statutes and its early teaching staff. What little is known of its early history is conveniently summarised in the Introduction which shows some close contact between Danish and Scottish scholars at this date. Copenhagen cannot be said to have made a major contribution to academic life in the later middle ages, but it retained its position as a small but valuable asset to northern intellectual life until the turbulence of the reformation period.

John M. Fletcher
Department of Modern Languages
University of Aston
Birmingham B4 7ET

Robert Feenstra and Cornelia M. Ridderikhoff (eds.), *Études néerlandaises de droit et d'histoire présentées à l'université d'Orléans pour le 750ᵉ anniversaire des enseignements juridiques*, Bulletin de la société archéologique et historique de l'Orléanais. Nouvelle série. Tome IX, no. 68, April, 1985.

In the late Middle Ages the University of Orléans was one of the most important law schools in Europe, noted in particular for its contribution to the development of the study of civil law. Among the many historians who have painstakingly reconstructed its past in recent years, Dutch scholars have been particularly prominent. This reflects the fact that the faculty played an important part in the establishment of Roman Law in the Low Countries through the influence of its professors as teachers and jurisconsultants. The present collection of essays is ample evidence that this enthusiasm of the

Dutch continues unabated. Indeed, it now extends beyond the late Middle Ages, for four of the thirteen articles deal with the centuries after 1500 when the faculty had lost its international élan but still played host (at least until the late-seventeenth century) to Dutch students. The two editors of this collection are themselves leading authorities on the faculty of law at Orléans. Professor Feenstra is a legal historian who has worked on the great thirteenth-century civilian Jacques de Révigny, while Professor Ridderikhoff is the author of a thesis on the early-sixteenth century professor and humanist Jean Pyrrhus d'Anglebermes. She is also co-editor responsible for the recent publication of the Procurator's Book of the German Nation 1444-1546. The essays which they have gathered together for this centenary publication relect their different interests. Half are devoted to noteworthy legal opinions espoused by particular Orléans professors, as revealed in surviving course transcripts; half can be broadly described as prosopographical. All are admirable examples of solid scholarship. None radically alters our vision of the faculty, but each is a useful addition to our still limited knowledge. Needless to say, this is not a collection for those who are seeking an introduction to the work that has been done on Orléans in the last fifty years. It is strictly for the informed *érudit*. Nevertheless, the tyro, anxious to know more about the recent scholarly activity of the Dutch in particular, could do no better than read the interesting introductory essay by Professor Feenstra, 'Etat des recherches menées depuis Meijers' (the great expert on law-teaching in thirteenth century Orléans).

L. W. B. Brockliss
Magdalen College, Oxford

Astrik L. Gabriel, *The University of Paris and its Hungarian Students and Masters in the Reign of Louis XII and François I.* Notre Dame, Indiana and Frankfurt am Main, 1986. Texts and Studies in the History of Mediaeval Education, eds. A. L. Gabriel and P. E. Beichner, no. XVII. ISBN: 3-72800536-8; $47 or DM 98. 238 pp.

To historians of the late-medieval university, Professor Gabriel's contribution to the study of the records of the German Nation at Paris needs no introduction. At present, he is engaged on an analysis of the hitherto unpublished *Liber Receptorum* of the Nation for the years 1494-1531 and the work under review is derived from his current research. The German Nation contained students not only from Germany itself but from every part of northern and eastern Europe, including a contingent from Gabriel's own original homeland, Hungary. Although the Hungarians formed only a small part of the Nation's members during this period, a mere twenty-four students out of some 600 registrands, Gabriel has decided, doubtless for sentimental reasons, to devote a separate volume to their history. This is essentially a prosopographical survey. The social background, educational history, and future career of each of the twenty-four is described as carefully as possible. Few in number as they are, the students are quite clearly a heterogeneous bunch. They originate from all parts of Hungary and Transylvania, are both rich and poor, and come to Paris at different points in their academic *peregrinatio*. Unfortunately, little can be uncovered about their later lives. The best documented figure is Blasius de Varda who stayed in Paris from 1515 to 1522, was an intimate acquaintance of the leading philosophers and theologians in the University, and returned to Hungary to become secretary to the primate, archbishop of Esztergom, in whose service he was still engaged in 1538. Understandably, the number of Hungarian students at Paris at any one moment was only a fraction of the total Magyar diaspora. At the most there were six Hungarians in the French capital in the early sixteenth century out of an expatriate contingent numbering between seventy and a hundred, chiefly to be found at Vienna and Cracow. Nevertheless, that even one or two students should have travelled so far is ample evidence of the intellectual importance of Paris at this date. If Gabriel's book only serves to remind us of this fact it will have provided a useful service. In fact, it does much more. Although ostensibly about his Hungarians, it is also a history of the German Nation *tout court*, the footnotes especially packed with details about students and masters from other countries. The book, then, is a mine of information. It must be added, too, that it is beautifully produced and illustrated. I have only one caveat, and that a minor one. Gabriel contends that the Hungarians disappear from Paris with the collapse of the Jagiellon kingdom after the battle of Mohács in 1526. He is doubtless correct, but he could have proved his point conclusively had he not only used the information in the *Liber Receptorum*, but had also searched for Hungarian students in the University's matriculation register which is complete from 1519 to 1553.

L. W. B. Brockliss
Magdalen College, Oxford

James K. Farge, *Orthodoxy and Reform in Early Reformation France. The Faculty of Theology of Paris 1500-1543*. Brill, Leiden, 1985. xii + 311 pp. $41.50. ISBN 90 04 07231 4.

When Luther and Eck failed to reach agreement in the fateful debate at Leipzig in July 1519, they both agreed to submit their position to the judgement of the universities of Erfurt and Paris. Both choices were understandable. Erfurt was a local German university with which neither Luther nor Eck was connected; the University of Paris, on the other hand, was recognised to be the international centre of theological studies, a position it had held from the time of Aquinas. Given this fact, Professor Farge's study of the Paris faculty in the first half of the sixteenth century is clearly a welcome addition to the plethora of recent studies on the early Reformation.

Indeed, it is surprising that the role of the faculty has never before been properly explored, for Professor Farge has been able to discover a wealth of hitherto unexamined material in Parisian libraries and archives. Above all, he has brought to our notice the value of the faculty's minute book as a source for studying the doctors' attitudes over the period. Although published in part by J. A. Clerval in 1917, the existence of these detailed registers of faculty opinion seem to have remained unknown to Reformation historians, and Professor Farge is to be commended for once more emphasising their importance.

Professor Farge's study is divided into two unconnected parts. The first provides a prosopographical account of the faculty's doctors between 1500 and 1536 in terms chiefly of their regional and social provenance, their educational background, literary output, and contribution to faculty life. The individual data on which this study is based has already appeared in detailed and comprehensive form in the author's earlier, *Biographical Register of Paris Doctors of Theology* (Toronto, 1980). On this occasion, he is content to present his findings in a dry, statistical manner which is seldom relieved by particular illustrations. In consequence, the reader quickly loses himself in the morass of tables and figures. He is left, too, with the feeling that much of the statistical analysis is energy misspent. As Professor Farge admits, it is extremely difficult to find out a great deal about all but a handful of his faculty doctors; their social background remains generally obscure and only the diocese of origin can be universally known. At the end of the day, all the prosopography really tells us is that the majority of doctors came from the Parisian basin and that few were going to receive plum jobs in the Church. Admittedly, this prosopographical information will become much more valuable when similar studies have been made of other theological schools in the Reformation era. At present, unfortunately, it is completely impossible to know whether the pattern of attendance at Paris was in any way typical.

The second and much longer part of the book deals with the faculty's reaction to the great religious debate of the age. This section in contrast is not just original but highly important. Professor Farge does not dramatically alter the traditional picture of the Paris doctors' role. This is still the faculty notorious not only for its opposition to Luther and Lutherans, but equally for its hostility to Biblical humanism: the persecuter of Reuchlin and Erasmus. However, by carefully delineating for the first time the doctors' response to the Reformers, Farge is able to paint the faculty in a far more positive and sympathetic light than hitherto. It has been incorrect, he insists, to see the faculty as obscurantist. Even discounting the handful of doctors who actively belonged to the reform movement (such as Lefèvre d'Étaples), there was always a majority in the faculty who recognised the existence of abuses in the Church which needed to be tackled. Only a few months after Luther nailed up his theses, the faculty was objecting in turn to the fraudulent claims of indulgence sellers (pp. 164-5). The faculty should be seen rather as a precursor of the Counter-Reformation, the doctors maintaining from the outset the unorthodoxy of Luther's theology and ecclesiology, and producing for the benefit of the faithful a series of unequivocal doctrinal statements, long before the promulgation of the faculty's 1543 Articles (pp. 208 *et seq.*). Moreover, the consistency and obduracy of the faculty is nothing if not heroic. While the cro:vn before the mid-1530s treated heresy lightly, the faculty continually recalled the king to his duty (often in no uncertain terms). The faculty might have been Gallican and Conciliarist in the main, but it was certainly no royal puppet. Indeed, even before the Reformation it had demonstrated its independence on a number of occasions, by refusing to support the French-controlled Council of Pisa (1512) and attacking the 1516 *Concordat.*

Evidently, in Farge's eyes, the faculty played an important part in keeping France a Catholic country. Along with the Parliament of Paris, if offered spiritually-aware Frenchmen a firm lead at a time when the crown preferred to see the Reformation as a political and diplomatic opportunity. Its power lay in the fact that it was a respected state institution. Contrary to the views of some historians, Francis I, says Farge, was not a Louis XVI with the absolute authority to form the minds as well as fleece the purses of his subjects. It was the faculty that was the spiritual conscience of the nation. On the other hand, Farge clearly shows there was a definite geographical limit to the extent of its moral authority. Although princes, prelates and theologians from all over Europe approached the faculty seeking arbitration of their theological and moral difficulties, they paid little attention to its decisions if judgement went against them. Luther paid no more heed to the faculty's censure of his opinions than the pope did to the judgement (albeit by a slight majority) in favour of Henry VIII's annulment. It is here (although Professor Farge does not say so) that the two halves of the book may perhaps be brought together. The Paris faculty in the first half of the sixteenth century was an institution of international importance but with a primarily regional clientele. Unlike the Society of Jesus at a later date it was not an international organisation with representatives at every court. It was really no more than an institution of Paris *curés* and canons relying on the historical power of its name to enforce its will. In an age of clientage, this was inevitably insufficient.

L. W. B. Brockliss
Magdalen College, Oxford

Acta Nationis Germanicae Iuristarum (1650-1709) a cura di Gilda Mantovani. Centro Per la Storia dell'Università di Padova, Fonti per la Storia dell'Università di Padova, vol. 9: Acta Nationis Germanicae II-v. Padua, Editrice Antenore, 1983. xvi + 656 pp.

In 1545 German students of the University of Padua decided to erect a new student club called *Inclyta Natio Germanica.* Of course, as at Bologna, there was already a German Nation. The *Universitas iuristarum* was organised into a *universitas iuristarum citramontanorum* and a *universitas iuristarum ultramontanorum.* Both *universitates* were subdivided into nations according to the 'nationality' of their members. By 1550 the principle of residence was used rather than that of birth. Among the ten nations of the ultramontane (or transalpine) university, i.e. the German, Bohemian, Hungarian, Polish, Provençal, Burgundian, Catalonian, Spanish, English-Scots, and Ultramarine (i.e. the Eastern Mediterranean area) the German nations had the most favoured position. The *Universitas artistarum* (*et medicorum*) was divided into seven nations, one ultramontane and six Italian.

The *universitates* and the nations were permanently confronted with clashes, quarrels, and general discord. Tension between Germans and Poles was frequent. The Germans, as we can read in their annals, felt neglected and misunderstood, and that their rights were being violated. Independent from the official German nation of the university, German students, both jurists and artists, and other students who felt close to them or had the same frustrations, met each other in German pubs and decided in 1545 to found a German club, called *Inclyta Natio Germanica*. This student club evolved its own organisation, with statutes, a matriculation roll, a chest and officers. The two official German *consiliarii* had the same function in the 'dissident' nation as in the official nation, and were assisted by two *procuratores*. In 1553 the artists separated from the arrogant and élistist jurists and founded a similar student club with statutes, a *matricula*, a chest and officers. These nations were recognised by the Doge and the Senate of the Venetian Republic and had to be accepted by the *Universitates*. New students could thus officially matriculate in the 'dissident' nations.[1] Their names were afterwards transcribed in the official rolls of the *Studium*. A similar phenomenon occurred in 1592 with the erection of the *Natio Regni Poloniae et Magni Ducatus Lithuaniae*. Their annals exist for the years 1592-1745.[2]

Already in 1545 the new German nation decided to keep a kind of diary of the most important events, the *Annales Inclytae Nationis Germanicae Iuristarum Patavinorum*. Only the first and the third book have survived. The first volume, 1545-1600, was edited in 1912 by B. Brugi.[3] The second volume, 1601-1649, is lost. The present edition contains the annals of 1650-1709. There is no trace of later annals.[4]

The reports are very annalistic detailing the most striking events which happened during the term of office of the *consiliarius*. Information is given about the working of the club, of its relations with the other nations (which are not always friendly) and with the university. The annals give us an insight into the impact and the influence of the Venetian government on the *Studium* from the sixteenth century onwards. The entries concerning religious questions are particularly interesting. The graduation of members is also registered, as is the acquisition of books for the nation's library and the nomination of new professors and officers. The annals are a prime source for the everyday life of the transalpine students in the Paduan university town, and for an understanding of the mentality of the German students. They are a faithful rendering of election quarrels, of financial problems, and of the attempt by a decaying nation to keep its prestige and prominent place in a university which was more and more losing its international character. Judging by the handwriting and the corruption of the proper names the text of these annals seems to have been written by an Italian scribe. In the index these corrupted names are corrected on the basis of other Paduan sources, in particular the matriculation rolls. However, the tables provided by the editor are rather too summary. Place names are not identified aned the modern equivalent not provided. The reader has to know the Italian version of the German or other place names to find them in the index. By going through the table I discovered not only Germans, Austrians, Hungarians, Swiss and Dutch students, but also *suppositi* from Burgundy, France, Spain, England, Sweden, Denmark, and Greece. Not all of them were members of the dissident nation, although the origins of its members were certainly less confined to the borders of the Holy Empire than those of the official German nation. According to the statutes of 1600, art. VIII

ad matriculam hanc et commoda nationis Germanos nostros tam superiores quam inferiores, Danos Praeterea Svecos, Borussos, Livonos, Boemos, Ungaros, Transylvanos, Moravos, Helvetios, Rhetos admittunto.[5]

The editor unfortunately provides very little of the historical context of these *acta*, the introduction being limited to a description of the manuscript and of the technical aspects of his editorial method. In the literature on the Paduan German nation (Brugi, Favaro, Premuda, Weigle, Knod, Luschin von Ebengreuth, Fitting, Rossetti, Den Tex, Poelhekke, and others) no mention is made of two German nations, an 'official' and a 'dissident'. Nor indeed did anyone suspect the existence of a specifically German nation of artists within a *Universitas artistarum* which had only one ultramontane and six Italian nations. The lack of sources on the nations before 1545 was not considered surprising, nor the fact that sources existed only for the German and Polish nations (besides some sources for the ultramarine nation of jurists).[6] The subject has now been elucidated in a convincing way by P. J. van Kessel in his Dutch dissertation.[7]

In reading the text I was struck by the resemblance of these annals to those of the German nation of the University of Orléans: the content of the stories, the mentality of the *suppositi*, the social status of the students, the painted armorial devices of the Prominent officers.[8] Incidentally, these devices can be very helpful for the identification of the students. The *Centro per la Storia dell'Università di Padova* is proving very active, and in the last few years many sources have been edited. We must hope that L. Rossetti and her team are persevering in the same way and that the promised source editions, in particular the matriculation rolls, will be edited soon. The Paduan sources are not only important for the history of the Italian universities but are crucial sources for a better understanding of the whole European university and scientific movement during the Early Modern Period.

Hilde de Ridder-Symoens
National Fund of Scientific Research — University of Ghent
Blandijnberg 2, B 9000 Gent (Belgium)
and Free University Amsterdam

1. Archivio Antico della Univ. di Padova, Cod. 459-462, 1545-1801.

2. *Ibid.*, Cod. 487-488. Cf. A. Brillo, *Gli stemmi degli studenti Polacchi nell'università di Padova* (Padua, 1933).

3. B. Brugi (ed.), *Atti della nazione germanica dei legisti nello Studio di Padova (1545-1609)* (Acta Nationis Germanicae Iuristarum II-1; Venice 1912).

4. Cf. G. Giomo, *L'archivio antico della università di Padova* (Venice 1893) and A. Luschin von Ebengreuth, 'Quellen zur Geschichte deutscher Rechtshörer in Italian', *Sitzungsberichte der kais. Akademie der Wissenschaften in Wien, Phil.-Hist. Klasse*, 113 (1887) 746-769; 124 (1891) 19-30.

5. Giomo, *op. cit.*, 50.

6. Giomo, *op. cit.*, 50-52, 84. Cf. note 4.

7. P. J. van Kessel, *Duitse studenten te Padua. De controverse Rome-Venetië en het protestantisme in de tijd der contra-reformatie* (Van Gorcum's Historische Bibliotheek, nr. 71; Assen 1963).

8. *Premier Livre des Procurateurs de la Nation Germanique de l'ancienne Université d'Orléans 1444-1546, Première Partie: Texte des rapports des Procurateurs*, éditée Par C. M. Ridderikhoff avec la collaboration de H. de Ridder-Symoens (Leiden 1971); *Deuxième Livre . . . 1547-1567, Première Partie: Texte des rapports des Procurateurs*, éditée Par C. M. Ridderikhoff (Leiden 1987, in press).

Christopher Brooke, *A History of Gonville and Caius College.* Woodbridge: The Boydell Press, 1985. xv + 354 pp. £19.50.

This is an excellent and valuable book. It can have been no easy matter to cover over six hundred years of college history in a reasonably concise way without sacrificing balance or depth, but insofar as it can ever be achieved, Christopher Brooke has managed it admirably. All the major happenings in the story of Caius are chronicled here; the achievements of its famous men are duly recorded; and there is a good deal of anecdotal material; but this is much more than a 'traditional' college history, and it wears its learning deceptively lightly. Every layer of college society is discussed, as well as its fabric, library, economics, religious life, and — most significant but most elusive of all subjects — its intellectual life. Moreover, all these are set in their proper contexts, so that the college is never viewed in isolation from its times and its several different environments. The book is founded upon a wide and incisive knowledge of all the relevant sources, both primary and secondary, supported by an understanding of the most recent historical scholarship in every period of the university's history. One valuable and hitherto unrevealed source for the seventeenth century is now made public, in the form of the correspondence of William Bagge, who was President (or vice-master) of Caius for a short while in the 1650s: this is full of details of college life in the period, and offers new insights into the state of Caius during the Interregnum under one of its most intriguing Masters, William Dell, the Independent preacher and forthright critic of the universities of his time.

As well as contributing to our understanding of times past, a college historian should not shirk his responsibility to be a chronicler of recent events. Professor Brooke has not been afraid to come right up to date, nor to tackle such delicate subjects as the dispute between the senior and junior fellows over aspects of college government in the early 1950s (the so-called 'Peasants' Revolt'). The author's deep affection for his college is evident, but he avoids sentimentality, and his judgements are never less than informed and appropriately critical. As a college history, it is a model of its kind; it could also serve as a useful introduction to much of the history of the University of Cambridge as a whole. Finally, the book demonstrates that it is still possible to write history which is readable as well as scholarly.

John Twigg
Queen's College
Cambridge CB3 9ET

J. C. T. Oates, *Cambridge University Library; a History. From the Beginnings to the Copyright Act of Queen Anne.* Cambridge University Press, 1986. xviii + 510 pp. £50.00. David McKitterick, *Cambridge University Library; a History. The Eighteenth and Nineteenth Centuries.* Cambridge University Press, 1986. xvii + 812 pp. £75.00.

Those with Oxford connections may be excused for imagining that library history revolves around Sir Thomas Bodley; these two magisterial volumes redress the balance for Cambridge. They trace the history of Cambridge University Library from its beginnings in the fourteenth century until the end of the nineteenth. Nothing comparable has preceded them and for this reason alone they are a welcome contribution to the history of Cambridge and to that of universities and libraries in general. The authors have worked end-on rather than in tandem and though it is not explicit that they shared a single brief, the presentation is similar. Oates has a long career in the Library behind him having joined it in 1936. McKitterick, a new-comer who generously acknowledges the work of his older colleague, has already made his own mark with papers on books and libraries in Cambridge. He has recently moved from the University Library to the librarianship of Trinity College.

Both volumes are soundly based on original sources particularly on the archives of the University and its Library. Unfortunately they lack a compendious bibliography and would have benefitted from the inclusion of a critical survey of their sources. Library history, of course, is not written solely from business papers; book-stock itself is another excellent quarry. Book-plates, other *ex libris*, annotations, notes of prices, old press-marks, bindings, traces of chain clasps, fore-edge titles and other scraps of evidence contribute to the story, and both authors use them. They have also read widely in secondary literature and Oates does not pull his punches when he finds error (cf. p. 430, n. 32 and p. 432, n. 37).

The origins are uncertain but during the latter half of the fourteenth century the University had a small collection of books in chests. The Old Schools were built over a long period but the wing which provided the original library room on its first floor, was under construction in 1420 and almost certainly in use by 1438. The Library slowly spread over the whole site from which it eventually moved it its present building in 1934. Without funds it relied on gifts and bequests some of which were substantial, and both authors discuss the more important ones in considerable detail, tracing the history of individual volumes, particularly manuscripts, and the use which scholars have made of them. Between 1530 and 1573 there was no book-related expenditure at all though small sums were spent on routine maintenance of the fabric. Not until the 1690s did the Library have its own endowment for book purchase but even the investment of Tobias Rustat's £1,000 capital was not as profitable at it might have been. Custody of the Library was entrusted to the University Chaplain until 1577 when a Grace authorised a salaried librarian, not always paid regularly however. The mid-seventeenth century saw an attempt to levy a charge on the colleges to augment his stipend of £3 6s. 8d. a year but it failed.

The early modern period poses two questions: what impact did the new learning and reformation have on the Library and, secondly, why did the Library apparently languish when prestigious development took place in Oxford. The new learning entered slowly, the Library not obtaining its first Greek texts until 1529, the gift of Bishop Tunstal. Oates ascribes the delay to the absence of any dominant figure in Cambridge. By 1557 the stock had dwindled to less than 200 volumes. Oates does not believe this was due to doctrinaire purges but rather to desuetude, lack of supervision and penury. A revival began in the 1570s under the régime of Andrew Perne and with benefactions from Archbishop Parker and others; but why did Cambridge lack a Bodley? Oates does not face this question squarely. Prestigious development needs benefactors and influence in high places; Cambridge had the misjudgement to back the Duke of Buckingham whose death brought plans to a premature end though his widow did give the Library Erpenius' oriental MSS. Next (as Leeds University discovered after opening its Brotherton Library) a new building can encourage further benefaction, nothing succeeding like success, and Oates neatly identifies a difficulty at Cambridge:

No procession of doctors however dignified their individual gaits could have survived in good order the passage down the narrow staircase from the Regent House . . . and up the turret-stair which led to the two rooms of the Library . . . (p. 156).

Furthermore the University was unable to buy the interests of some citizens in the site which it favoured for library development. The University even failed to make one long-term gain out of Parliament for it had to return the archiepiscopal library to Lambeth in 1664 in exchange for Richard Holdsworth's collection.

The award of copyright deposit privilege promised great things to a library which still relied on gifts and bequests. Hopes were fulfilled only slowly. The book trade was dilatory and the University treated its privilege capriciously. Not until the Copyright Agency was founded in 1863, largely the brainchild of Panizzi rather than either university, did efficiency begin to intrude. Meanwhile the eighteenth century had begun auspiciously with the gift of Bishop Moore's library, purchased for the University by George I, in McKitterick's view a political act to secure support for the Hanoverians (he does not quite elicit Oxford toryism at that time). The gift almost trebled library stock and consequently posed immense administrative problems, compounded by the appointment of a *protobibliothecarious* as well as a librarian. The early nineteenth century saw the unedifying spectacle of some members, their families and friends using the Library as a circulating library for novels. The mid-nineteenth century brought reform, some income and the librarianships of Mayor and Bradshaw together with a shift in power from college to university. The Library stood to gain but its restricted though conveniently central site prevented spectacular development; *Fachbibliotheken* arose as faculties and departments developed subject-based collections.

No summary can do justice to the detail in these two volumes. The modern mind boggles at Richard Bentley borrowing the Codex Bezae for five years or so. Doubts arise, however, over the authors' method; both have worked chronologically and so any thematic approach has to be through the indexes. McKitterick's indexer has not served him well, scattering thematic headings throughout the alphabet and unhelpfully hiding 'finance' under 'money' and 'capitation tax'. There is imbalance, too. Oates devotes three chapters to the mid-seventeenth century librarian Abraham Whelock, some of which would have been better reserved for a paper on philology. Similarly McKitterick's chapters on Bishop Moore and his library drift away from the central theme. Library stock receives greater attention than library management. The role of college libraries is perhaps underplayed; one recalls Parker's MSS. at Corpus and Whelock bustling between the University Library and college libraries both for his own research and on behalf of others. Undergraduates were excluded from the University Library and could be unwelcome in college ones, and McKitterick discusses the report of the University Commissioners on college libraries and books for undergraduates; revision of the undergraduate curriculum implied parallel revision of library facilities.

The two volumes are a signal achievement. They are well-printed and have useful plans as well as illustrations, but Oates and McKitterick might just remember when they sip a well-earned morning coffee that Mocha is on the Red Sea, not the Persian Gulf (Oates, p. 289)!

P. S. Morrish
Brotherton Library
University of Leeds

P. M. Harman, ed., *Wranglers and Physicists. Studies on Cambridge Physics in the Nineteenth Century.* Manchester: Manchester University Press, 1985. viii + 261 pp. £27.50.

In March 1984 the Wordsworth Hotel at Grasmere was host to an international seminar on Cambridge mathematical physics in the nineteenth century. Eight of the papers given at the meeting, together with a helpful linking introductory essay by the editor, are now published as *Wranglers and Physicists*. As the title suggests, the disparate, and often technically-demanding, contributions have the common theme of the way in which British physics acquired a distinctive character from the Cambridge mathematical education of the majority of its practitioners. For example, the Cambridge Mathematical Tripos emphasised optics, mechanical analogies and explanations involving an ether. Indeed, historians of science have quite commonly referred to the 'Cambridge School' of Green, Stokes, Kelvin, Maxwell and Larmor, all of whom had been senior wranglers. Nearly half of the physics chairholders in British universities after 1850 had taken the Cambridge Mathematical Tripos. The emphasis that this honours degree placed upon 'mixed mathematics', of solving problems rather than being concerned with mathematical rigour, was effective as a route into physics because of the weight it gave to the description and analysis of physical phenomena — particularly to optics. The wave theory of light adopted by its practitioners became a model for the analysis of heat, electricity and magnetism in the hands of later wranglers and their tutors. Not until the 1890s, when the Natural Science Tripos (NST, founded 1851) was reformed, did the Cavendish laboratory begin to figure prominently in the training of British physicists and the Mathematical Tripos became devoted exclusively to the training of pure mathematicians.

However, as David Wilson, the previous author of a valuable study of the NST (*Hist. Studies Physical Sciences*, 12 (1980), 325-71) shows in an excellent comparison between physics education at Cambridge, Edinburgh and Glasgow, four of the strongest Cambridge physics graduates, Thomson, Tait, Steele and Maxwell, had taken their first degrees at Scottish universities, where the senior wranglers Hugh Blackburn and Philip Kelland taught in the 1840s. Wilson stresses the necessity of recognising 'regional and institutional variation within the history of scientific ideas' and argues persuasively that significant elements of Scottish influence can be detected in individuals of the Cambridge group — for example, the different physics styles of Stokes and William Thomson can be attributed to the latter's education at Glasgow under William Meikleham, whom Wilson rescues from obscurity. In a separate essay on Maxwell, Peter Harman also agrees that the Scottish tradition of analogical physics played a formative role in shaping Cambridge mathematical physics in the 1840s.

Although most essays in the book on Thomson, Maxwell, integral theorems and electrodynamics are mathematical and 'internal' in scope, two other essays are concerned with an educational context. In a highly original contribution, Crosbie Smith argues that there was a peculiarly Cambridge school of geology, made up of the wranglers Sedgwick, Whewell and William Hopkins (the most important of the priviate coaches of wranglers) who deployed a structuralist 'geometrical' way of thinking about stratigraphy, as opposed to the organic, palaeontological way stressed by their contemporaries. He emphasises that Hopkins's geological papers must not be ignored when considering the development of mathematical physics at Cambridge. Finally, in an analytical and bibliographical *tour de force*, Ivor Grattan-Guinness examines Cambridge as a centre of mathematical research and textbook writing between 1815 and 1840, when it was particularly influenced (though selectively) by French mathematical traditions. As a prolegomena to further research Grattan-Guinness raises a number of stimulating questions concerning *Denkweisen* — the different methods and styles of working in mathematics and mathematical physics in different countries, notably France, England, Scotland and Ireland.

In so far as universities cannot be divorced from the ideas they disseminate, *Wranglers and Physicists* will be of as much value to historians of education as to the historians of science it primarily addresses.

W. H. Brock
Victorian Studies Centre
University of Leicester

J. T. D. Hall, *The Tounis College. An Anthology of Edinburgh University Student Journals, 1823-1923.* Edinburgh, Friends of Edinburgh University Library, 1985. 298 pp.

Student magazines are an essential source for the history of student life in modern universities, and their appearance is itself a symptom of the intensification of student consciousness. All four Scottish universities began continuous publication of such a magazine in the 1880s, and the Edinburgh version, *The Student*, dating from 1887, provides over half the extracts in this anthology. Most of the rest date from the 1820s and 1830s, and only a few pages cover the years between 1839 and 1887.

This hiatus in student journalism naturally reduces the value of the collection for historians, and the format itself has many drawbacks. The editor provides useful and accurate contextual information, but has little to say about wider questions of university history, and many of the extracts are chosen for their literary or picturesque quality, or their connection with authors like Stevenson and Conan Doyle, rather than for the light which they throw on student conditions. Moreover, the editor is committed to the view that 'many of the pleasures and tribulations of student life are one and the same through the years', and this has probably influenced the choice of items. Even so, the observant reader can see that student life in the 1820s had much in common with patterns of general sociability among middle-class youth in the city, while from the 1880s it took on a more inward-looking and corporate character.

The historian trying to explain this change will need to look at the news items in magazines as well as the features, and to allow for the fact that editorial cliques were often unrepresentative, and for the imitative influence of current journalistic conventions on style and content. But such historians will in any case seek out the originals. This collection is directed to a non-specialist market, and certainly provides much agreeable reading, and much incidental information about such matters as the development of athletics, the impact of the admission of women, the effects of the First World War, and the rituals which surrounded that Scottish peculiarity, the rectorial election.

R. D. Anderson
Department of History
University of Edinburgh
Edinburgh EH8 9JY

Ferdinand Seibt (ed.), *Die Teilung der Prager Universität 1882 und die intellektuelle Desintegration in den böhmischen Ländern*, Munich: Oldenbourg, 1984. 220 pp.
Acta Universitatis Carolinae. Historia Universitatis Carolinae Pragensis. Vol. XXII (1982), fasc.1. 152 pp. Kčs.15.

The Charles University of Prague has had a very fissiparous history. Sixty years after its foundation in 1348, the German majority of its students seceded and set up the university of Leipzig across the Saxon border (cf. F. Šmahel's article, *History of Universities* iv (1984), pp. 153-66). In the next century a separate Jesuit academy was established as rival to the decayed and Czech-dominated Carolinum; a further sixty years later the two were forcibly merged, and the resultant Carolo-Ferdinandeum pursued a steady, if largely unremarkable and provincial evolution into the age of nationalism. There then took place developments which leave the observer with a distinct sense of *déjà vu*. First, in 1882, the Czech majority of staff and students seceded, by imperial decree, to create a separate and rival Carolinum. Sixty years on once more the two Prague universities were again forcibly reduced to one: in 1939 the Nazis closed the Czech establishment; in 1945 the tables were turned, with the suppression of the German establishment and the explusion of its staff and students.

The injustices of 1939 and 1945 still lie too close for scholarly appraisal. Until recently that also held true for the events of 1882, which had given academic expresion to the polarity of nationalities in Bohemia. But these two centenary collections, the one a volume of papers produced for a gathering of the Collegium Carolinum, the West German descendant of Sudeten-German academic historiography, the other an issue of the highly meritorious journal *Historia Universitatis Carolinae Pragensis* (hereafter *HUCP*), edited by the archives division of today's Carolinum (and how many other universities do as much to cultivate their past?), show that mature judgements can now be passed on them. One writer alone among the twenty-four on view exhibits serious *ressentiment* — and the veteran Václav Vaněček's rather graceless polemic in *HUCP*, since it rehearses the arguments he had already deployed for a similar anniversary fifty years earlier, serves merely to underline how fraught the whole subject used to be. The contributors concentrate on the debates and campaigns which immediately preceded the division of the University, on the practical implementation of the change, and on its impact by the end of the century or so (a few look beyond). Although neither book provides an adequate synthesis of its conclusions, they are clearly in substantial agreement.

The division of the Carolinum in 1882, well-known as one of the most significant political compromises struck in the last decades of the Habsburg Empire (it formed part of the log-rolling whereby Minister President Taaffe secured his long-standing 'Iron Ring' against the Liberals), emerges here as a genuine cultural compromise too. Both sides were prepared for it: the Czechs through the powerful development of their national educational movement inside and outside the University during the 1860s and 1870s; the Bohemian Germans by the growing isolation and introversion of their national community. These preconditions are ably survey ed by J. Havránek in *HUCP*, who follows the Czech programme from its faltering dreams of 1848 — when students needed the help of Palacký even to compose a Czech-language petition — to its clear numerical predominance among pupils and its substantial body of lecturers by the 1870s, and shows how German resistance was orchestrated mainly, not by Sudeten professors, but by immigrant academics and by the provincial *Statthalter*. And both sides derived considerable benefit: the Czechs with the confirmation of their University as a fully-fledged Bohemian institution (foreshadowing their claim after the First World War that the Carolinum had always been a *Landesuniversität*, never dependent upon the Empire); the Germans by avoiding the fate of minority status within a single academic body.

Thus the actual transition proceeded smoothly, helped no doubt by the comparative tranquillity of Bohemian politics at the time and by Emperor Francis Joseph's personal determination to press ahead (he sealed the decision, *motu proprio*, with an 'Allerhöchste Entschliessung'). In fact things proved something of an anti-climax. Several good articles here show how creative energies flagged during the 1880s, whether among jurists and philosophers as a whole (H. Slapnicka and E. Schmidt-Hartmann in the Seibt volume), or in individuals who, like the pioneer of Czech chemistry, Vojtěch Šafařík, adapted poorly to the new enviroment (L. Niklíček *et. al.* in *HUCP*). In particular, Czech scholarship was temporarily derailed by the affair of the 'Manuscripts', whose authenticity — sacrosanct to the older generation of patriots — could now (ironically) be impugned from a securer base by the young 'realists' of the new Philosophical Faculty, led by Jan Gebauer 'valuably appreciated by T. Syllaba in *HUCP*) and T. G. Masaryk. Nor was medicine, embroiled — as L. Hlaváčková shows in *HUCP* — in the construction of new buildings, quick to throw up another Purkyně.

Meanwhile the German University suffered from declining morale as student numbers fell (at one stage its Philosophical Faculty had two teachers for every three pupils), and failed to take advantage of the admirable research opportunities which were furnished as a corollary of this.

One crucial intellectual implication of the 1882 decision is repeatedly alluded to in these volumes. The division of the Carolinum proved workable because the divorced parties agreed not to meet in future; co-existence increasingly rested on mutual ignorance. The integrative function of the university, which in other parts of the Habsburg realm and beyond could still be sustained, even created from scratch — as at Czernowitz (examined in a guest appearance for the Seibt volume by E. Turczynski) amid the very different circumstances of the Bukovina — was replaced in Bohemia by a disintegrative one. Another set of implications, however, is neglected, for the two branches of the reconstituted Carolinum continued to operate within the larger intellectual context of the western Habsburg lands as a whole. That dimension has hardly been touched on here, though Ernst Mach was a leading light of the University at the time of its bifurcation (which indeed he helped to prepare), and figures of established or rising international stature, like Gindely and Masaryk, were heavily involved in it. What was Bohemia's academic contribution to the Austrian *fin de siècle* and the new currents of thought which it engendered? How far did the restructuring of university life in Prague affect that contribution? Such questions, prompted by the present collections, are not directly addressed in them.

R. J. W. Evans
Brasenose College, Oxford

Portsmouth Record Series. Records of University Adult Education 1886-1939. A Calendar compiled by Edwin Welch. Portsmouth, n.d., £22.50.

The Council of the City of Portsmouth should be congratulated on the production of this handsome volume, part of a series aimed at making 'the written sources of Portsmouth history widely available', while helping 'to set a new pattern for the publication of local records in Great Britain' (p. 226). This vision is especially commendable in the study of the history of adult education. Following the general studies produced by J. F. C. Harrison and Welch and John Burrows on adult education in London, and Stuart Marriott, future work will, to an increasing extent, entail greater dependence on local sources of the type described in the Portsmouth volume, while the nature of the available local material underlines the need for comparative work.

The Cambridge university extension centre at Portsmouth was of no special distinction. Its two local organisers during its early years, Frederick Blake and J. Herbert Fisher, argued in 1899 (Appendix III) that the centre's 'non-achievement of anything startling' was mainly due to the nature of the population in a garrison town, 'largely composed of the naval and military element . . . one of the worst kind of elements from which to draw an audience sufficiently interested in work of this kind'. The same seemed to apply to the civilians employed by the Dockyard who, 'after their duties there do not seem to interest themselves much in higher education'. Their impresssions are confirmed by the short history of the Portsmouth branch of the Workers' Educational Association. Founded in September, 1906, the Association's first branch in the Southern District, it rapidly declined, and was terminated in 1916. Consequently, except for students of local history, the story of adult education at Portsmouth would appear best suitable as part of a comparative analysis, combining the study of a number of local extension centres.

There is no shortage of fascinating themes which emerge, however briefly, from the necessarily short descriptions of the documentation (mainly from the Cambridge University Archives) included by Welch in this calendar, for instance, the manner in which class relations were reflected in the centre's operation and administration. In this context one may find interesting the reference to a confession by a working man who had attended the first extension course at Portsmouth: 'I feel somewhat ashamed of my ignorance when in the society of the more educated' (1e), or the undertones in J. Herbert Fisher's 1927 comment on the students of tutorial classes who 'would not be too happy in a University Extension Class, because in the latter the numbers are usually larger, and they would not, therefore, be able to hear their own voice to the same extent, and thus not be able to impress some of their fellow students' (Appendix V). Other themes are the relatively large proportion of women students who attended extension courses compared to tutorial classes, as well as the more general issue of the relations between the extension and other adult education agencies. The perceived changes in the demand for courses on certain subjects following the first world war (73e, and Appendix V).

Technically, the calendar is virtually faultless. Edwin Welch, currently Archivist to the North-West Territories of Canada, has executed his task with admirable thoroughness. The description of the various sources is clear, accurate, and sufficently detailed to give the scholar a solid enough grip on the material without reproducing it word for word. One might have wished for a better introduction which could have taken into account some of the recent literature on the extension movement. For instance, Welch's treatment of the Oxford and London extensions is extremely sketchy especially in view of the aforementioned need for comparative studies. Suggestive analysis is offered on some points such as the relation between student recruitment and the availability of public transport or the tendency of friends and neighbours to attend the same classes, while a major issue such as the self-perceived failure of the extension movement to attract sufficiently large number of working class students is only briefly mentioned. But all this is of little consequence compared to the obvious merits of this splendid work.

Alon Kadish
History Department
Hebrew University
Jerusalem, Israel

Geoffrey J. Giles, *Students and National Socialism in Germany*. Princeton University Press, 1985. 360 pp. $47.50.

Geoffrey Giles' book, *Students and National Socialism in Germany*, has essentially two stories to tell: the rapid success of the Nazis among German university students (Giles opens with the statement that the German Students' Union was the first national organisation of any type to be won over by the Nazis) and the subsequent failure of the Nazi student organisations to make radical changes in the universities during the Third Reich. In telling these two stories, Giles focuses on the University of Hamburg, where he has done impressive archival work. The local Hamburg story smoothly dovetails with national events, and Giles moves ably back and forth between the two.

Giles's discussion of the local and national scences may, however, be too seamless. Giles has selected Hamburg as a case study, but he has devoted little attention to the singularity of his case. The University of Hamburg, founded in 1919 in the aftermath of the First World War, was a modern university in a commercial city without the long university traditions of Heidelberg, Berlin or Munich. As a newcomer, the university was unable to draw the national student bodies that other universities did. Thus its students relate closely to the social structure of Hamburg itself, and Giles has missed an opportunity to examine that link. The university also selected a more liberal faculty than most other universities, so that Hamburg's faculty included such important liberals as Albrecht Mendelssohn Bartholdy and Ernst Cassirer, and the university's catalogue reflects the liberal bent of the faculty, listing courses on English liberal philosophers and a selection of seminars on the French Enlightenment. Giles mentions Nazi student complaints about being taught by Jews in Hamburg, but he has not dealt with the paradox of a right-wing student body in the proximity of a relatively liberal faculty. One would like to know how they interacted. Giles has convincingly argued that the Nazis did as well among Hamburg students as elsewhere, but intriguing questions remain about how that occurred and what it meant.

The most fascinating and original part of Giles's book is the second part of his narrative, depicting the failure of the Nazi student movement to realise any of its ambitious plans to alter the structure of German education. Those plans were frustrated for a number of reasons, all carefully detailed by Giles.

But most interesting is the fact that the Nazi hierarchy, including the Reich Education Minister Bernhard Rust, cared little for the universities or university students; their thoughts were elsewhere. Professor Giles has produced for us another of those ironies that pervade the history of Nazism: he has depicted a social group in which the Nazis did extremely well but for whom the Nazi leaders had little sympathy. This is not merely the familiar question of old élites and a new radicalism, although that enters significantly into Giles's discussion of the Nazi student organisation and the old fraternities. It has much more to do with the variety of expectations the Nazis seemed to elicit with their flexible agenda. One is forced by Giles's account to ask, as one must always ask, how the Nazis were able to raise the expectations they did.

If I have not provided a full summary of Giles's argument, it is because Giles has written his book with an attractive pluralism of causality. His book involves a complicated mixture of sociological analysis, a careful following of events, and a series of brilliant biographical sketches; and Giles gracefully pulls the various elements of his account together into an elegant narrative structure. Giles has added most to our understanding of the supposed Nazi social revolution of the thirties, providing a significant example of its paralysis; but for the historian of the university, he has provided an excellent analysis of a strange episode in the career of the modern German university.

Carl Landauer
McGill University